[illegible]
erat impeditus in [illegible] ecclesie [illegible]
in presencia p(re)d(ict)i alii consistunt [illegible]
Senonen(sis) dioc(esis) in capella dom(us) [illegible] Templi [illegible]
in capella, et ostendit sibi crucem in qua erat ymago (Christ)i, et dixit sibi q(uod)
sup(er) vestes pro reverencia. Requisitus si fr(atr)es ordinis Templi cum recipiuntur
negatione predicta et cum bono modo, dixit causa q(uod) de abnegatione Crucifixi
[illegible] Interrogatus dixit se nescire. It(em) dixit Interrogatus si credere q(uod) p(ro) illi[illegible]
ent Interrogatus dixit [illegible] Interrog(atus) annus [illegible] erat q(ua)n(do) ipse fuit recept(us) in d(i)c(t)o ordine
ar cu(m) p(rese)n(t)ibus. Interrog(atus) [illegible] et si aliq(ui)d in ea immisceat falsitatis vel consensu[illegible]
[illegible] ea pro veritate dixerat et si aliqd in ea immisceat falsitatis vel consensu
[illegible] ea pro veritate dixerat et omnem aliam heresim in [illegible] manibus abiurare et
sup(er) scripturas, p(e)c(c)atum et omne [illegible] et ecclesiasticis sacramentis. Item eadem die in [illegible]
[illegible] fratrum et [illegible] Templi per fratrem Robertum de [illegible] ordinis
recept(us) in fratrem ordinis [illegible] Templi [illegible] in qua imago erat in illa cruce depi[cta]
[illegible] dixit sibi q(uod) oportebat eum negare ill[illegible] [illegible] si interrogaret a quoc[umque]
[illegible] ac fratrem recept(um) dixit q(uod) sic et [illegible] si interrogaret
[illegible] sup(er) manum mea. Et cum fratrem [illegible]
sup(er) crucem. Et dixit recepto [illegible] spuas sup(er) [illegible] ordinis q(uo)n recipiuntur [illegible]
[illegible] dixit se nescire aliud scire. Requisitus si alii [illegible] modum et [illegible]
[illegible] no. Post [illegible] eidem fratri [illegible] restituentes [illegible]
[illegible] ipsum ad [illegible] Qui frater Hugo predictus Jura[vit]
corporaliter tacto libro modo et forma [illegible] ordinis
[illegible] eum in [illegible] ordinis [illegible] depicta precepit [illegible]
[illegible] et ostensa [illegible] cruce in q(ua) erat ymago Crucifixi depicta precepit [illegible]
[illegible] et ostensa [illegible] cruce nolunt spuere. Interrog(atus) utrum osculat(us)
[illegible] q(uod) spueret sup(er) [illegible] cruce [illegible]
[illegible] receptis [illegible] ordinis [illegible] cuilibet
[illegible] receptis dixit q(uod) ipsis receptis [illegible] q(uod) abnegatione p(e)c(c)atum qua fecit [illegible]
[illegible] sius d(i)c(t)i ordinis. Dixit causa [illegible] suam q(uod) abnegationem [illegible]
[illegible] ordinis. Requisitus utrum aliqui de receptis [illegible] facere p(e)c(c)atum [illegible]
[illegible] ordinis. Requisitus utrum aliqui [illegible] vel ultra mare qui fuerunt
[illegible] aliquis illud p(e)c(c)atum comisit [illegible] q(uod) recipiatur ita dixit se credere
[illegible] Requisitus utrum credit q(uod) recipiatur ita dixit [illegible]
[illegible] illos qui [illegible] Interrog(atus) [illegible] etatis erat
[illegible] loci et remansit ipsi fratri [illegible] ipsi capud. Interrog(atus) [illegible]
[illegible] d(i)c(t)i loci et remansit ipsi fratri [illegible] et quorundam aliorum Notarii [illegible]
[illegible] [illegible] et quorundam [illegible] formidine
[illegible] aliam ut [illegible] formidine

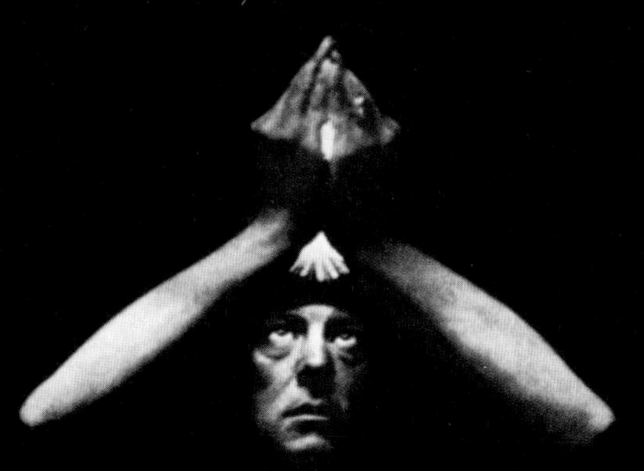

THE HIDDEN WORLD OF SECRET SOCIETIES

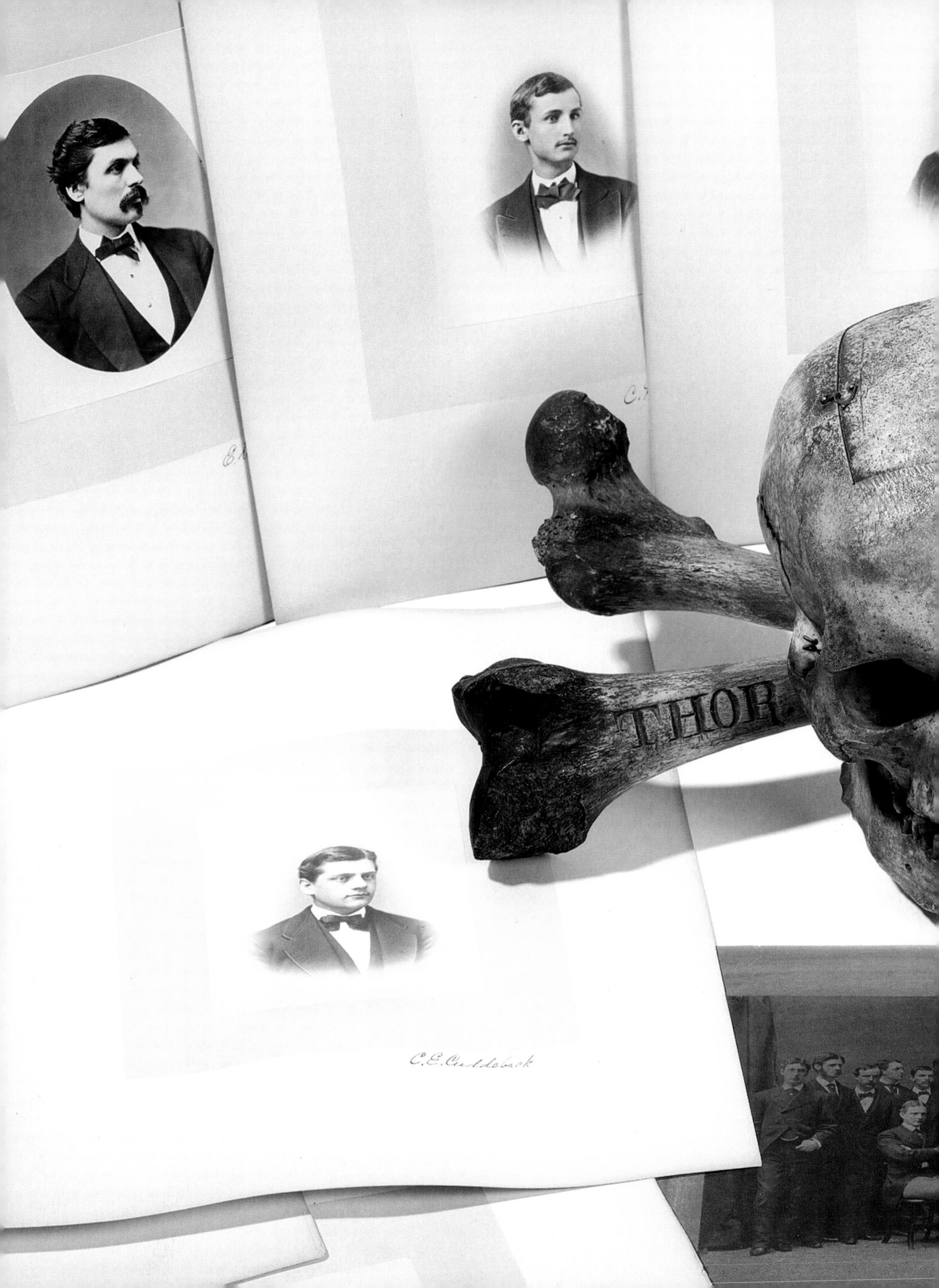
THOR
C.E.Cuddeback

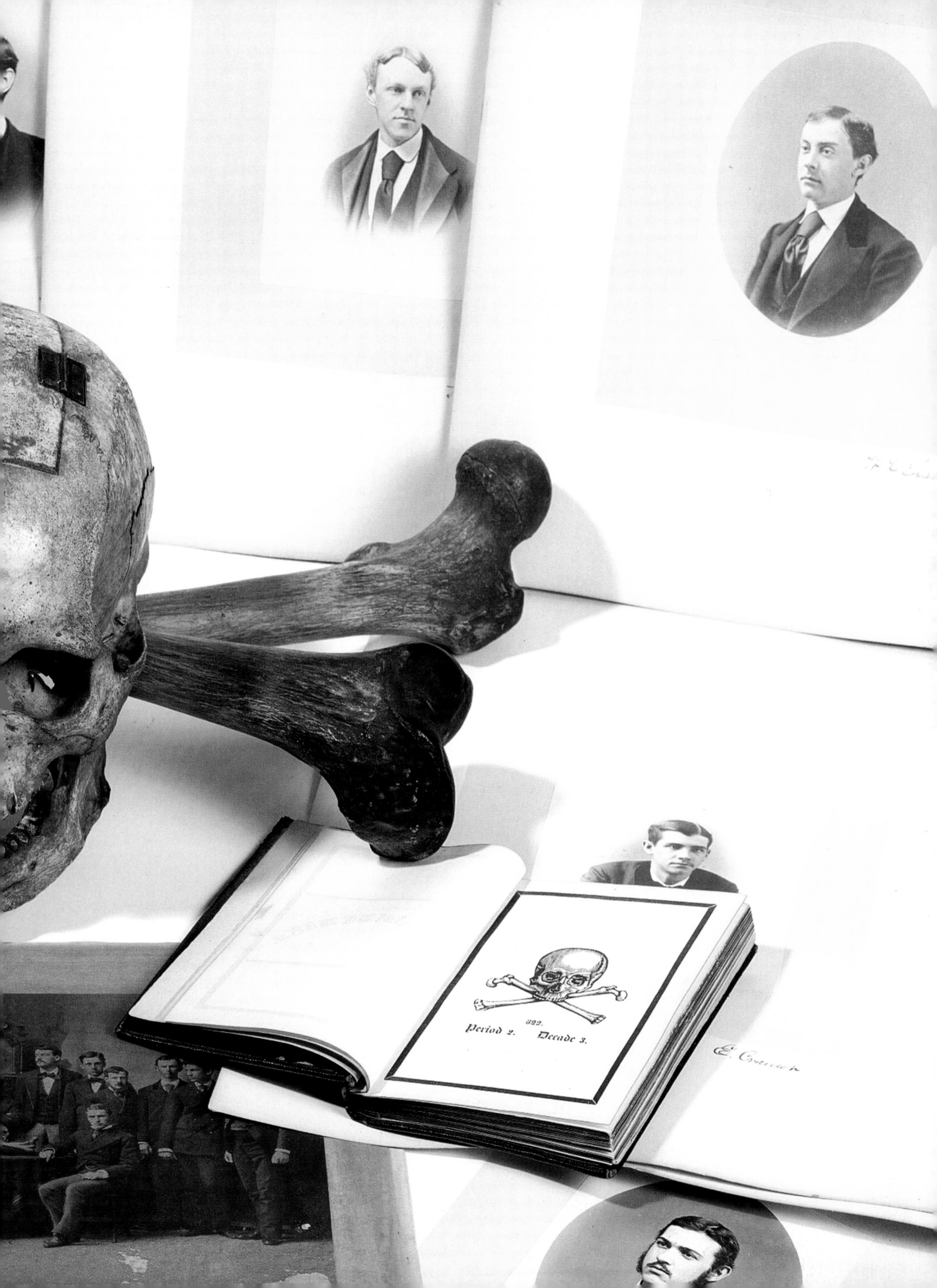
322.
Period 2. Decade 3.

Special thanks to Christine Austin, Katherine Barnet, Jeremy Biloon, Stephanie Braga, Jim Childs, Susan Chodakiewicz, Rose Cirrincione, Lauren Hall Clark, Jacqueline Fitzgerald, Christine Font, Jenna Goldberg, Hillary Hirsch, Amy Mangus, Robert Marasco, Kimberly Marshall, Amy Migliaccio, Nina Mistry, Dave Rozzelle, Adriana Tierno, Alex Voznesenskiy, Vanessa Wu

Published by LIFE BOOKS, an imprint of Time Home Entertainment Inc.
135 West 50th Street
New York, New York 10020

ISBN 13: 978-1-60320-226-8
ISBN 10: 1-60320-226-9
Library of Congress Control Number: 2012934747

We welcome your comments and suggestions about LIFE BOOKS. Please write to us at:
LIFE BOOKS
Attention: Book Editors
PO Box 11016
Des Moines, IA 50336-1016

If you would like to order any of our hardcover Collector's Edition books, please call us at: 1-800-327-6388 (Monday through Friday, 7:00 a.m.–8:00 p.m. or Saturday, 7:00 a.m.–6:00 p.m. Central Time).

Endpapers A parchment page from *Processus Contra Templarios.* Published in limited edition by the Vatican in 2007, this is a replica of the long-lost official transcript, with Pope Clement V's verdict, of the 1308 trial of the Knights Templar on charges of heresy. As you'll learn in our pages, Clement put down the Templars and was instrumental in having many of the order's leaders killed. Nothing is easy in the secret world. Photograph by Eric Vandeville/Gamma/Getty

Page 1 Portrait of Aleister Crowley, courtesy Harry Price Library, University of London

Previous spread An 1872 ballot box, and other materials, from Yale's secretive Skull and Bones society. Photograph by Christie's/AP

This spread Copies of the Vatican-published replicas of *Processus Contra Templarios.* Photograph by Eric Vandeville/Gamma/Getty

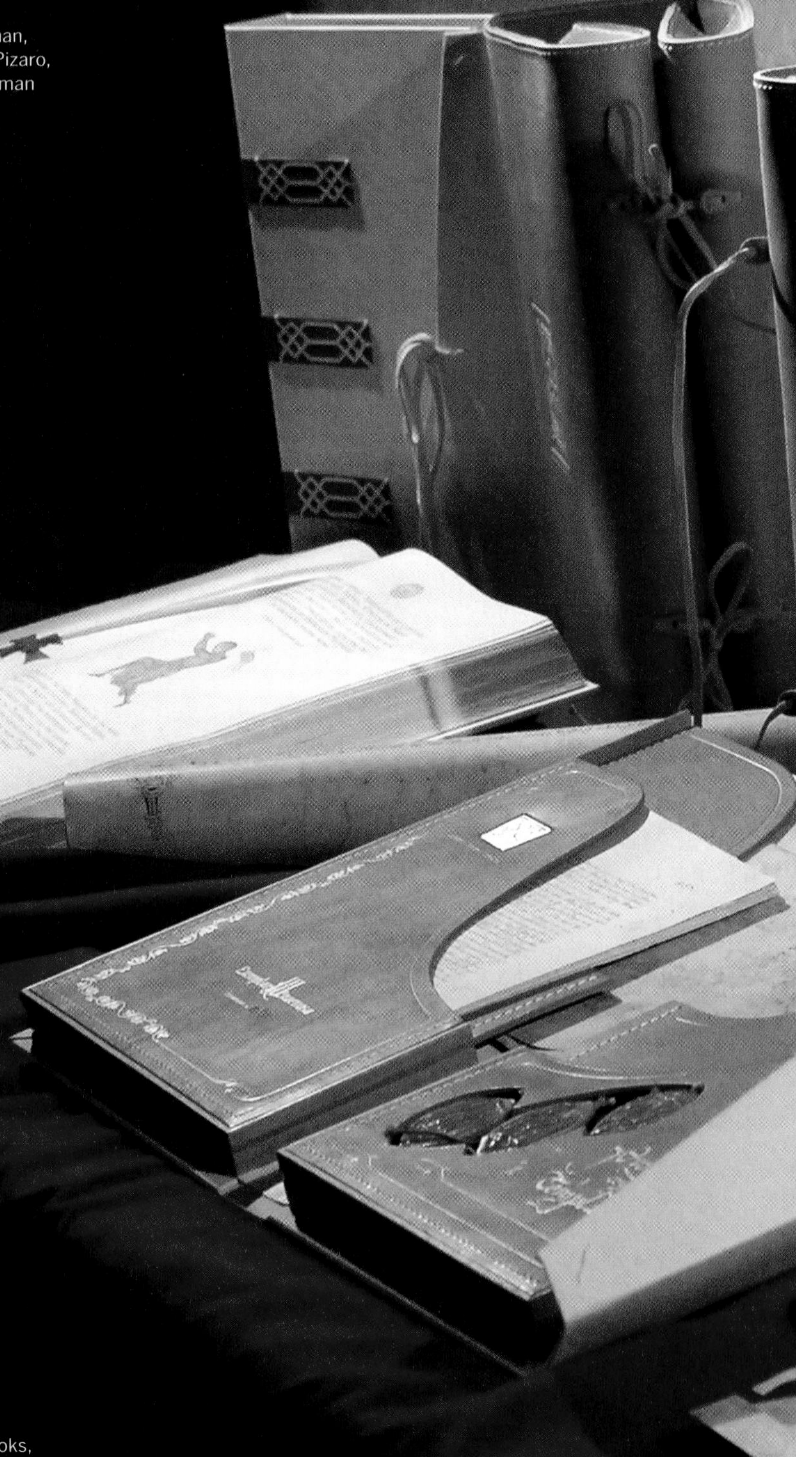

THE HIDDEN WORLD OF SECRET SOCIETIES

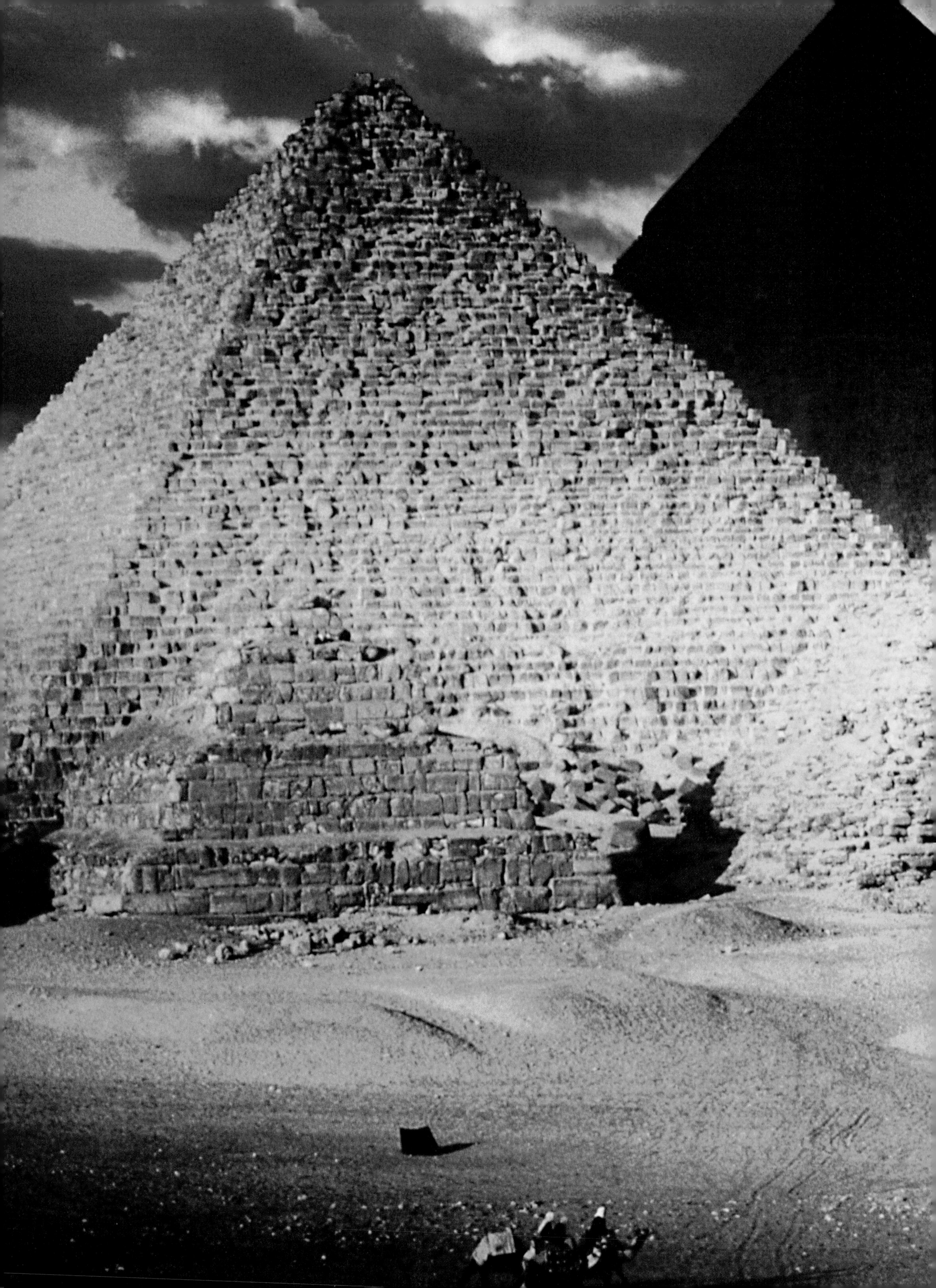

Introduction

WHAT'S ALL THIS ABOUT PYRAMIDS AND TRIANGLES?

THERE ARE THREE massive pyramids outside Cairo, Egypt, each of them climbing toward heaven, and one of them climbing higher than its brethren. The Great Pyramid of Khufu is the oldest of the Seven Wonders of the World, and the only ancient Wonder still standing. Fans of pyramidic symbolism will tell you that this cannot be by accident. The edifice endures, they are sure, for a profound reason.

JEAN-PIERRE LESCOURRET/CORBIS

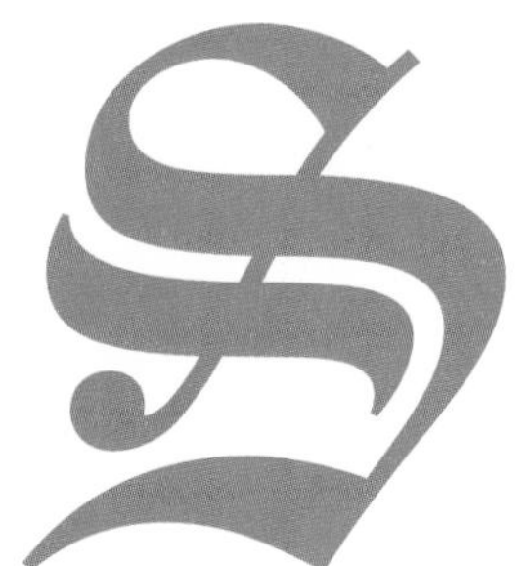*hhhhhhh.*

Don't tell a soul, but what you beheld on page six, which is of course the Great Pyramid at Giza, means much beyond what is immediately apparent in the photograph. Sure, as you know, it's a tomb: The famous Egyptian pharaoh Khufu, sometimes called Cheops, was supposed to be interred here (his remains have never been found), and in his day (circa 2551–2528 B.C.) he wanted a memorial beyond all others. So he ordered his people to erect in his honor what would become, after 20 years of toil, the tallest building on earth (it would retain that distinction for nearly 4,000 years). To get to such a height (481 feet), the pyramid shape was practical: a really solid foundation, a large base of more than 13 acres, and then sides that taper upwards. It can't fall over.

But it was more than just practical. It was, to those who were in the know (Khufu certainly among them), highly symbolic. A pyramid quite obviously resembles a mountain, and going to the mountaintop for guidance, whether in a pantheistic, polytheistic or monotheistic culture, is a journey worth taking. In this quest, the pilgrim ascends; in Egyptian culture, the king was given a leg up in reaching the gods above. At the top—a place that might be visited physically by climbing the 91 steps of a pyramid such as the one at Chichén Itzá in Mexico—or simply by contemplating any pyramidical structure from afar, one might find spiritual enlightenment. The pyramid, reaching up, seeks to unite the earthly and the divine. The summit is the point of connection.

People other than the pharaohs or the Maya of the Yucatán Peninsula interpreted the pyramid and its triangular shape differently. Pagans viewed a downward-pointing triangle as a symbol of the feminine, and an upward-pointing one as masculine. Other ascriptions, by the ancient Greeks, the early Christians and so many more, can be readily apprehended. A triangle was a physical representation of the sacred number three—a representation of family (father, mother and child, or the male and female and their ability to procreate); or the Father, the Son and the Holy Spirit; or the sky, the earth and all creatures living thereupon; or marriage (a union when two become one); or conversely an idea that one, perhaps God, becomes all; or even the Robert Frost angle: a road not

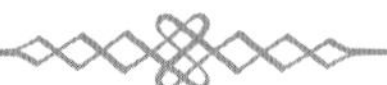

EL CASTILLO, nearly a hundred feet high, is the dominant structure in Chichén Itzá in Mexico. Outside Khartoum, Sudan, there are more than 200 pyramids in the ruins of the ancient city of Meroe.

JEAN-PIERRE LESCOURRET/CORBIS

ANDREW MCCONNELL/ROBERT HARDING/CORBIS

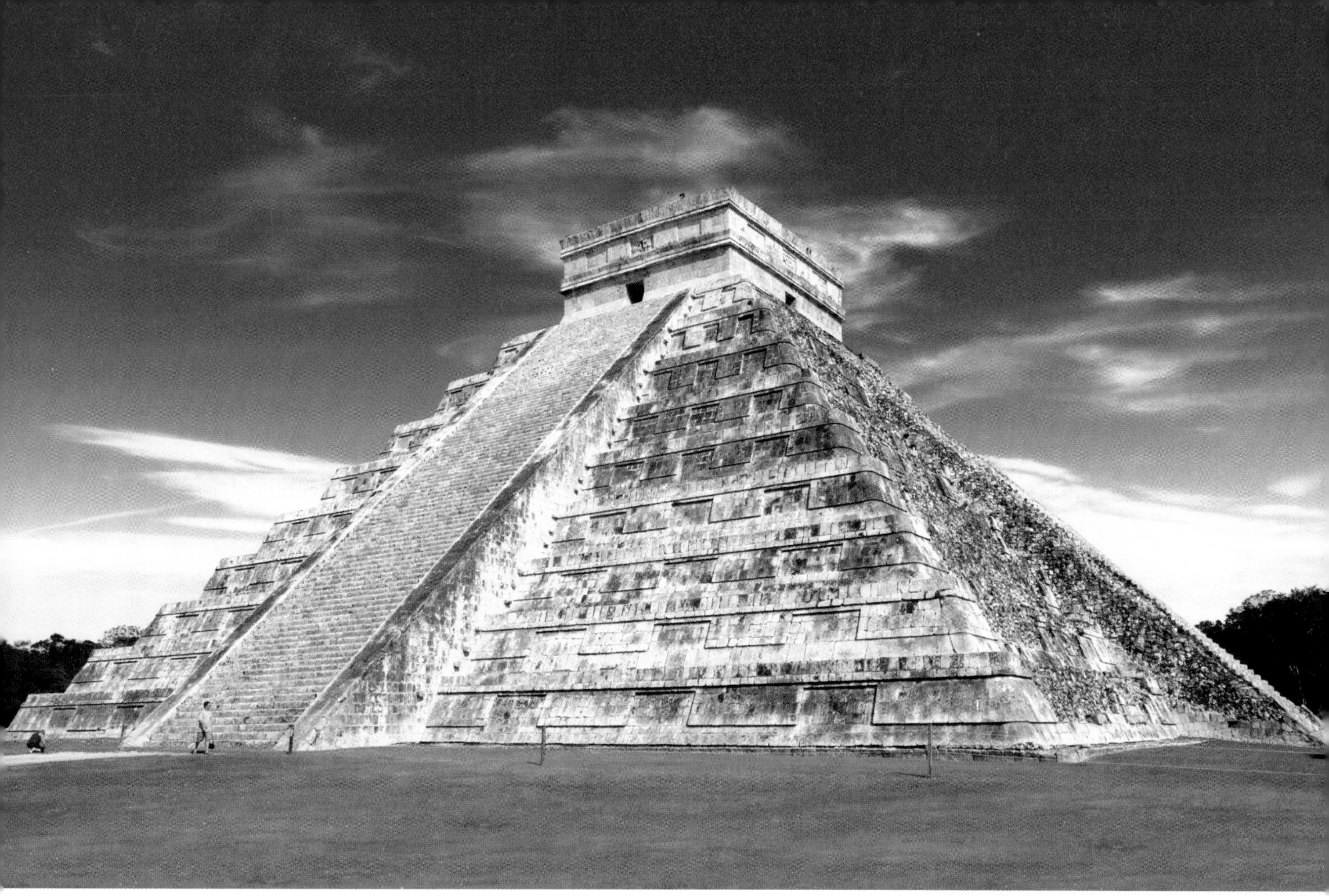

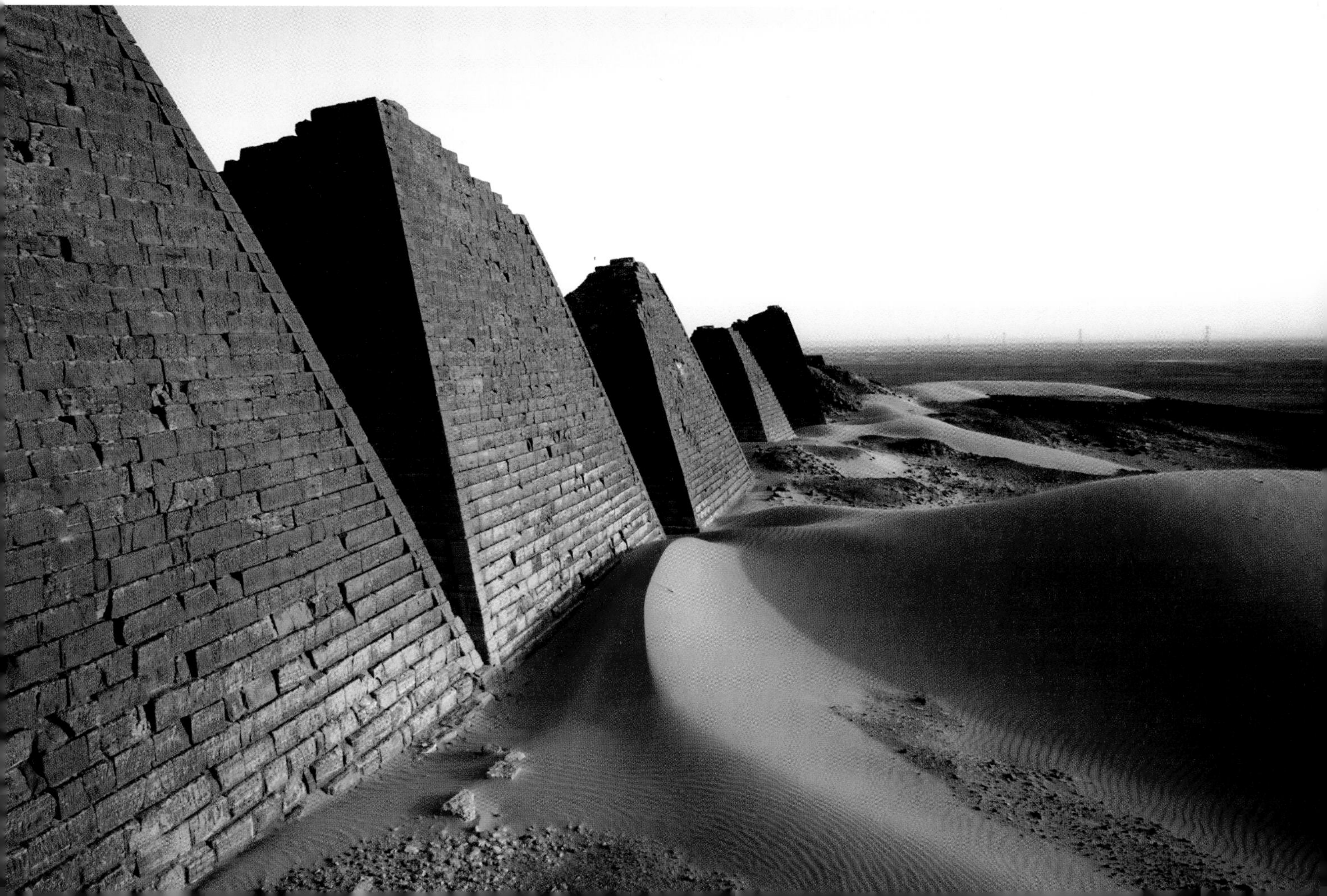

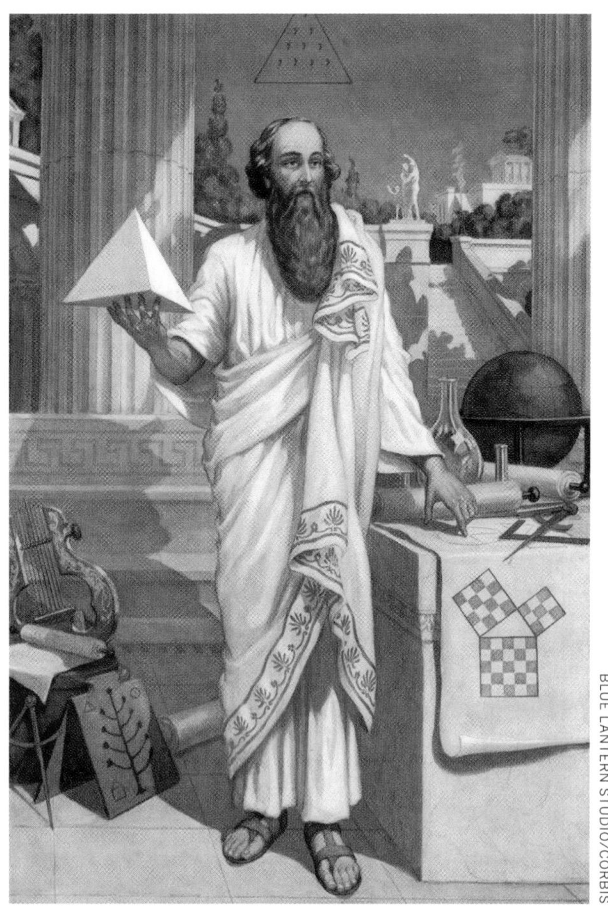
BLUE LANTERN STUDIO/CORBIS

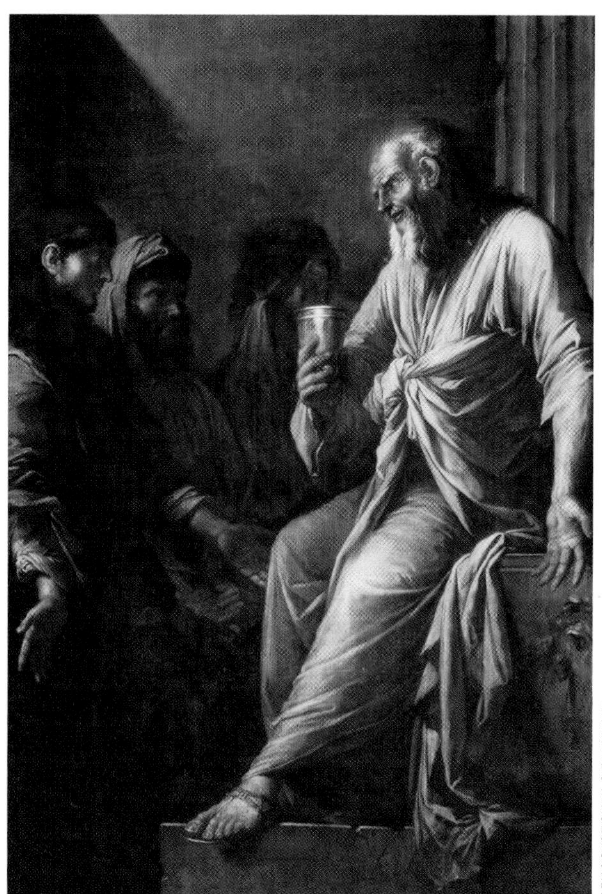
CHRISTIE'S IMAGES/CORBIS

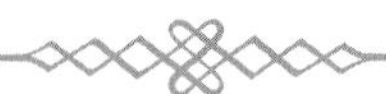

PYTHAGORAS (left) was a man of mathematics and interconnectivity, and therefore an inspiration for scientists and societies that followed. Socrates was a deep thinker—too deep, perhaps, for his own good.

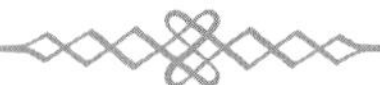

taken, wherein we are always at a certain point in life and must choose which way to go.

Most of this triangular imagery is for the good, some of it is holy, and much of it was appropriated by one secret society or another through the centuries (and also by the United States of America, on the back of the dollar bill). Other societies took other symbols—the Christian cross was on the mantle of the Knights Templar; the swastika has meant something through the years to one culture or another; the "all-seeing eye," most often associated with the Illuminati is also on the dollar bill—but the point here is symbology and fraternity, and nothing dominates that discussion like the pyramid or triangle. This is about a signaling. Whether we are signaling to God, whether He is signaling to us, whether we are signaling to Nature, whether Nature is signaling to us, or whether we are signaling to one another, the message is: *I get it. I'm in. I'm with you. I've got your back. You can count on me.*

The New York Yankees of the world's secret societies are perhaps the Freemasons (or Masons). They have long had as their uppermost symbol (of many, including things like beehives), the triangle. The Masonic interpretation of the three-sided polygon will be parsed later in these pages. The point just now is: These signs and symbols have been intended, since time immemorial, to mean something to someone, and to bind someone to someone else. They have served to unite the secret-bearers, who then, once joined as like-thinkers, did good works or bad (the Ku Klux Klan chose triangular hoods). You'll see a lot of signs and symbols in the pages ahead. When you do . . .

Shhhhhhh.

As will be made clear in this book, there have been and are many different levels of secrecy, from strictly secret to hardly secret, in the history of secret societies. And there are many different levels of weirdness, from barely to extremely. Having said that: If half of what you read on the pages forthcoming is true, we are living in a bizarre and dangerous world. (Which of course we are.)

If *most* of it is true, then immediately beware.

Even, in cases: Be afraid. Be very afraid.

Now, is that the right tone? Certainly we at LIFE Books are not here to make sport of secret societies. We are not about to bite the hand that feeds us, with this particular volume. Some of us on the staff have belonged to more or less secret societies ourselves (Yo, Casque and Gauntlet!). And one of the reasons for writing and publishing this book is: Secret societies are very cool. They always have been—that's what makes them enticing and sometimes worth joining. They are inherently inscrutable, intimidating, unsettling, sexy and, therefore, taken altogether, a whole lot of fun to try to figure out. Ask Dan Brown. Also, for us at LIFE: They present a visual challenge, which we always love, because many of them, by virtue of their secrecy, don't offer themselves eagerly to photography.

The challenge having been thrown down by these many clubs, associations, mobs, "councils" and "commissions," we said to ourselves: Okay, let's see what we can find.

You, dear reader, have in your hands a 128-page book filled with pictures. What do you think? You, as if presiding at a closed-door conclave, can be the ultimate judge.

What we have found in looking at the universe of secret societies is that there exist (or once existed) associations of various degrees of seriousness: movements of significance, benevolence, malevolence or simply bonhomie. That seems to be the bottom line when looking at secret societies. Each of them has a linear raison d'être, and whether that is seen as worthwhile (even with such societies as the Klan) rests entirely in the mind of the beholder.

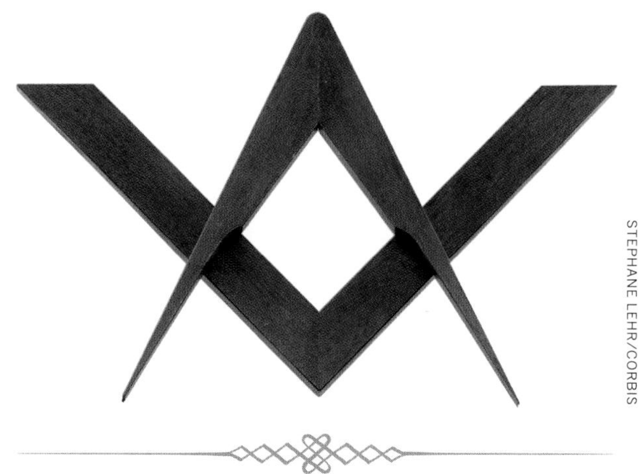

STEPHANE LEHR/CORBIS

THE TRIANGLE has long represented the Deity in symbolic form. That is what the Masons and many other societies have seen in it, and why they consider it essential.

We also found that the tradition of secret societies is older than Methuselah, and some of the institutions that we rightly revere today in the cultural, religious or political mainstream grew from societies that were once, by necessity, secret. What was the most successful secret society of the first, second and third centuries A.D.? Well, that would be Christianity. There you go.

This is an interesting subject, and not just from an "oh wow!" perspective.

Then again, it sure is "oh wow!" at regular turns.

The 19th century historian Charles William Heckethorn spilled an awful lot of ink on this subject when he published two large volumes of *The Secret Societies of All Ages and Countries* in 1875 and 1896, and his initial Author's Introduction remains a useful framing device:

"1. *Intelligibility and Nature of Secret Societies*—Secret Societies once were as necessary as open societies: the tree presupposes a root. Beside the empire of Might, the idols of fortune, the fetishes of superstition, there must in every age and state have existed a place where the empire of Might was at an end, where the idols were no longer worshipped, where the fetishes were derided. Such a place was the closet of the philosopher, the temple of the priest, the subterranean cave of the sectary.

"2. *Classification of Secret Societies*—Secret societies may be classed under the following heads: 1. Religious: such as the Egyptian or Eleusinian Mysteries. 2. Military: Knights Templars. 3. Judiciary: Vehmgerichte. 4. Scientific: Alchymists.

5. Civil: Freemasons. 6. Political: Carbonari. 7. Anti-Social: Garduna. But the line of division is not always strictly defined . . ."

And Heckethorn goes on and on.

He does so authoritatively, and he's dead right: The line of division is not always strictly defined—the militaristic Knights Templar had a fierce religious component, for instance—and the overarching principle that unifies the classifications is, as Heckethorn says, a response to authority and orthodoxy. The secret folk figured they simply *had* to do this. They were compelled to think and feel this way, and therefore they needed to go underground, because to exist aboveground would have led to an end, or at least to big trouble.

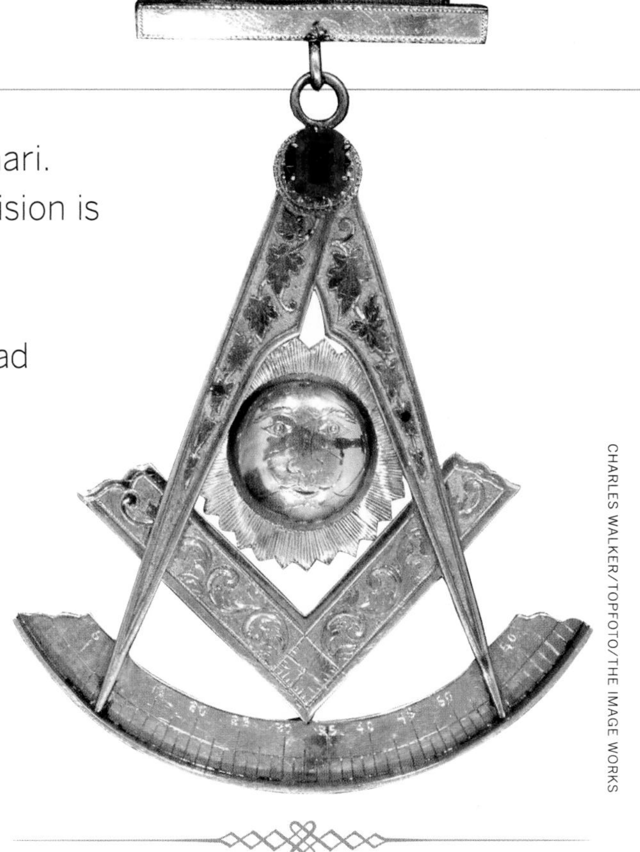

CHARLES WALKER/TOPFOTO/THE IMAGE WORKS

THE MASONIC SQUARE and compass, architect's tools, represent restraint, order, skill and knowledge. Without their use, a whole form—a consubstantiated life—cannot be made.

Consider, to return to the provocative example put forth earlier, the Christian movement: A zealot in what we now call the Holy Land had been crucified. But this, his followers felt, was no ordinary zealot. In his person and in his teachings he was extraordinary—a philosopher king and even a holy man. In fact, the Son of God. In the decades after Jesus, the Gospel writers Mark, Matthew and Luke constructed their biographies, the disciple Peter made his way to Rome, and the convert Paul spread the word. The cult of Christ grew stronger in the shadows. In many parts of the Roman Empire, it was deadly dangerous to be a Christian, and only martyrs openly professed themselves. Religious services were held in the dark, communicants whispering their prayers. In relatively short order (three centuries not being an undue period of time for the growth of an institution as mighty as Christianity), Jesus' importance in civilized society was manifest, and in A.D. 313, Constantine, who would himself become a convert, issued the Edict of Milan, which proclaimed religious tolerance in Rome and essentially allowed and encouraged his empire to become Christian.

No other secret societies are or have been the equal of Christianity (although more than a couple, including the recently famous Opus Dei, have been

Christian). But they have moved about furtively and in clandestine fashion. They have gathered themselves, always feeling on the outs and, as said at the beginning, *in the know.* They have recruited like-minded members by whispering.

Shhhhhhh.

What secret societies have hid from through the centuries were, as Charles Heckethorn says, religious, military, judicial, scientific, civil, political or social establishments (which is essentially the complete menu). They have had, in each case, their reasons to hide—and some of them still do today.

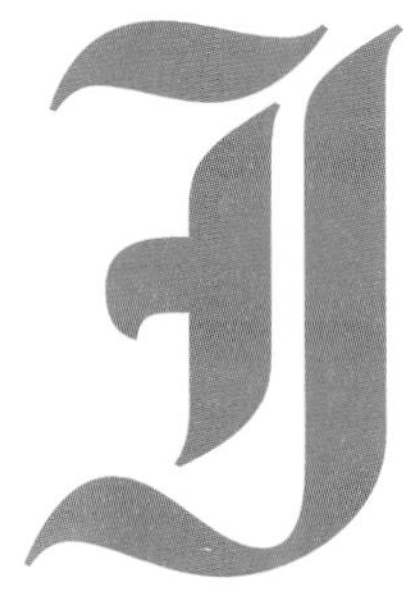

mplicit in Heckethorn: We can suppose that ever since Eve said "*Psst*—try the apple?" people have been attempting to keep secrets from figures of authority and power. It is human nature. We do not know which Neanderthal tribes were particularly inclined to such subterfuge, but we can assume there were some. Hunting, gathering, cooking a nice meal, piling up goods, cheering for a sports team and forming a secret club: These are very high on the homo scale, and probably always have been.

There is an exotic word, *chthonic,* that derives from the Greek and means "under the earth." It is regularly applied to ancient cults that existed in opposition to the then standard view of the world, a view that involved a pantheon of gods, headed by Zeus, who existed on Mount Olympus. The dissidents in these chthonic organizations met and reveled in hard-to-find spaces, unwittingly establishing rules of decorum for all secret societies to follow. Ben Franklin's Freemasons, Rudolf Hess's Thules, Henry Kissinger's Bohemian Grove buddies and Ralph Kramden's Raccoons all owe a debt of gratitude to the chthonic cults, at least in terms of how a secret society might reasonably (so to speak) disport. These organizations much enjoyed their private rituals and dances. A hallmark handshake is presupposed, as are symbols—pyramids, triangles and such.

We don't know a whole lot about the various chthonic cults, but we do understand their Greek descendant societies, the *mysteria,* or so-called "mystery religions." (Our word *mystery* derives from the Greek *myein,* which means, interestingly for our current purposes, "to initiate.") These were gatherings of people that were seen, by their participants, as elevated above others, more important than, for instance, general—public—religious observances. The conclaves involved teachings, dances, hymns and prayers exclusive to their memberships. The Eleusinian Mysteries, begun in 700 B.C. and

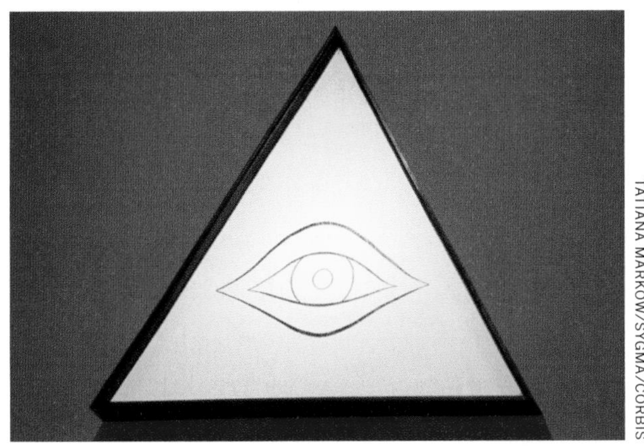
TATIANA MARKOW/SYGMA/CORBIS

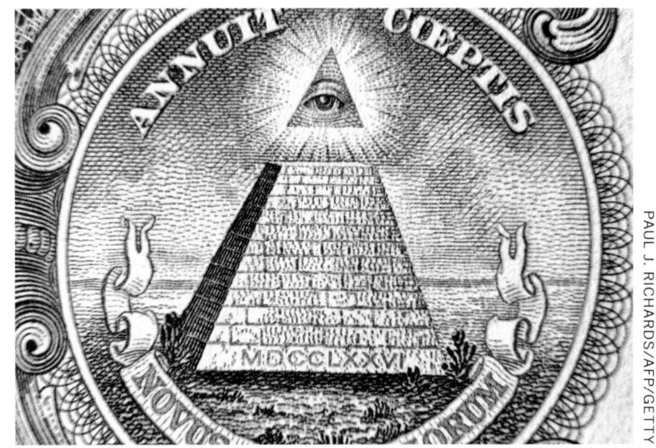

PAUL J. RICHARDS/AFP/GETTY

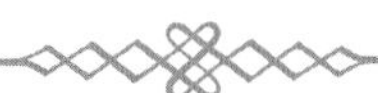

IT IS CALLED the all-seeing eye, or the Eye of Providence, and, often ensconced in a triangle, is usually interpreted as God peering over his creation. It has been important to the Illuminati, the Masons and the United States of America. It graces our nation's Great Seal and the reverse side of our dollar bill.

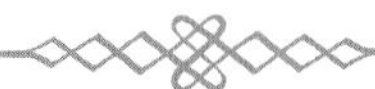

in existence for more than a millennium (until Emperor Theodosius I suppressed non-Christian religions), are perhaps the best known today. The Apollonian Oracle at Delphi, with its high priestess Pythia, was a related society, and would be referenced by the secretive Templars, Masons, Rosicrucians and others.

What did these mystery religions care about? For the most part, good things, such as spiritual growth. And untouchable things, such as life after death.

Do understand: It was not just the plebeian class that was drawn to these secret societies. The intelligentsia not only joined them, they inspired them. Pythagoras was a philosopher born circa 570 B.C. in Samos, and his brilliant blend of mathematical genius and mysticism was intoxicating to many. In his wake grew the Pythagorean Brotherhood: Members swore a solemn oath on the *tetractys*, a sacred triangle; signed over all their worldly goods; assumed a five-year vow of silence; and dedicated themselves to social and political reform.

The Pythagoreans cherished several notions, including the immortality of the soul, the value of virtue and the importance of rationality: that mathematical science, especially as evinced in geometry and trigonometry, underpins our world.

Born a century after Pythagoras was Socrates, and his experience as well as that of Pythagoras shows that almost as quickly as secret societies established themselves as a religious element in Greek culture, they branched out beyond a discussion of God alone to philosophy (more generally) and to science. Socrates, according to his student Plato, said that virtue certainly could be attained from Nature, but also by initiation. He was all-in on virtue, a principal tenet of the mystery religions. In fact, he extolled virtue above all—even above state. He would be condemned for this unwavering faith. According to Plato, he once said, "And I conceive that the founders of the mysteries had a real meaning and were not mere triflers when they intimated in a figure long ago that he who passes unsanctified and uninitiated into the world below will live in a slough, but that he who arrives there after initiation and purification will dwell with the gods. For 'many,' as they say in the mysteries, 'are the thyrsus bearers, but few are the mystics'—meaning, as I interpret the words, the true philosophers." Those around him were disquieted by these "mysteries," and so they arrested Socrates, charged him with blasphemy and corrupting the young, and they convicted and killed him. (Well, actually: They asked, rather forcefully, that he kill himself. He did so, with a potion of tea laced with hemlock.)

As we see, although the operative word is, of course, *secret,* its synonymous partner in this story is *mystery.* By the time the Templars, who were united as a militaristic club by their monasticism and sense of chivalry, were hacking people apart in the Christian Crusades of the 11th and 12th centuries, they were fully out in the open, certainly—but they still harbored secrets. The Templars were bloody-minded folk, as were the Hashishin (the Assassins), the Garduna, the Thuggee, the Tongs, the Black Hand, the Knights of the Golden Circle, the Klan, the Irish Republican Brotherhood (which later evolved into the Irish Republican Army), the Thule Society and the Mafia. The Sons of Liberty was a political secret society before our Revolutionary War brought it into the light of day. Also taking themselves seriously indeed were the Illuminati, the Masons, the Rosicrucians: We'll meet them all soon. Then you had your weirdo cults; we'll meet them too. On college campuses beginning in the 19th century, social organizations formed in emulation of these many legendary groups, and hijinks became part of the secret society modus operandi. Some kids never grow up, and so today we have the Bohemian Club. It is for, *ahem,* adults.

Now we will begin to roll out these many societies, in all their strangeness. Remember: Whatever you learn, beginning as your turn the page . . . *Shhhhhhh.*

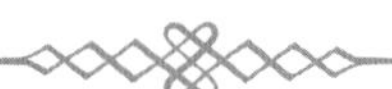

MODERNISM: At the Louvre Museum in Paris, a glass pyramid glows. In San Francisco, the Transamerica Pyramid stretches toward the sky, just as Khufu's pyramid at Giza continues to each day.

ARNAUD CHICUREL/HEMIS/CORBIS

BOB ROWAN/PROGRESSIVE IMAGE/CORBIS

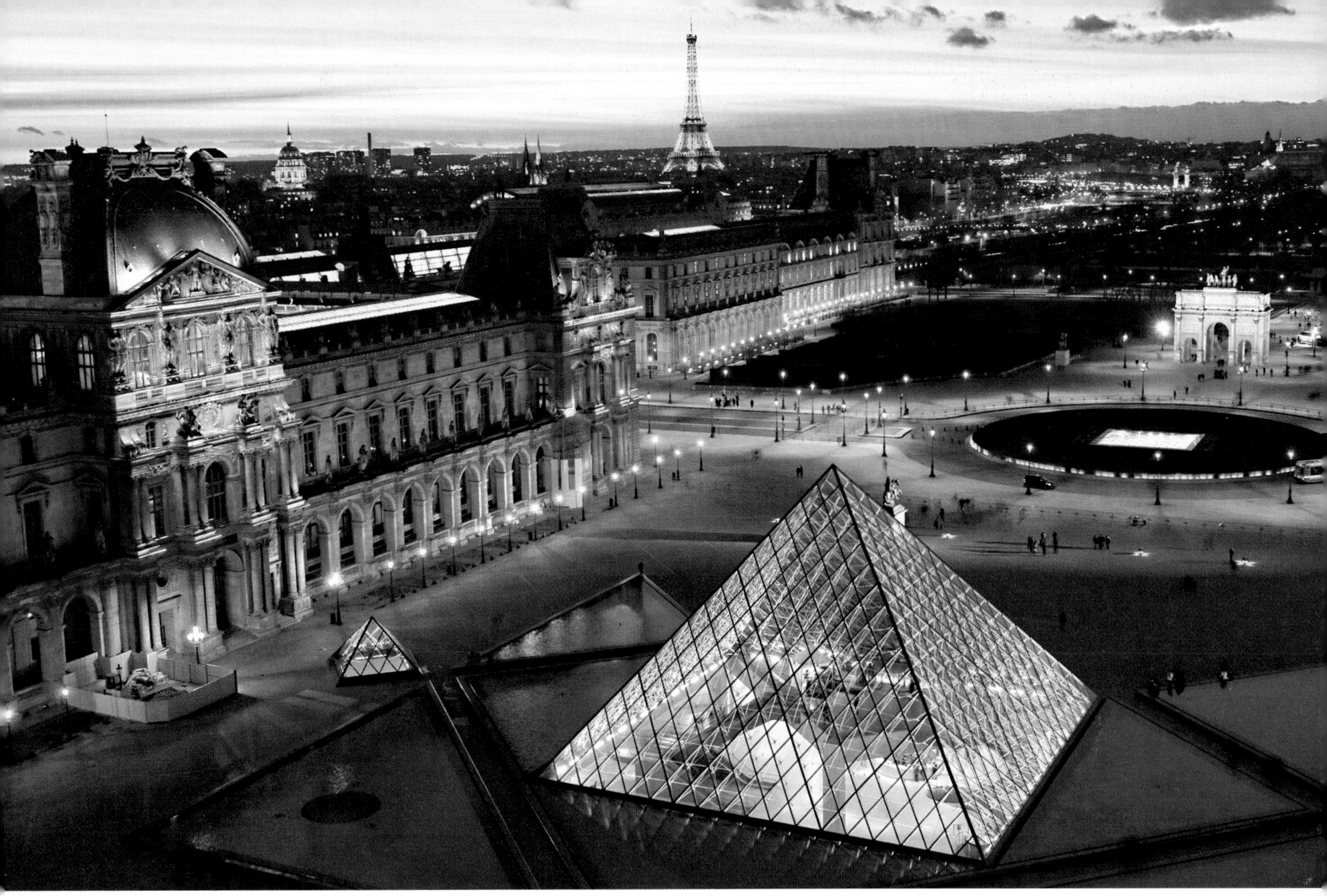

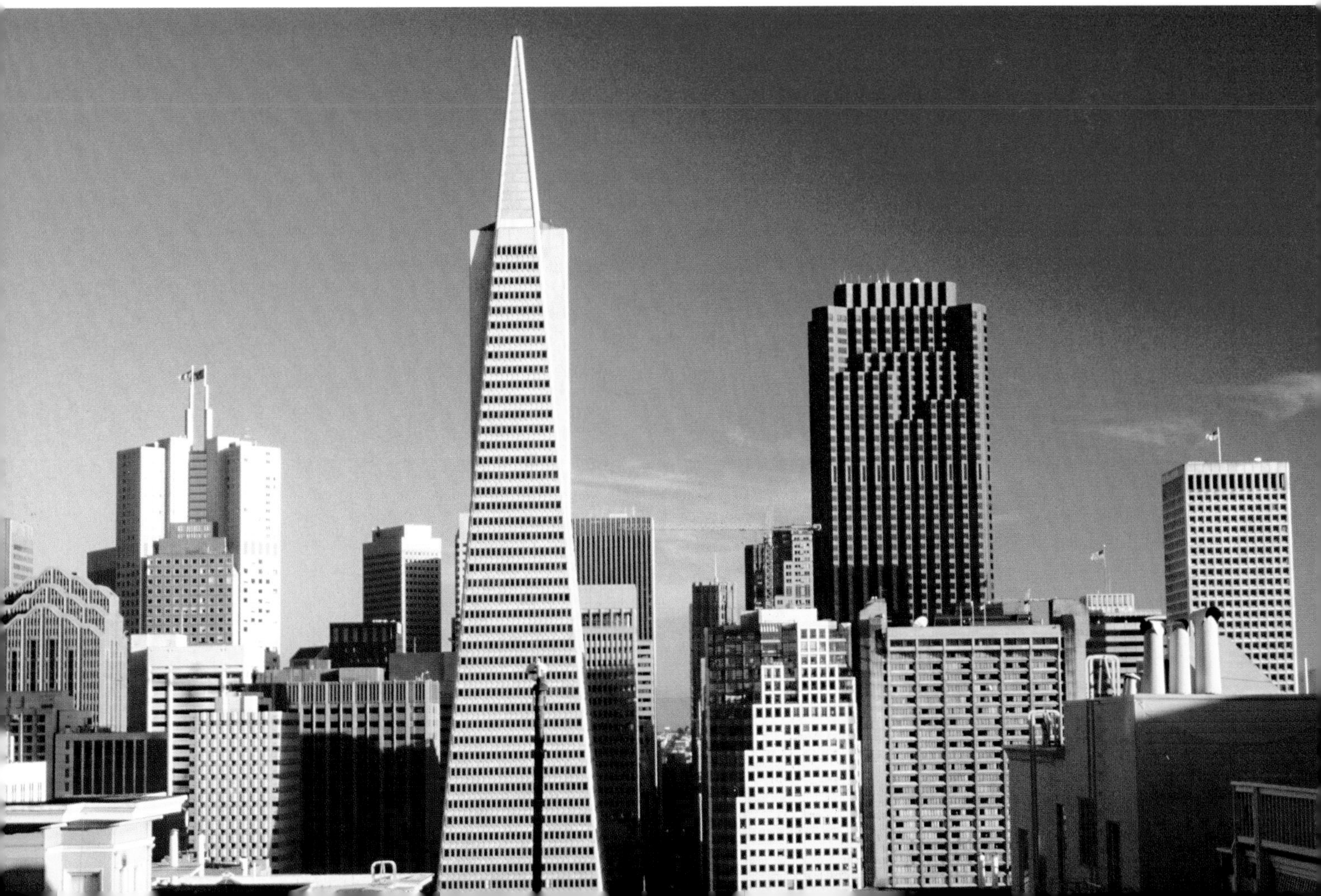

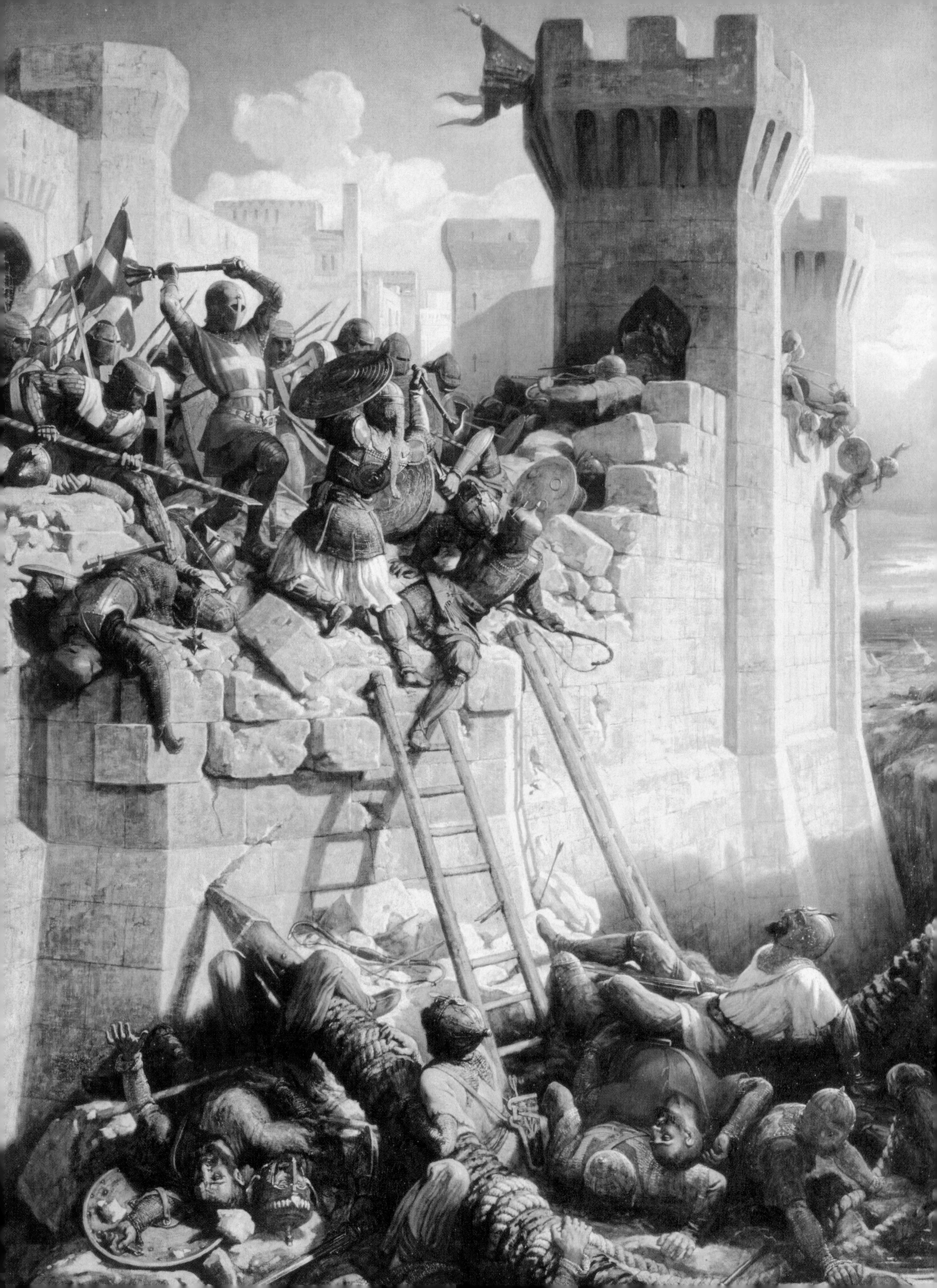

Chapter 1

BACK IN THE DAY

THIS 19TH CENTURY painting depicts a very bad 13th century day for the Knights Templar, of whom we will learn much more beginning on page 24. They were energetic Christian warriors during the Crusades and had several military triumphs in the Middle East beginning in the second half of the 1100s. But by now the Muslims are on the move against the Templars, and are here storming their headquarters in Acre. After that fortress falls in 1291, the Templars retreat to Cyprus and their end is nigh. As soon as they are gone—within only two centuries of their founding—legends of their secrets begin to rise. They become more famous in afterlife than they were in life itself.

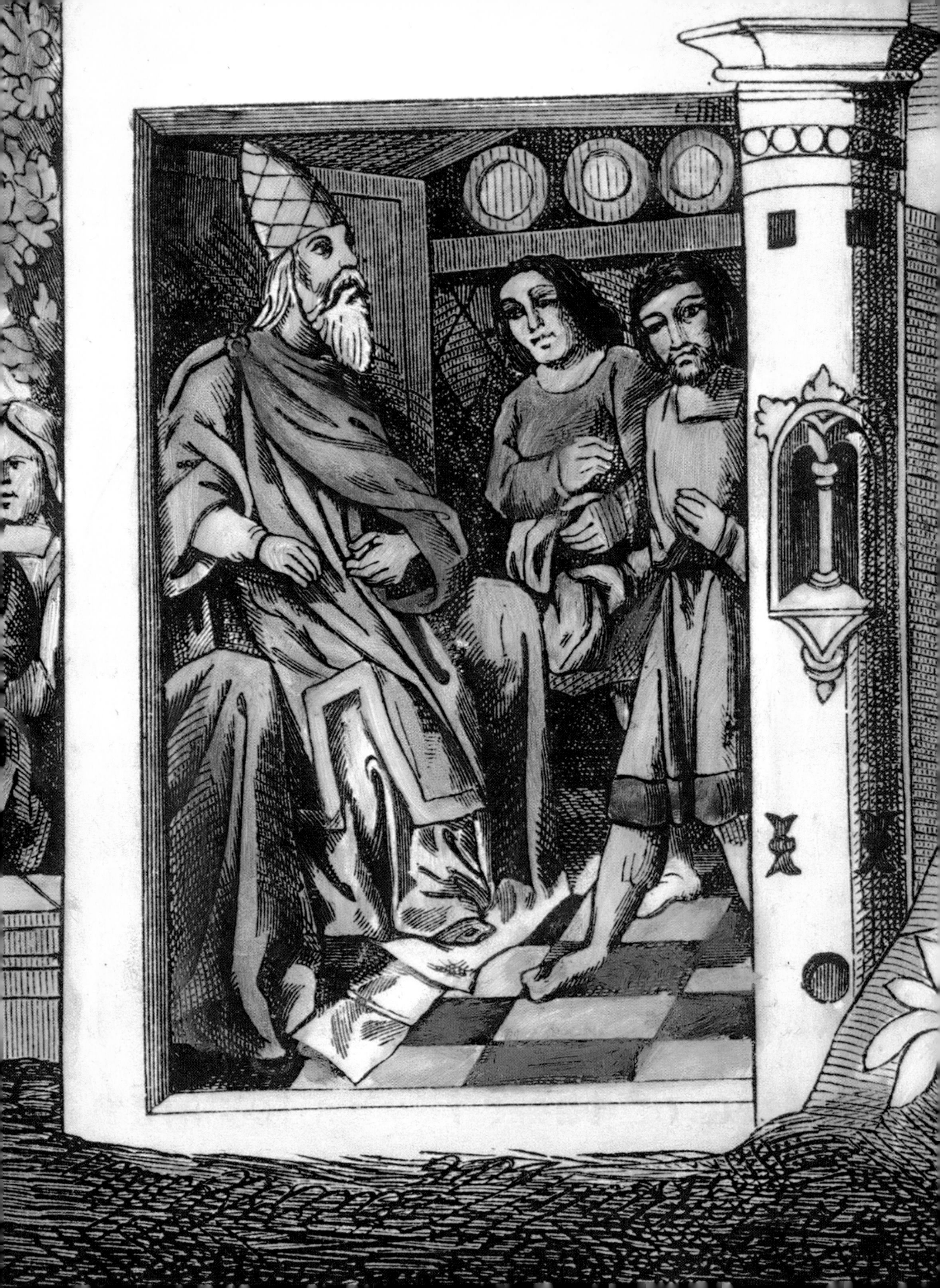

The Assassins

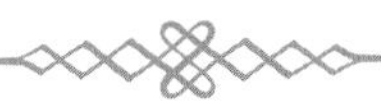

Now then, if you have not done so already, check your belief systems at the door. The world you are about to enter is more packed with mythologies than King Arthur's Camelot. Also, the rules and traditions of secret societies—benevolent or malevolent—are generally uniform, and later-forming societies have sought credibility by linking, either philosophically or genealogically, to those of yore.

As our book's introduction implies, there were hundreds if not thousands of ancient secret societies, most of them unknown to us, but we have to start somewhere in this survey and it is good to start with the Assassins. They are a fascinating and historically durable entry, which is to say: They really existed, and exerted real power and influence. In fact, if some secret societies aficionados are to be believed, the Assassins' heritage endures in the present day, handed down through the Templars, thence the neo-Templars and the Masons, and all the many who have claimed association with the Masons.

Much of their legend—secret initiations, hashish eating, obsessive devotion to their leader, a general wantonness (the Assassins' Creed: "Nothing is true, everything is permitted")—was largely built by their enemies in the schismatic Islamic world of the 11th, 12th and 13th centuries, then reached the wider world beyond Persia when such as Marco Polo brought back the wild tales.

The group's founder was named Hasan-i Sabbah, whose headquarters were in a fortress named Alamut in the mountains of northern Persia. The name *Hashishin* would be corrupted in English as "assassin"; they gave us the word. How and why? Well, Hasan had many enemies but few soldiers. He pioneered a means of warfare wherein stealth killings substituted for larger operations. As Bernard Lewis wrote in *The Assassins: A Radical Sect in Islam,* "Hasan found a new way, by which a small force, disciplined and devoted, could strike effectively against an overwhelmingly superior enemy."

The Hashishin were not done in by Islamic rivals but by the Mongol hordes that overran Persia in the 13th century. By then, the Assassins had established a reputation that would inform all secret societies to follow.

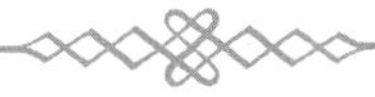

HASAN-I SABBAH gives instructions—or perhaps secrets—to his devoted followers at Alamut. It was alleged that he had his men under some kind of spell, perhaps enforced by drugs, and that they would willingly martyr themselves by plunging from the parapets if Hasan asked—which he would sometimes do for effect. He and all subsequent leaders of the Assassins would be known throughout the Middle East as the Old Man of the Mountain, and this too added to the group's intimidating legend because it made the organization's otherwise-unnamed leader seem immortal.

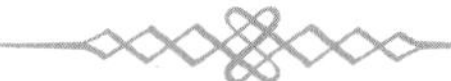

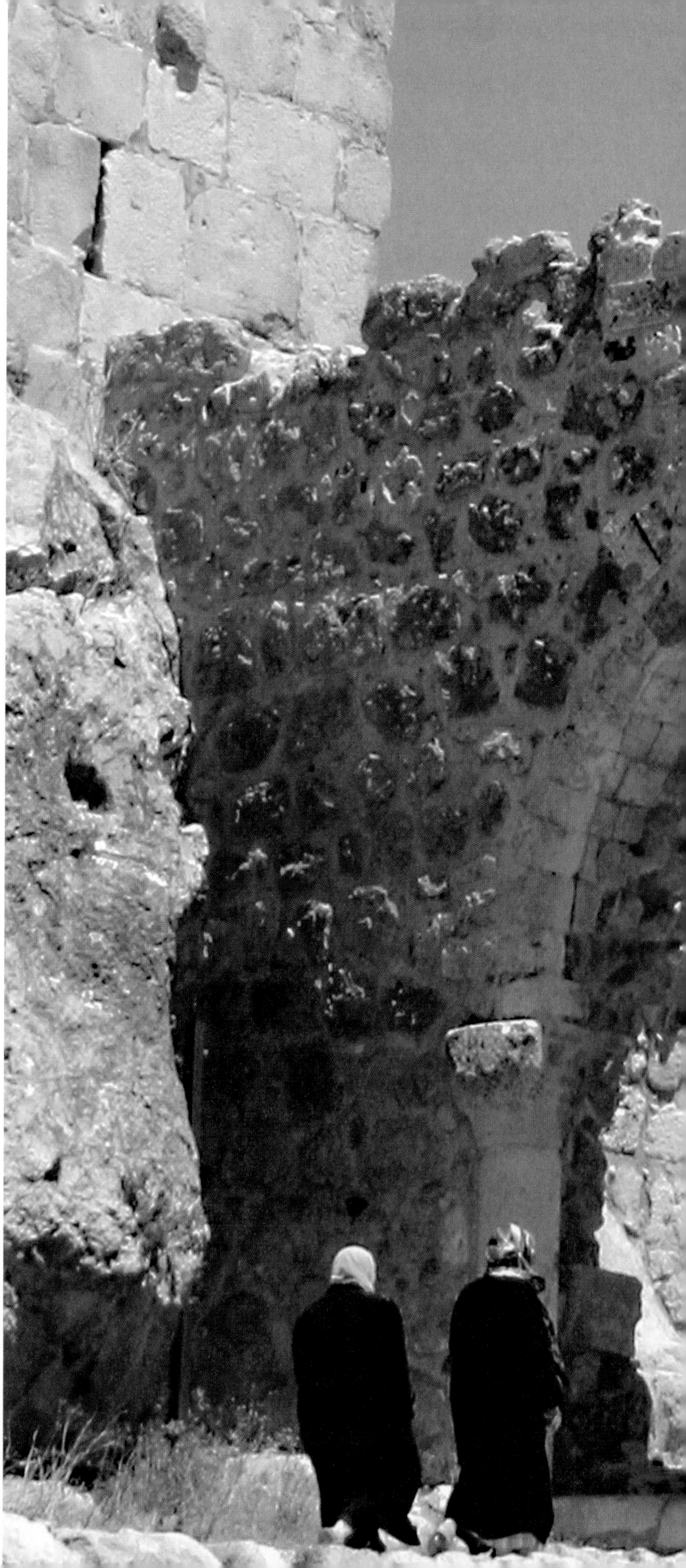

TWO WOMEN approach the main gate of Masyaf citadel in western Syria; the pathway to the formidable castle has been cleared during modern-day restoration and excavation work, and the site is open to tourists and scholars interested in the Assassins. The Byzantines were the first to build here, but it was the Assassins of the 12th century who greatly enlarged the fortress. Among their improvements was a grand throne room, from which the Old Man of the Mountain would preside. In 1256, the Mongols, under direction from Genghis Khan's grandson Hulagu, razed the fortifications.

REUTERS/CORBIS

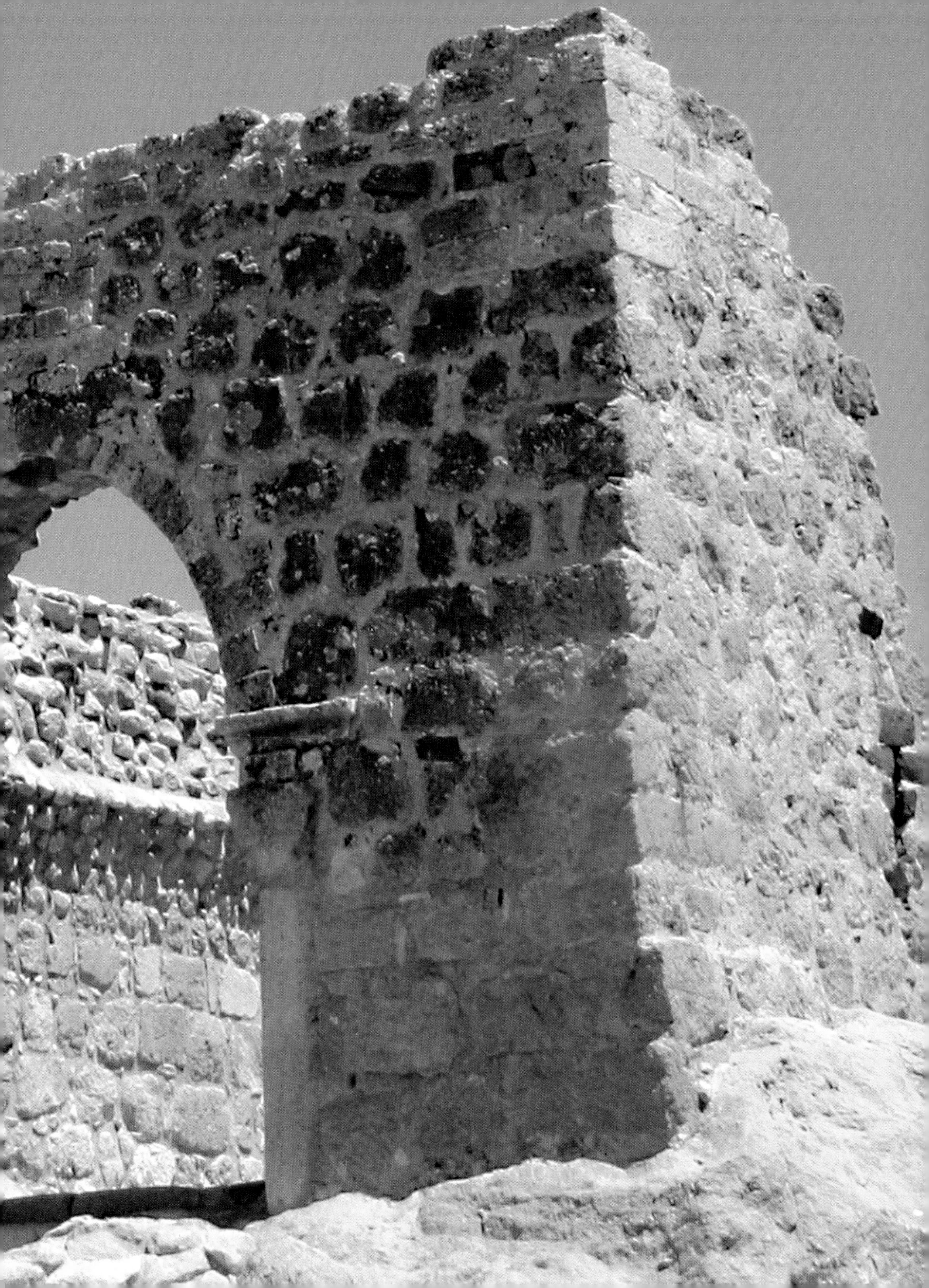

The Knights Templar

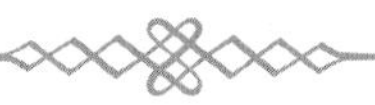

As with the Assassins, whom they certainly met during the tumultuous 12th and 13th centuries in the Holy Land, the Knights Templar had both a religious aspect and a militaristic one.

Europeans all, the first nine knights came together in Jerusalem circa 1118–1119 to protect Christian pilgrims. Their base was in the Temple Mount compound, and they dubbed themselves the Poor Fellow-Soldiers of Christ and of the Temple of Solomon. Their vows were of chastity, obedience and poverty, but this last soon yielded as their reputation grew, their ranks swelled (to a thousand "brother knights" and thousands more of lesser ranks) and contributions from back home to fund their Crusading efforts against the Muslims made them a mighty (and mighty rich) army. Their renown and influence—and holdings—spread throughout Europe as well as in the Holy Land. Then came their end. In 1187, Saladin's Islamic warriors captured Jerusalem. It was retaken in 1229 but fell again in 1244. The Templars set up headquarters in Acre, but that fell, too, in 1291 (please see painting, page 18). They fought on, but within a decade were routed.

When the Holy Land was lost, the Templars became vulnerable to their foes; and one who moved against them was King Philip IV of France, who conspired with Pope Clement V in declaring the Templars heretics. Charges started flying: They were sexual perverts; they were occultists, Satanists; they worshipped not Christ but the demon Baphomet; they had conspired with Islam. (In fact, they were cordial with the Assassins, but that group was hardly as engaged in the Crusades as were other Islamist sects.) Philip had the Templars in France rounded up; around 60 would be executed, most prominent among them the order's last Grand Master, Jacques de Molay, whose death in 1314 marks the end of the Templars.

Once they'd been branded as bizarre during their persecution in France, the rumors of plots and subplots proliferated. Today, many people believe the Templars' treasure (and maybe the Ark of the Covenant or the Holy Grail) is buried in Jerusalem, that survivors fled to Scotland and set up shop there or that the Templars discovered America. The Templars rival the Freemasons as the most famous secret society of all time.

And they probably weren't a secret society at all but just a military outfit. And even if they were: They closed up shop early in the 14th century.

OPPOSITE: Jacques de Molay, sporting the Templar insignia of a red cross on a field of white, was burned at the stake in France in 1314, two years after Pope Clement was forced by King Philip to dissolve the order.

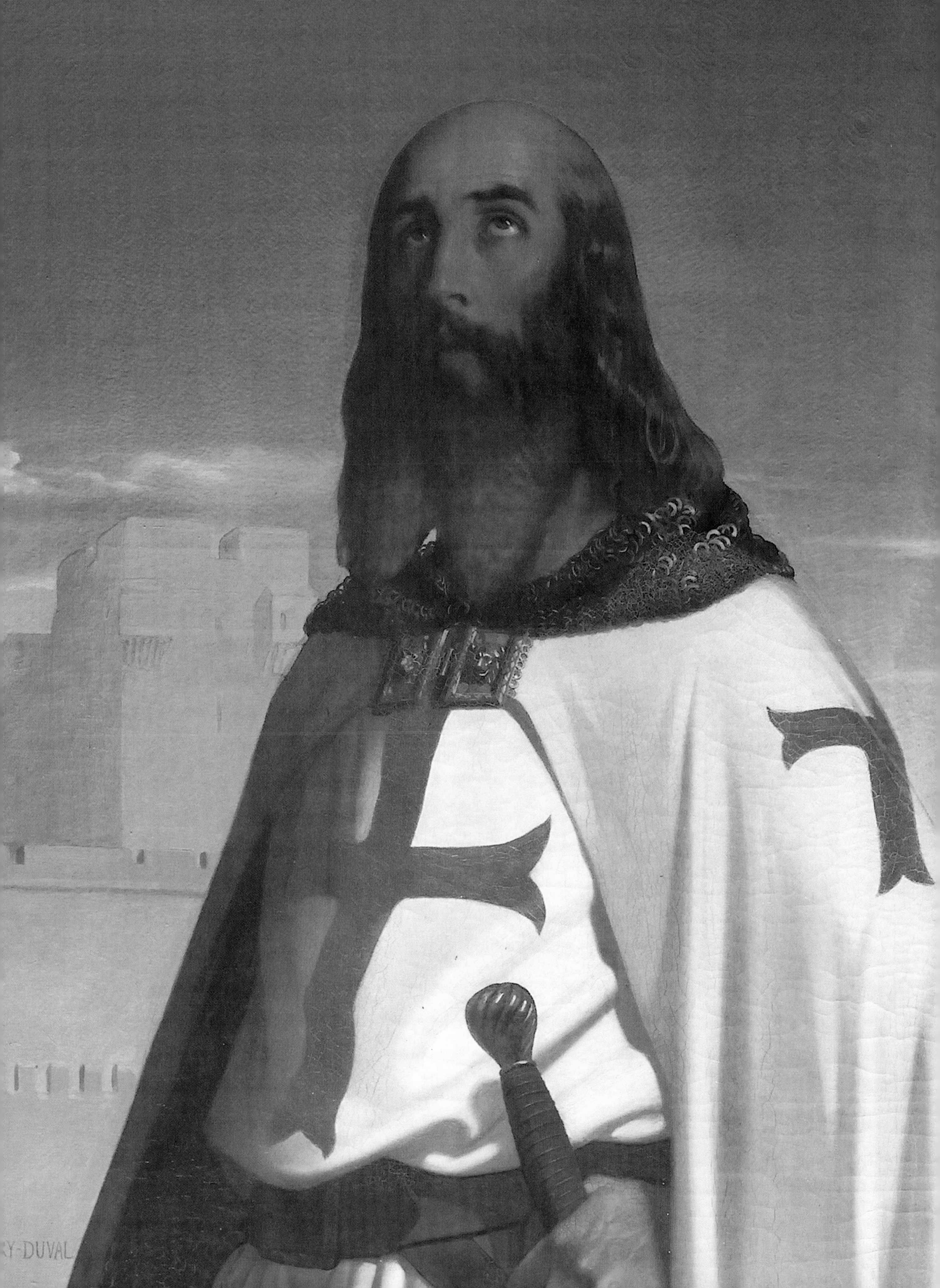
RY-DUVAL

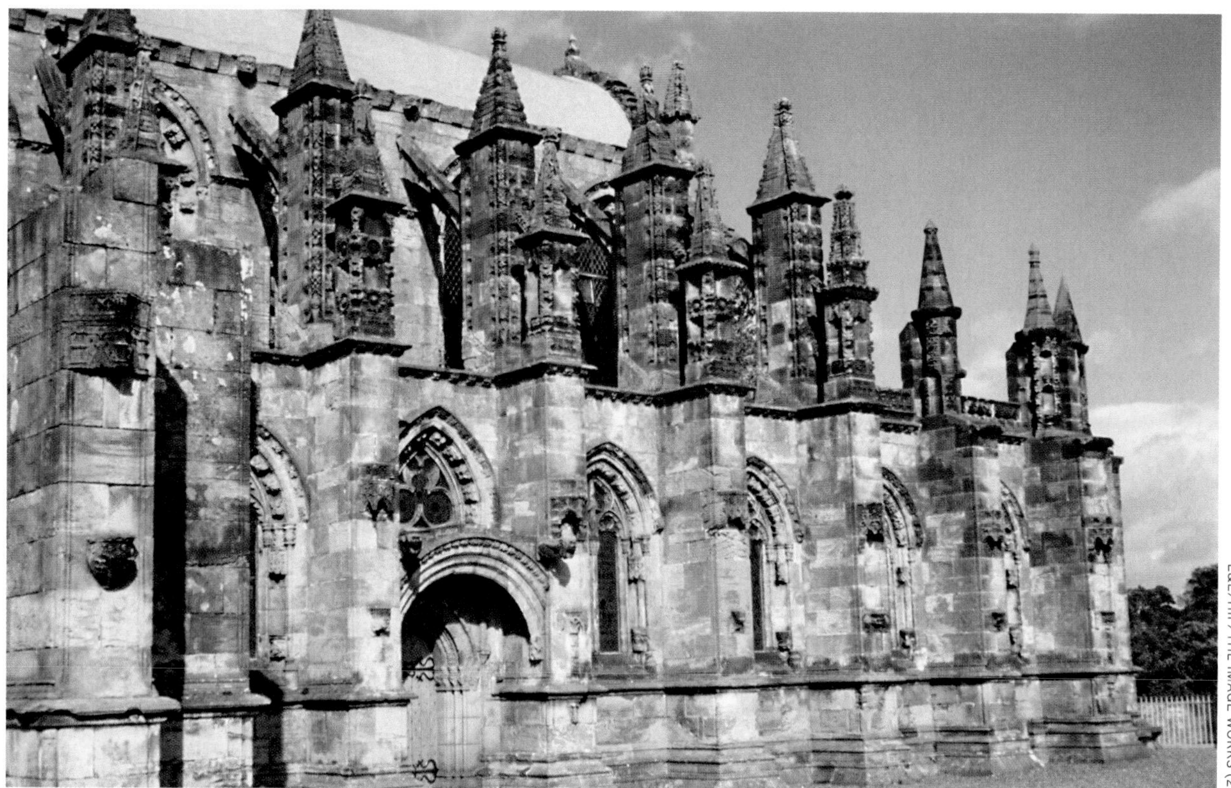

E&E/HIP/THE IMAGE WORKS (2)

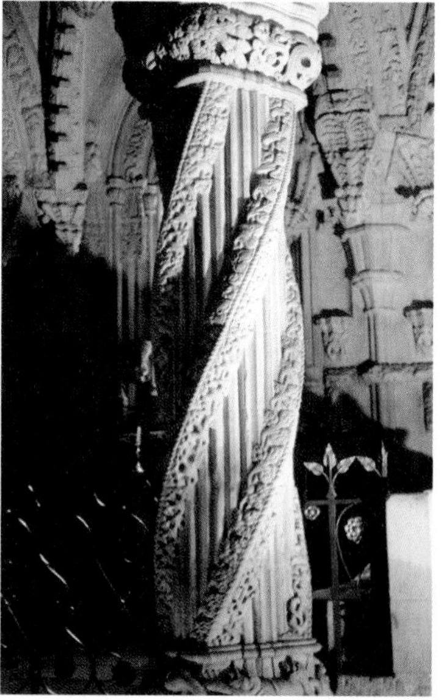

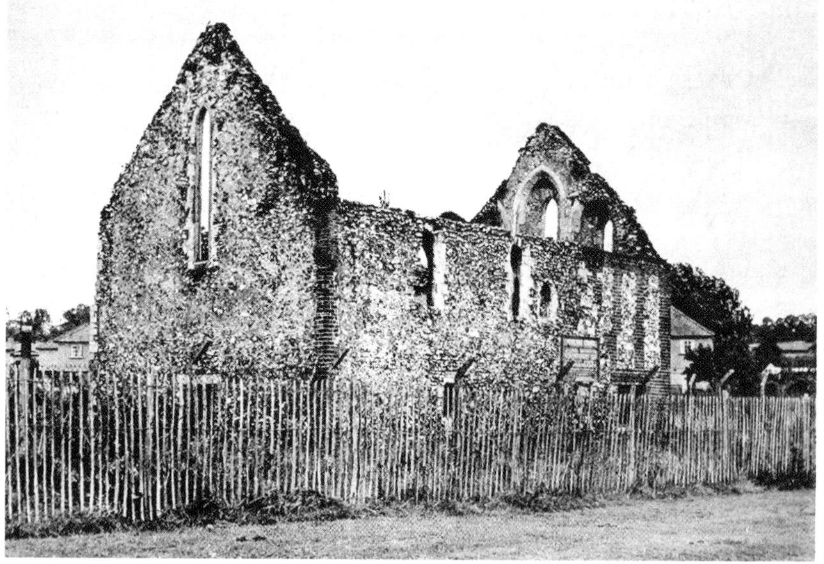

MARY EVANS/THE IMAGE WORKS

SOME SAY the use of advanced construction techniques in medieval buildings purportedly associated with the Templars is evidence of the order's influence on Freemasonry—perhaps evidence of a four-century secret link between the two groups—but these edifices stood more probably as evidence of Templar wealth. Opposite is an authentic one, in Tomar, Portugal: The Convent of the Knights of Christ and Templar Castle. Above, right: Also real, ruins of the 12th century Moor Hall Chapel in Harefield, England, which had been a hospice and place of worship for knights of the Middle Ages (and has since been razed). The final two pictures are of Rosslyn Chapel in Scotland, which is part of the Templar exodus myth and to many Dan Brown fans, the resting place of the Holy Grail.

OCEAN/CORBIS

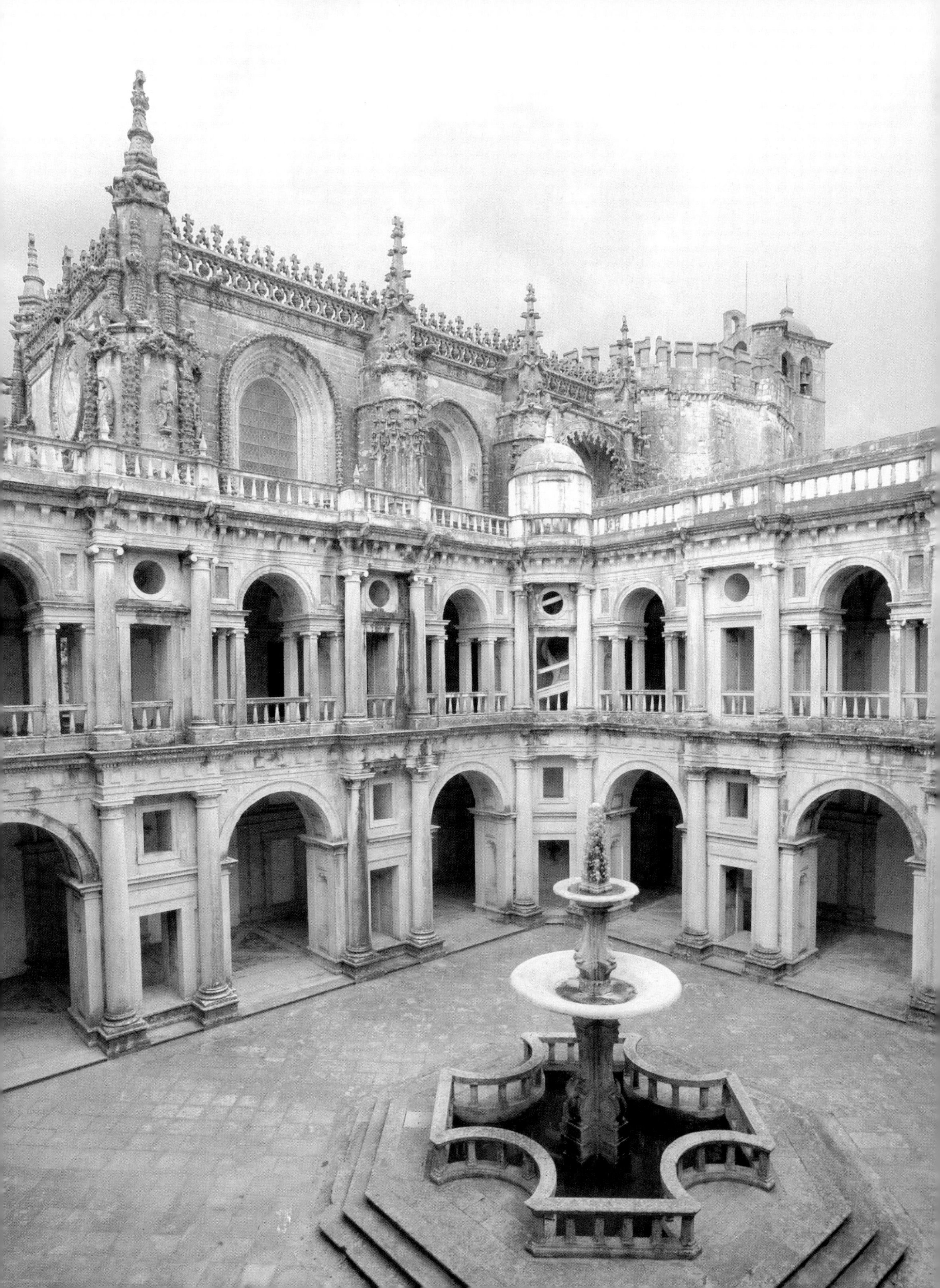

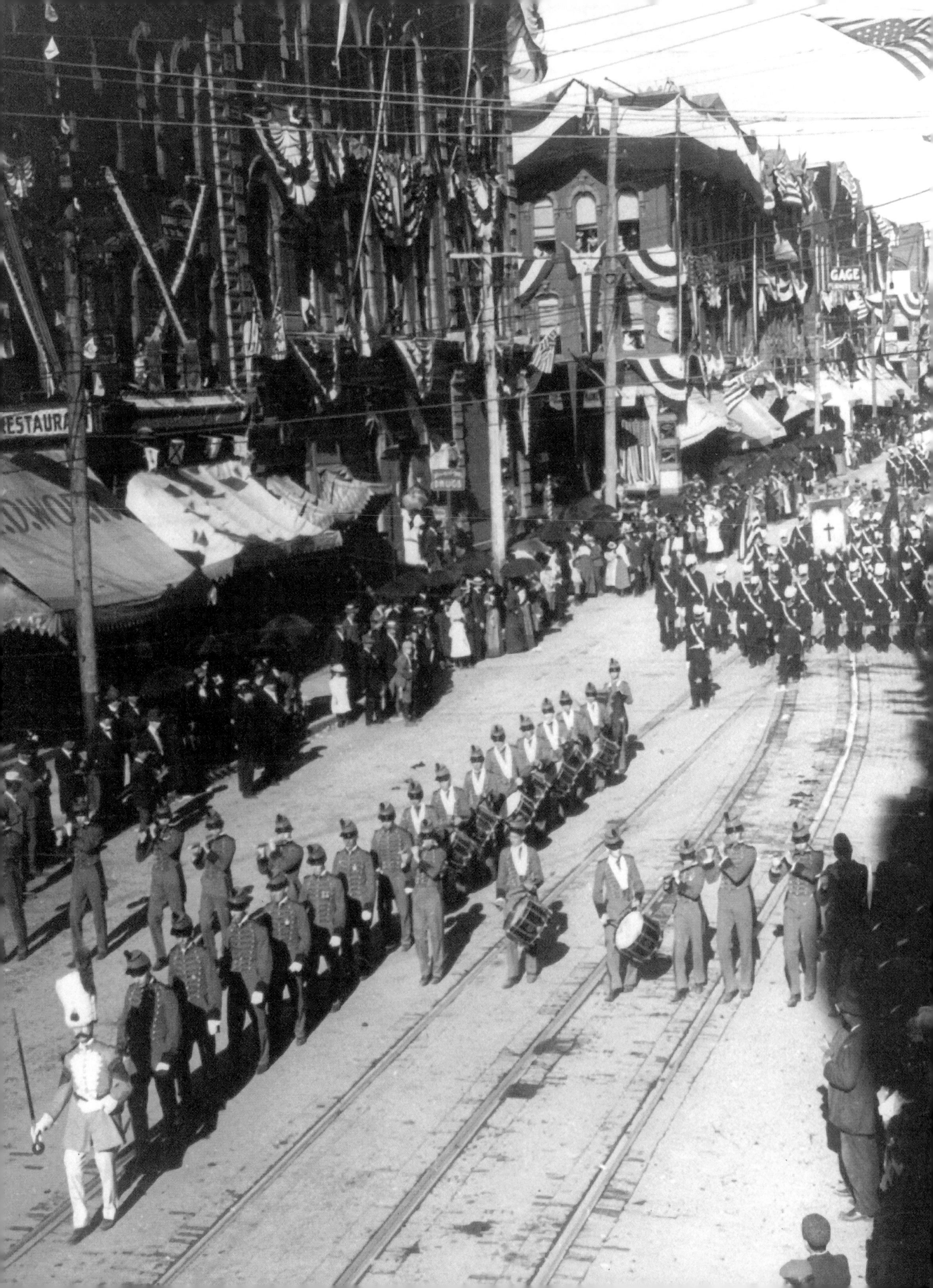
GAGE

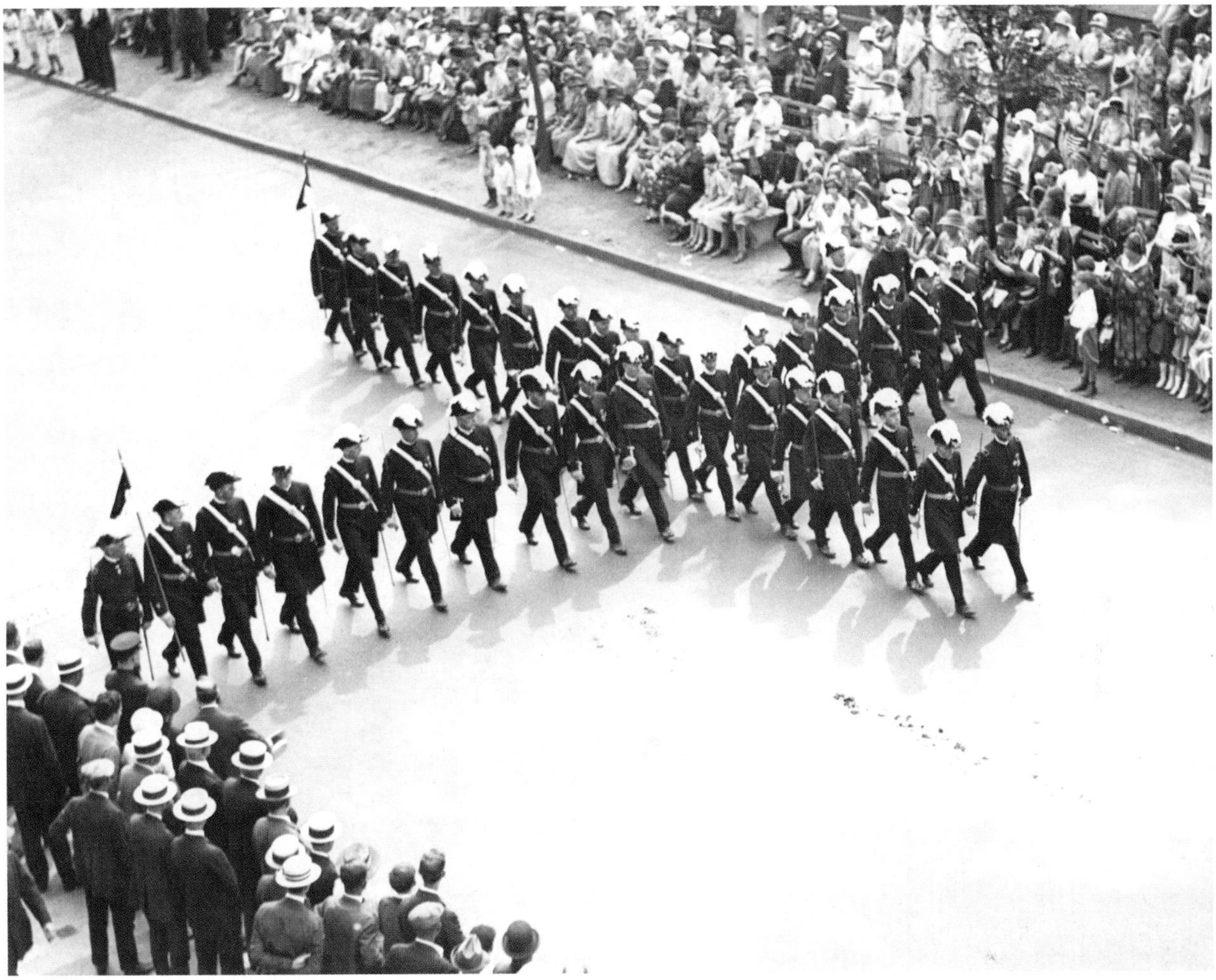

THE TEMPLARS LIVE! Or do they? One of the strangest of the plethora of strange parts to this story is the claim by many Masonic and other organizations to be directly descended from the Templars. Rosslyn Chapel, which we visited on the pages immediately previous, is perhaps the most famous physical representation referenced in the survivors' stories, but it represents a very shakily built bridge indeed between the Templars and the Freemasons. The way the story goes: Templar refugees landed in Scotland, probably with treasure, and continued to practice Templar traditions in secret, even as they fought alongside the Scots against the British. A prominent Scottish Templar family down the decades was the Sinclairs, and in the mid 14th century William Sinclair built Rosslyn Chapel. Its unfinished state is due to its purposeful resemblance to the Temple in Jerusalem (say the theorists) or to the fact that the Sinclairs went broke (say others). William Sinclair was the founder of the Freemasons who continued Templar work in secret until they came above board—were discovered, so to speak—in the 18th century. Meantime, William's descendant Henry made a voyage to America (predating Columbus), and he and his men brought Templarism to the New World, and perhaps buried artifacts from Jerusalem in a mysterious pit on Oak Island in Nova Scotia. All of this represents a very big "Wow," and has spawned something larger than a cottage industry in Templar/Freemason theory: histories, biographies, novels, movies. The *Wow* has been reflected in the flesh since the rise of Masonry by groups that freely celebrate their actual or philosophic Templar heritage. On the opposite page, members of an order of Masonic Knights Templar march in a parade in Jamestown, New York, on August 14, 1897. Above: A group of 20th century Knights Templar in full uniform march in a cross formation on Fifth Avenue in New York City circa 1930. They are part of a parade of 15,000 who sing the hymn "Onward, Christian Soldiers" as they proceed.

GRANGER

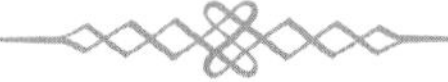

HERE, WE see members of an order of Masonic Knights Templar in the early 20th century. The regalia of Masons, who claim spiritual descent from the medieval knights, often include—and proudly—Templar insignia, such as the red and white banner. Influential in the Mason-Templar linkage was a 1738 speech by Andrew Michael Ramsay, a man designated as Grand Orator of a lodge in Paris. His "Apology for the Free and Accepted Masons" included the declaration that Crusaders were Masons as well as Templars, and that the secret words of Freemasonry had their origins in the watchwords of military camps in the Holy Land. The speech was quickly translated into English, and members of Masonic organizations in England, upon reading it, said to themselves: "Ah, of course."

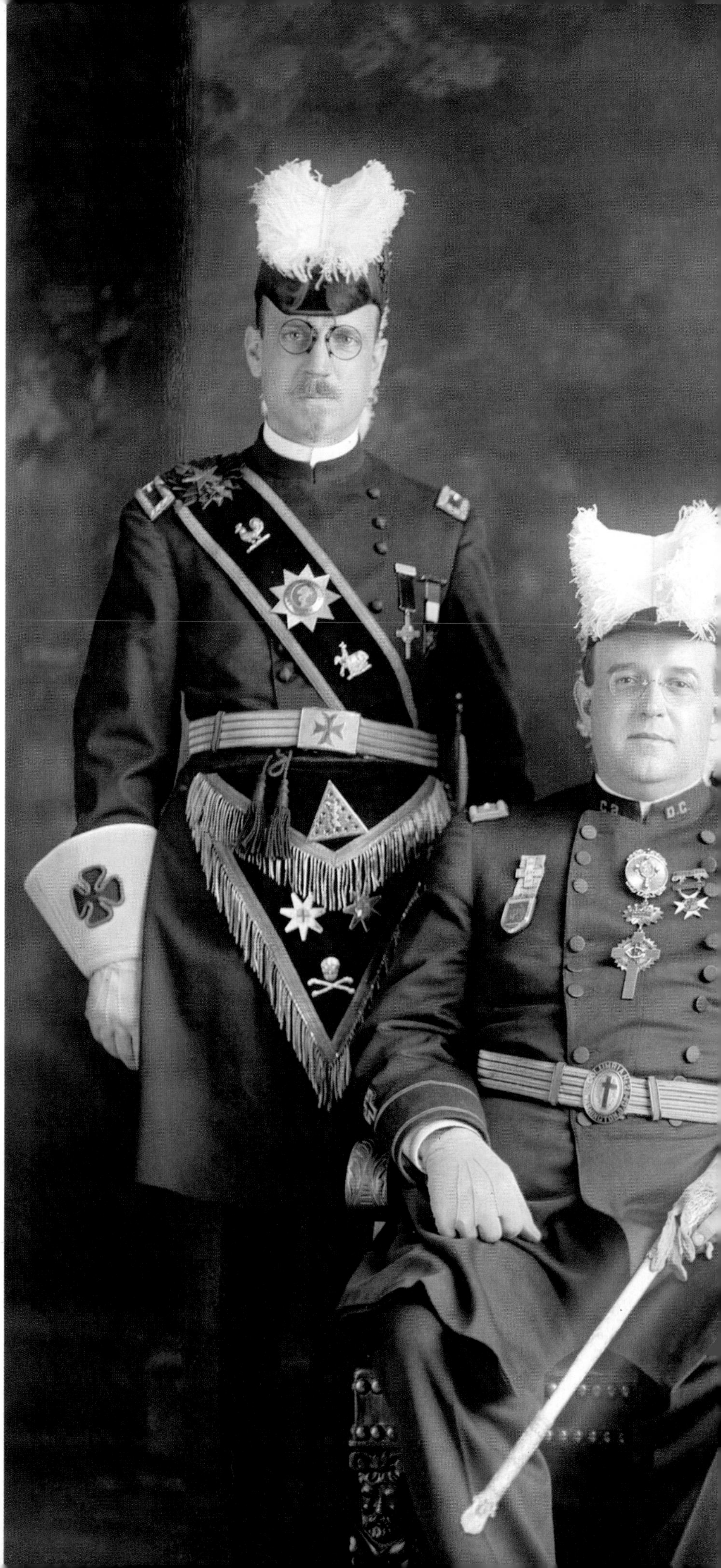

GRANGER

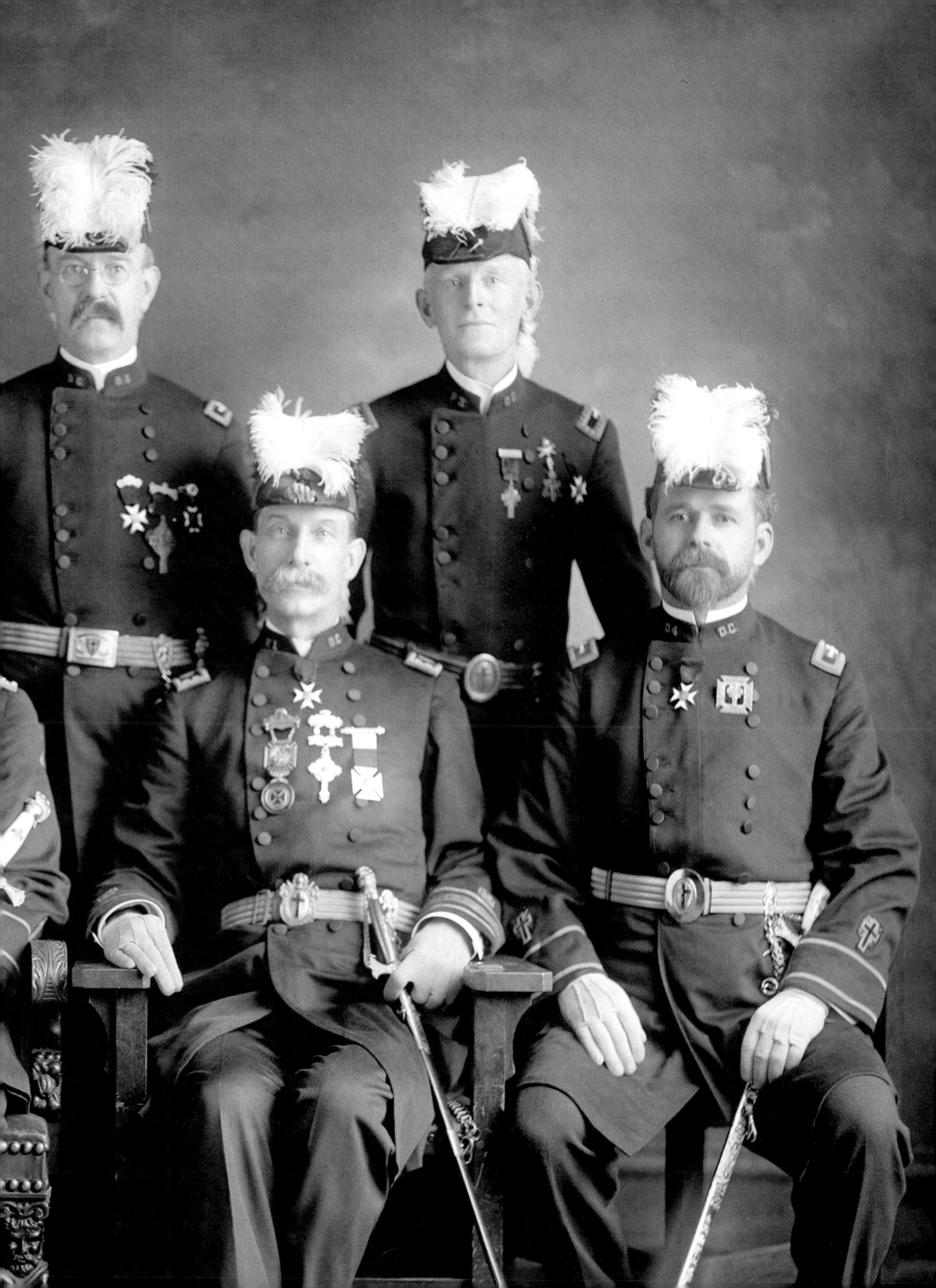

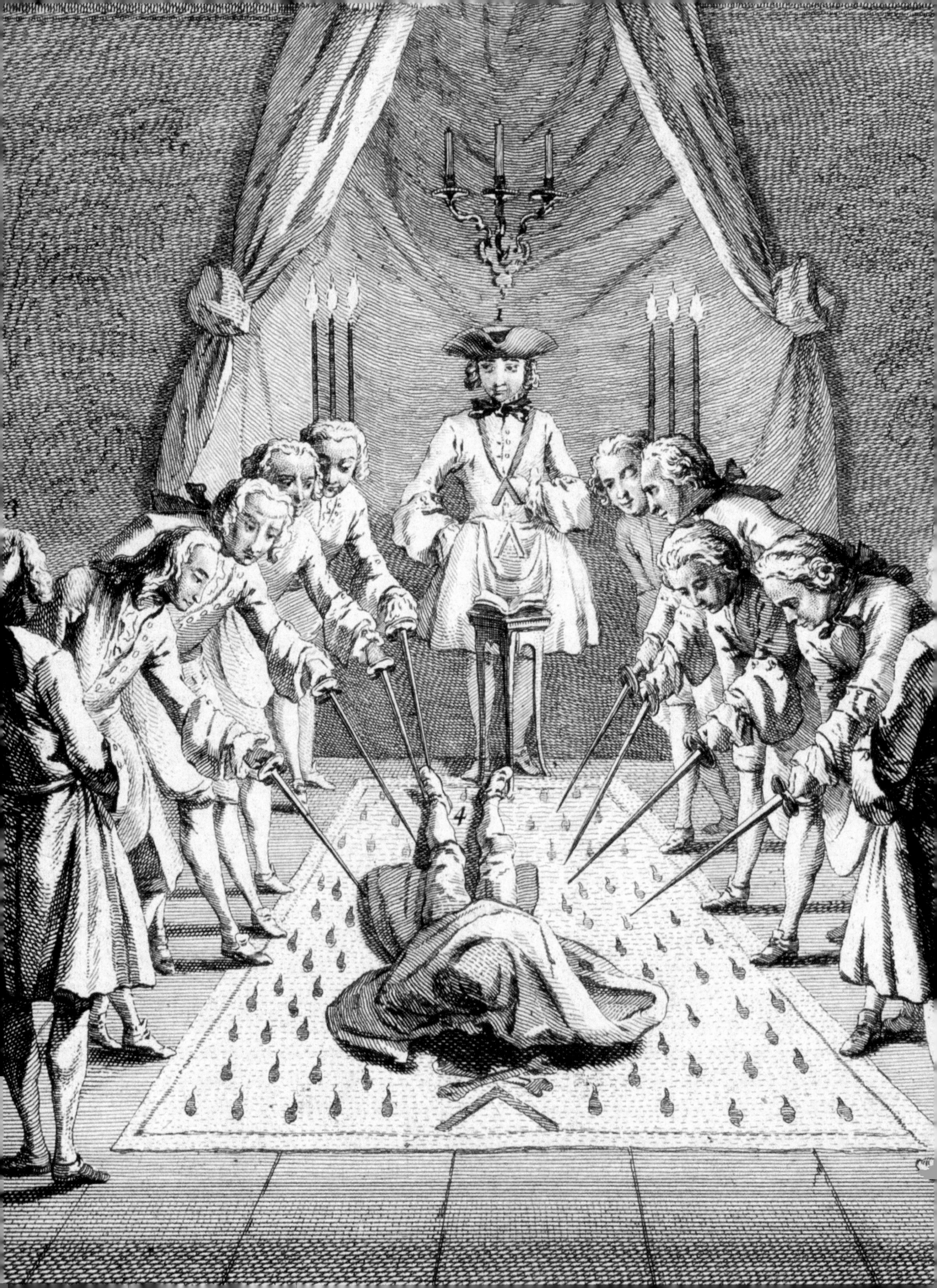
4

The Freemasons

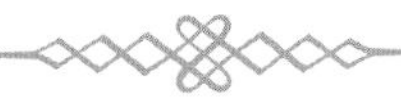

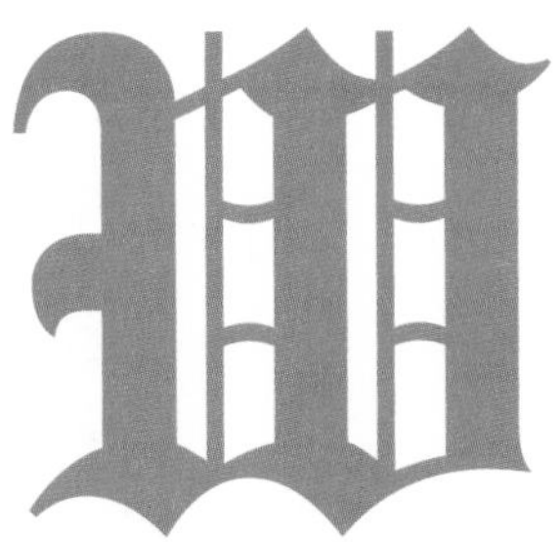

We've just learned about the Templars and their ensuing ties to the Masons, and this should be a seamless and uncomplicated transition. But nothing is seamless and uncomplicated in the world of secret societies, so please continue to pay close attention. You will be rewarded with illumination (which also happens to be the promise of many of these societies).

One of the confusions is that Masonry—or at least elements of Masonry—not only associated itself with the Templars but with just about any prior society or story that stood for "good": Many were inspired by the Pythagoreans and their belief that numbers reflected the harmony of the universe. Then there was Hiram Abiff, a master builder who, for work on behalf of the great Solomon, oversaw 183,600 craftsmen and laborers in raising a temple to God and a palace for the kings of Israel. One day, three rebels from his crew accosted Hiram and tried to force him to reveal the password of the master's degree. He refused. A man with a gauge struck him in the throat. Hiram remained stoically mum. The second man, brandishing a square, struck him in the breast. He staggered on, and was killed by the third man, who had a maul. The Masons regard Hiram as their great martyr, and as a lesson on the value of protecting valuable secrets.

Going further back, it has been proposed by a few that Adam himself was the first Mason, and that the sect's hallmark apron represents the fig leaf. Remarkable.

All this began as basically a labor union for stoneworkers in the 14th century. The term *freemason* begins to appear circa 1375 in London city records, referencing highly skilled masons who were allowed to travel the country working on the most splendid projects—castles, cathedrals and such—when the norm was to shackle the working class to localities. In short order, the freemasons learned to enjoy and protect their privilege, organizing themselves into local "lodges" that admitted the talented elite and that led them to protect their membership through codes and secret handshakes. As the Masons became *the* club to join, their membership grew far beyond actual masons—princes, philosophers, clergymen and aristocrats clamored for membership, and were allowed in—and their mission changed. The Masons became known as tolerant and open-minded and convivial, dedicated to doing "good." Who wouldn't be proud to join?

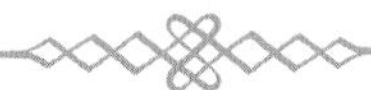

OPPOSITE is an 18th century engraving of the initiation of a Master Mason with his fellow Freemasons attending. The basis of Freemasonry, as a craftsmen's society, was laid in the 14th century, but the Masons' rise as something other—and more—began many years later.

STAPLETON COLLECTION/CORBIS

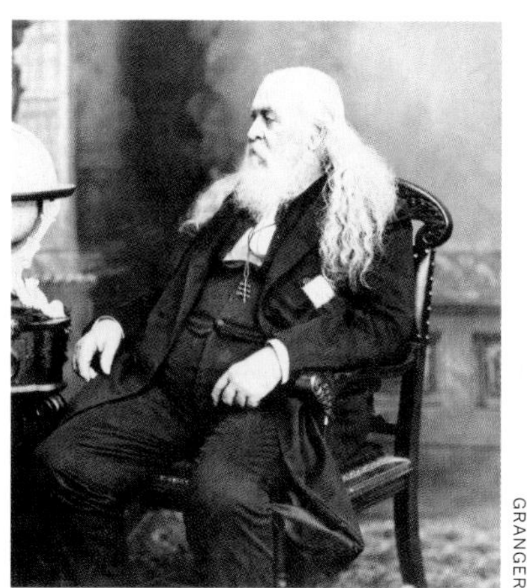
GRANGER

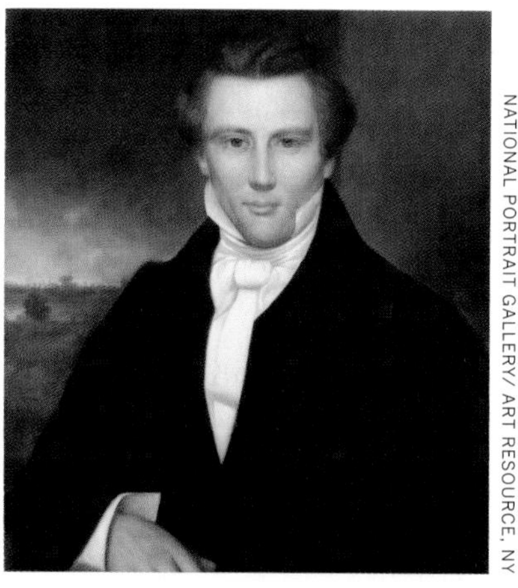
NATIONAL PORTRAIT GALLERY/ ART RESOURCE, NY

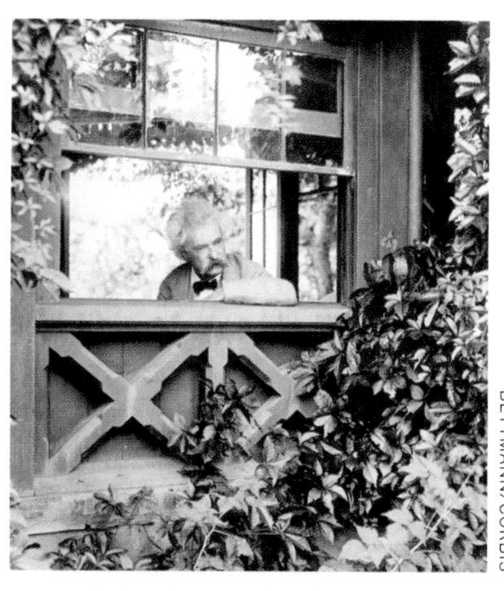
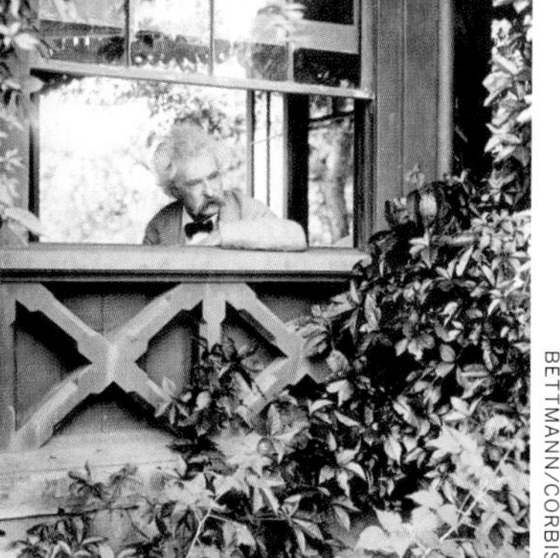
BETTMANN/CORBIS

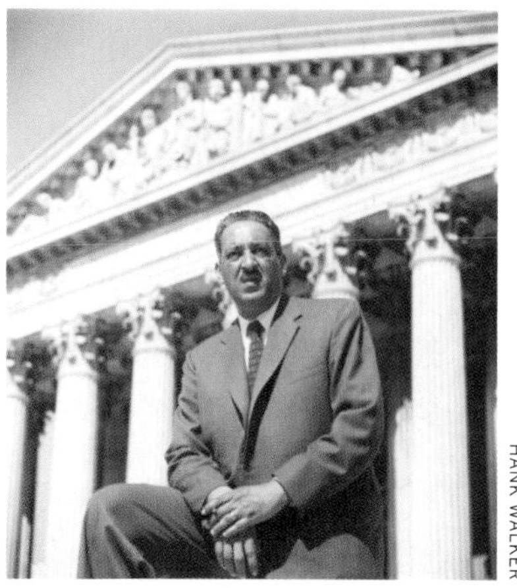
HANK WALKER

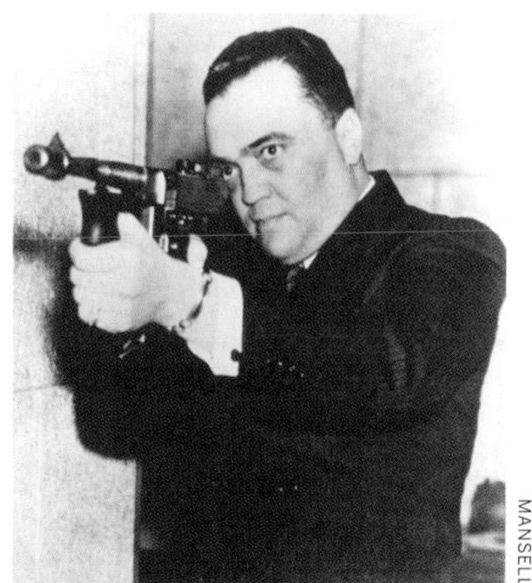
MANSELL

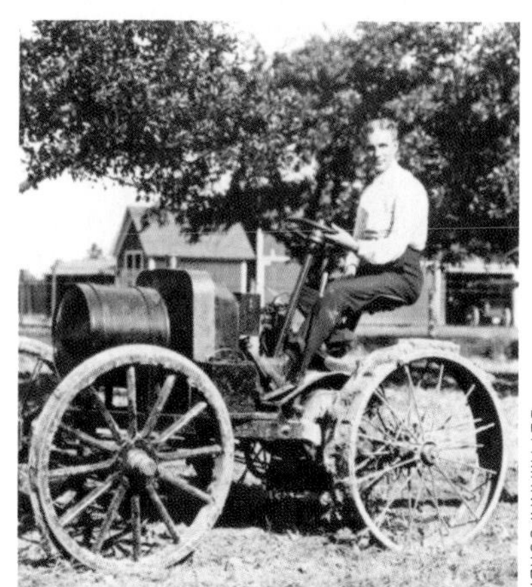
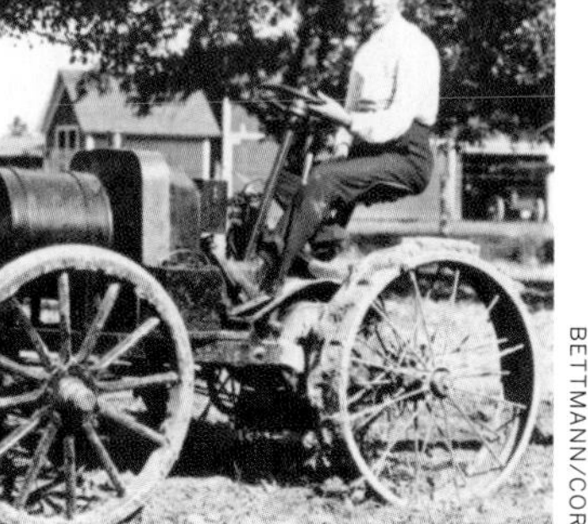
BETTMANN/CORBIS

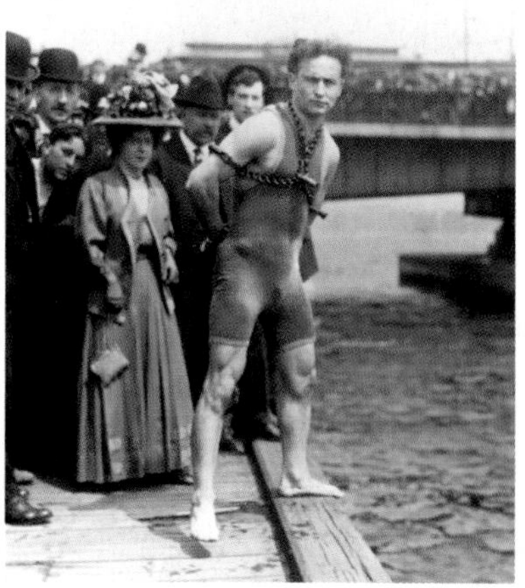
CORBIS

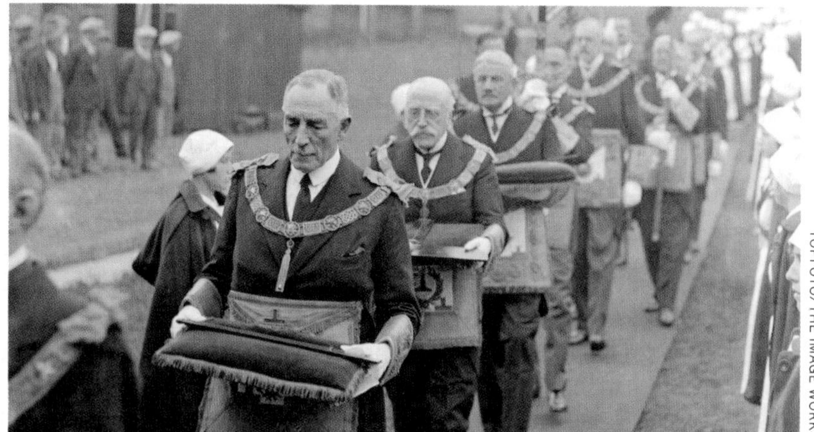
TOPFOTO/THE IMAGE WORKS

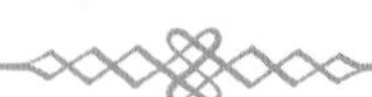

IT'S GOOD to be a Mason, and here we have a gallery, clockwise from top left: Albert Pike (1809–1891), American lawyer and poet; Joseph Smith (1805–1844), founder of Mormonism; the writer Mark Twain; the automaker Henry Ford; Lord Ampthill during a full Masonic ceremony at the laying of the foundation stone of the New Hospital in Alton, Hampshire, England, in 1929; magician Harry Houdini, ready to dive into the water in Boston in 1906; U.S. Supreme Court Justice Thurgood Marshall. In the center of the page: FBI chief J. Edgar Hoover. Opposite: The very impressive Chicago Masonic Temple, which was built in 1891–1892 and demolished in 1939. On the pages immediately following: On November 12, 1897, the Masonic Grand Lodge of Arizona meets in a cave in the mine of the Copper Queen Consolidated Mining Company in Bisbee.

GRANGER

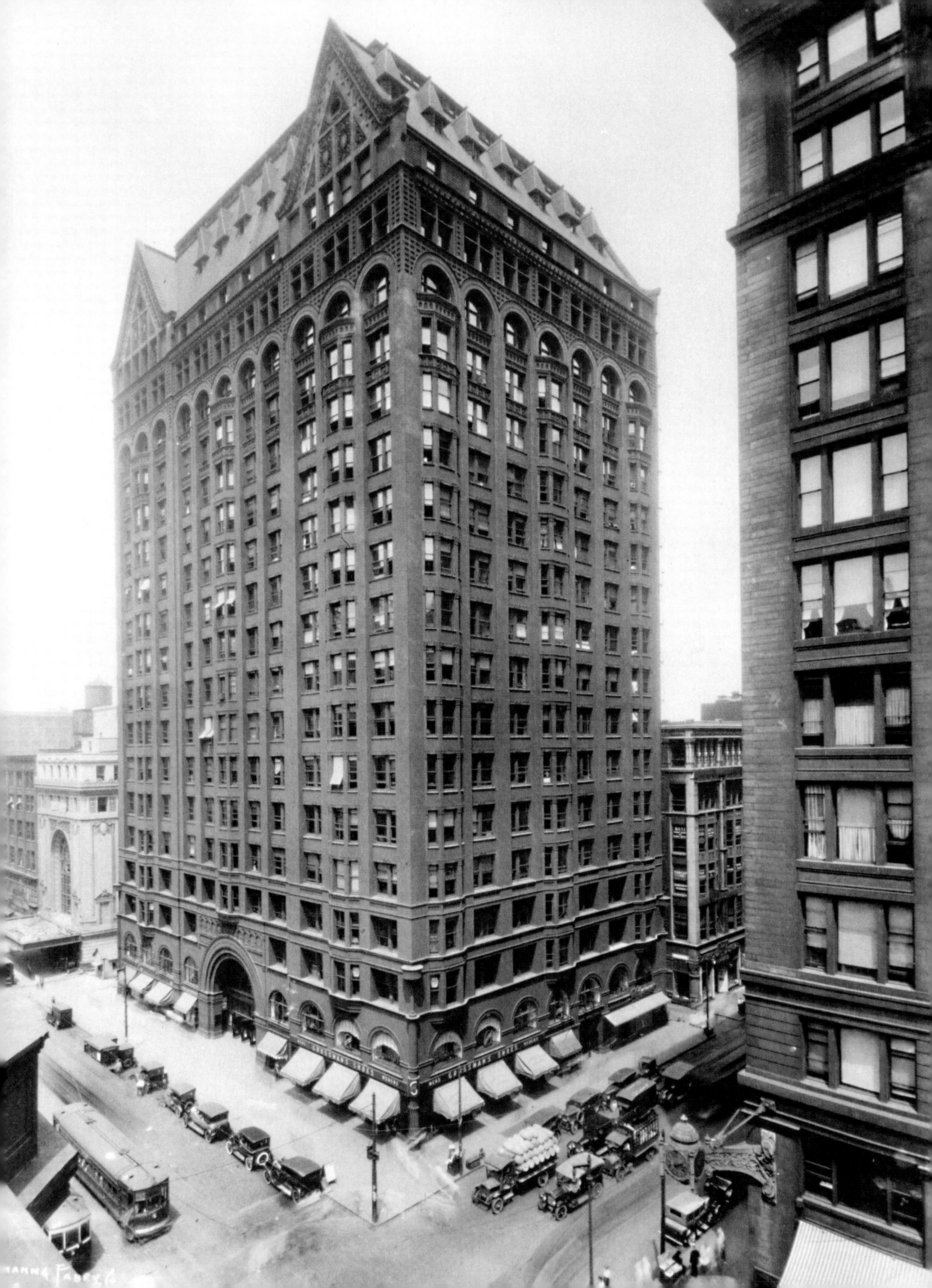
GROSSMAN'S SHOES
WOMENS
MENS
GROSSMAN'S SHOES

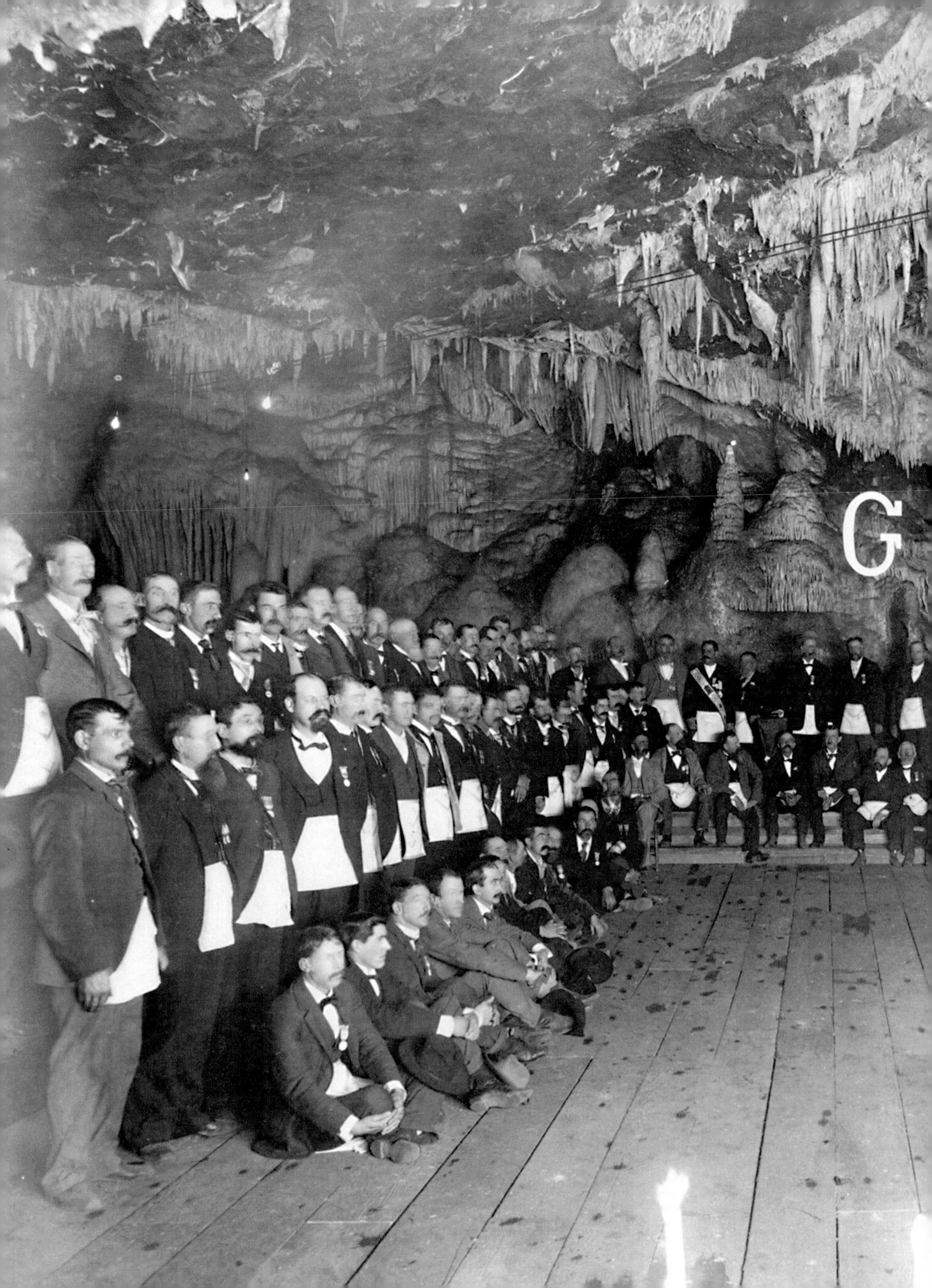
G

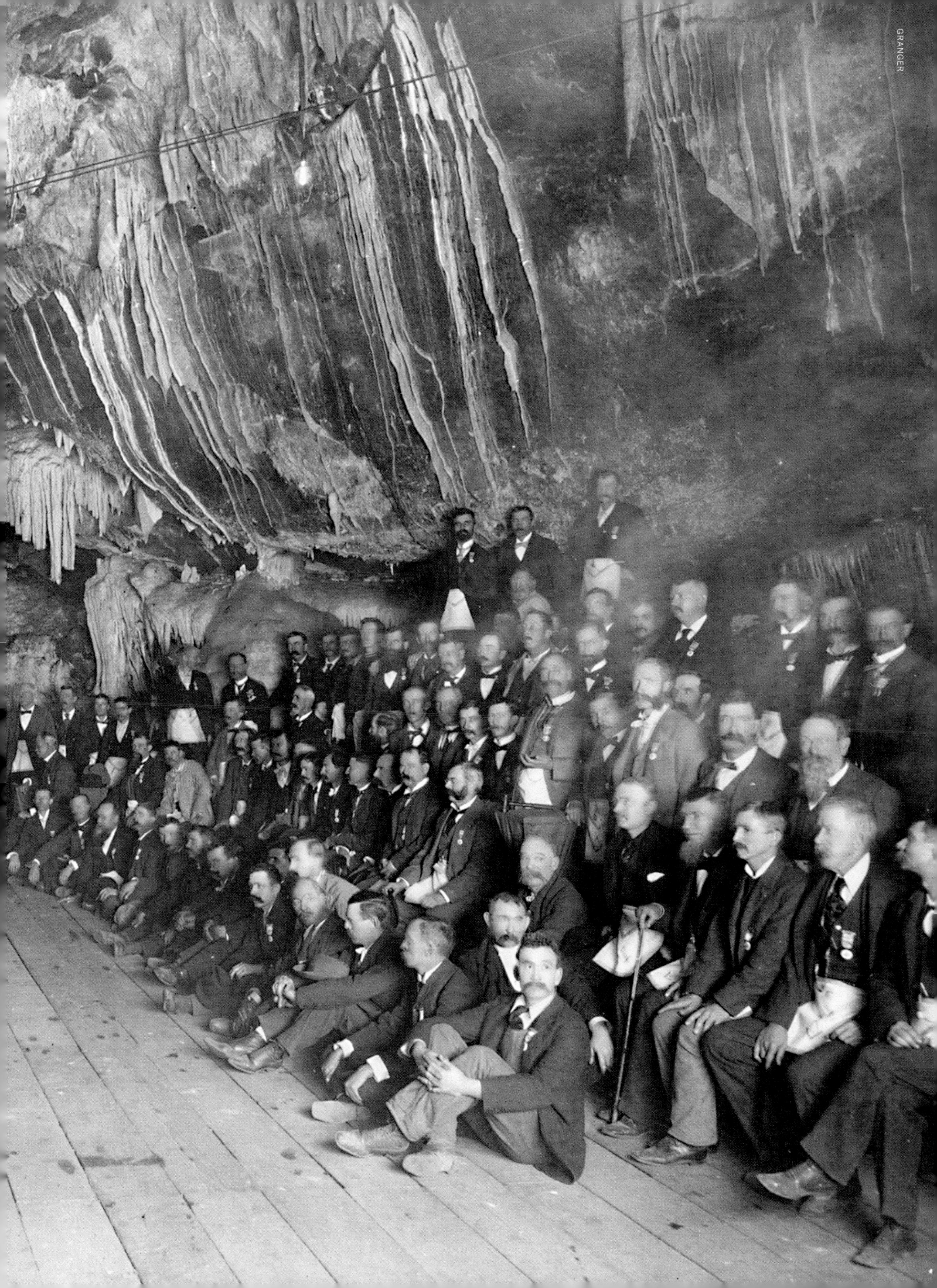

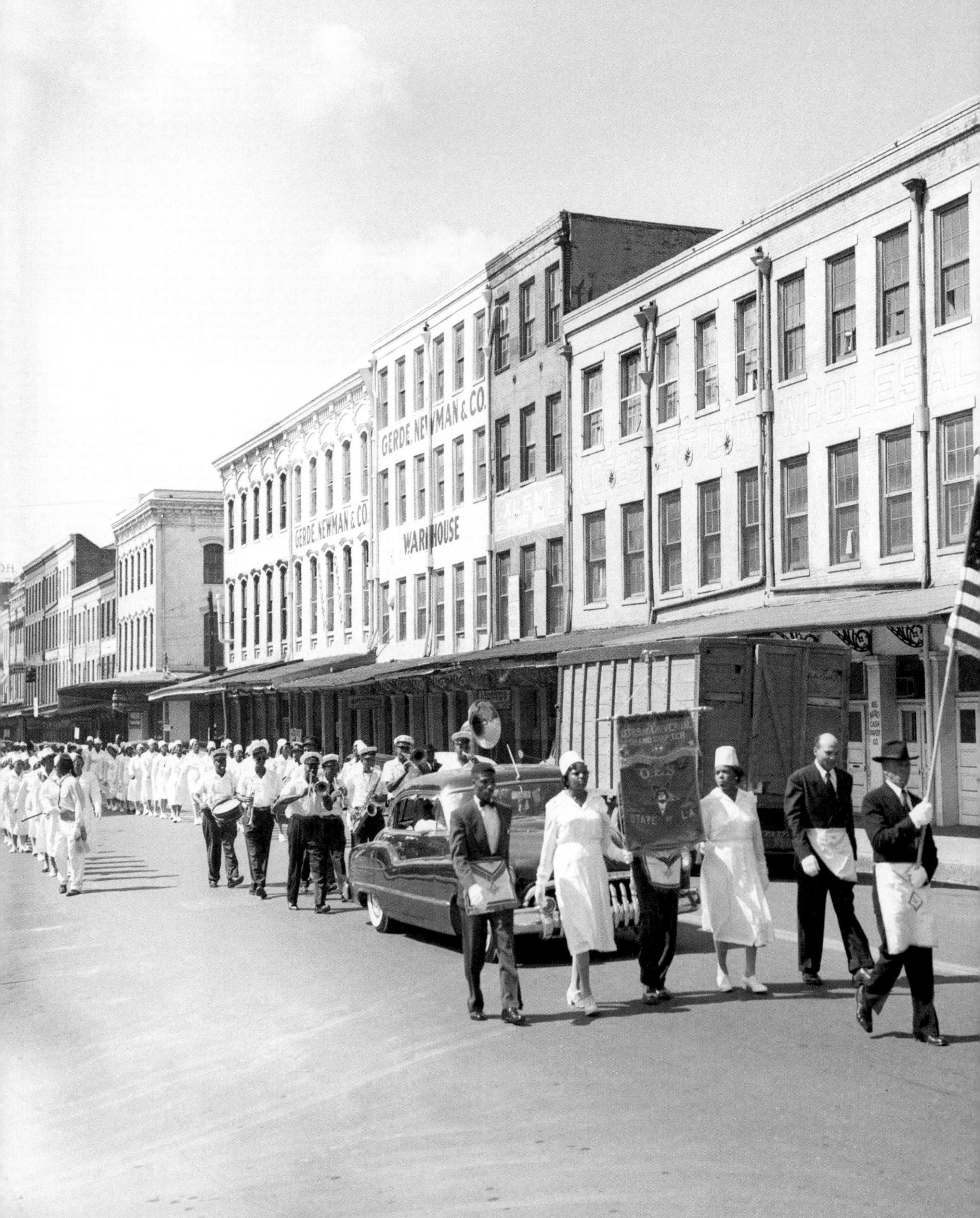
GERDE, NEWMAN & CO.
GERDE, NEWMAN & CO.
WHOLESAL

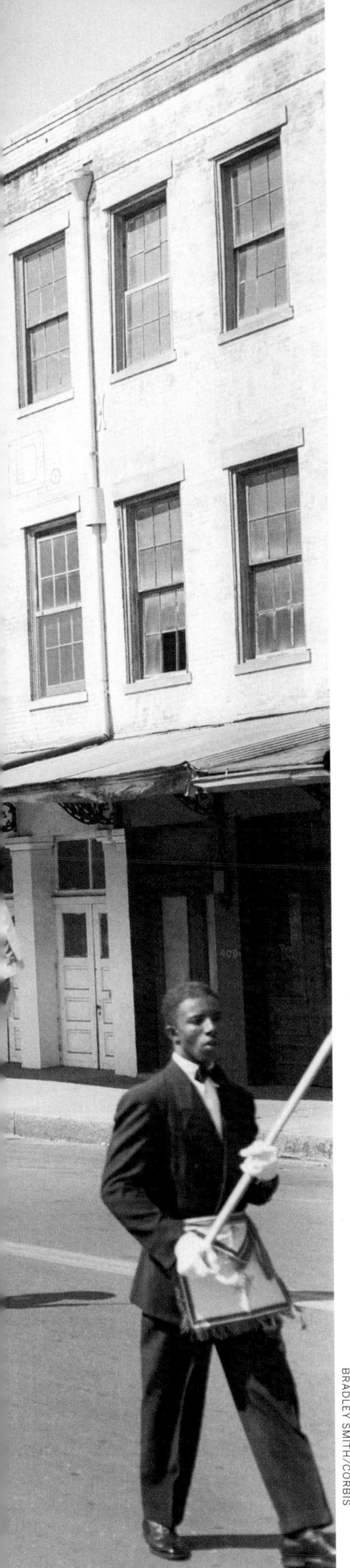

BRADLEY SMITH/CORBIS

COME ONE, COME ALL? Well, sort of. At left, we have, circa 1950 in New Orleans, a parade with the Daughters of the Universal Chapter of the Order of the Eastern Star. Below, left: An African American man wearing a Kossuth-style hat, Masonic sash and apron, and an Independent Order of Odd Fellows collar. Right: An American Freemason circa 1850. In 1785, a German Mason wrote, "The hearts of Freemasons are certainly open to women, but the Lodges are closed to them"—and that about said it as far as generally accepted policy. Nevertheless, in France at that approximate time, the notion of "Adoptive Masonry," in which female lodges affiliated with male ones, became a big thing; "Everybody participates," wrote Queen Marie Antoinette with approval in 1781. In America, the Order of the Eastern Star, founded in 1867 for female relatives of Freemasons, followed the Adoptive Masonry model and remains strong today. Another question in America, of course, as the Masonic movement grew larger in the 17th and 18th centuries

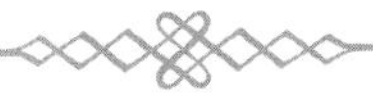

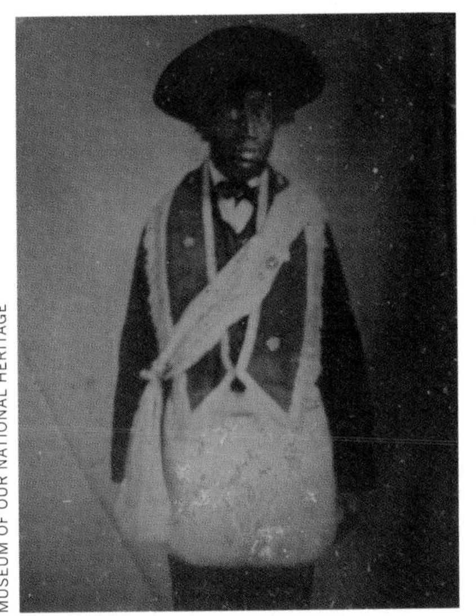

MUSEUM OF OUR NATIONAL HERITAGE

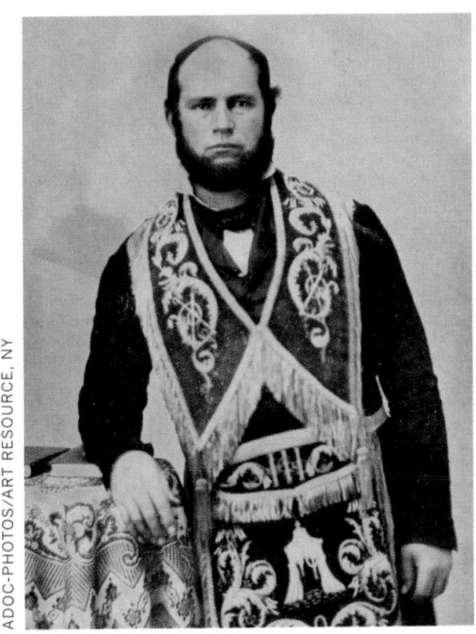

ADOC-PHOTOS/ART RESOURCE, NY

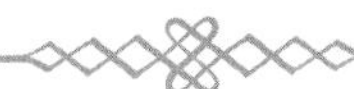

was: What about African American men? As might be expected, most were excluded from white lodges. Prince Hall was a Boston clergyman who is seen by many historians as one of the most influential African Americans in the formative years of our nation; there are claims that, among other things, he fought in the Revolutionary War. He was an abolitionist and leader of a free black community in Boston and hoped to gain for his local brethren acceptance in such societal bastions as schools, the military and, yes, Freemasonry. Although he'd been rejected by the American Freemasons, he still believed in the fraternity's principles and goals and gained entry into a British lodge in Boston in 1775. Subsequently, he founded the African Grand Lodge of North America and was unanimously elected its Grand Master—a post he held until his death in 1807. Prince Hall Masonry burgeoned outside the mainstream, and eventually there were African American lodges in every state of the Union.

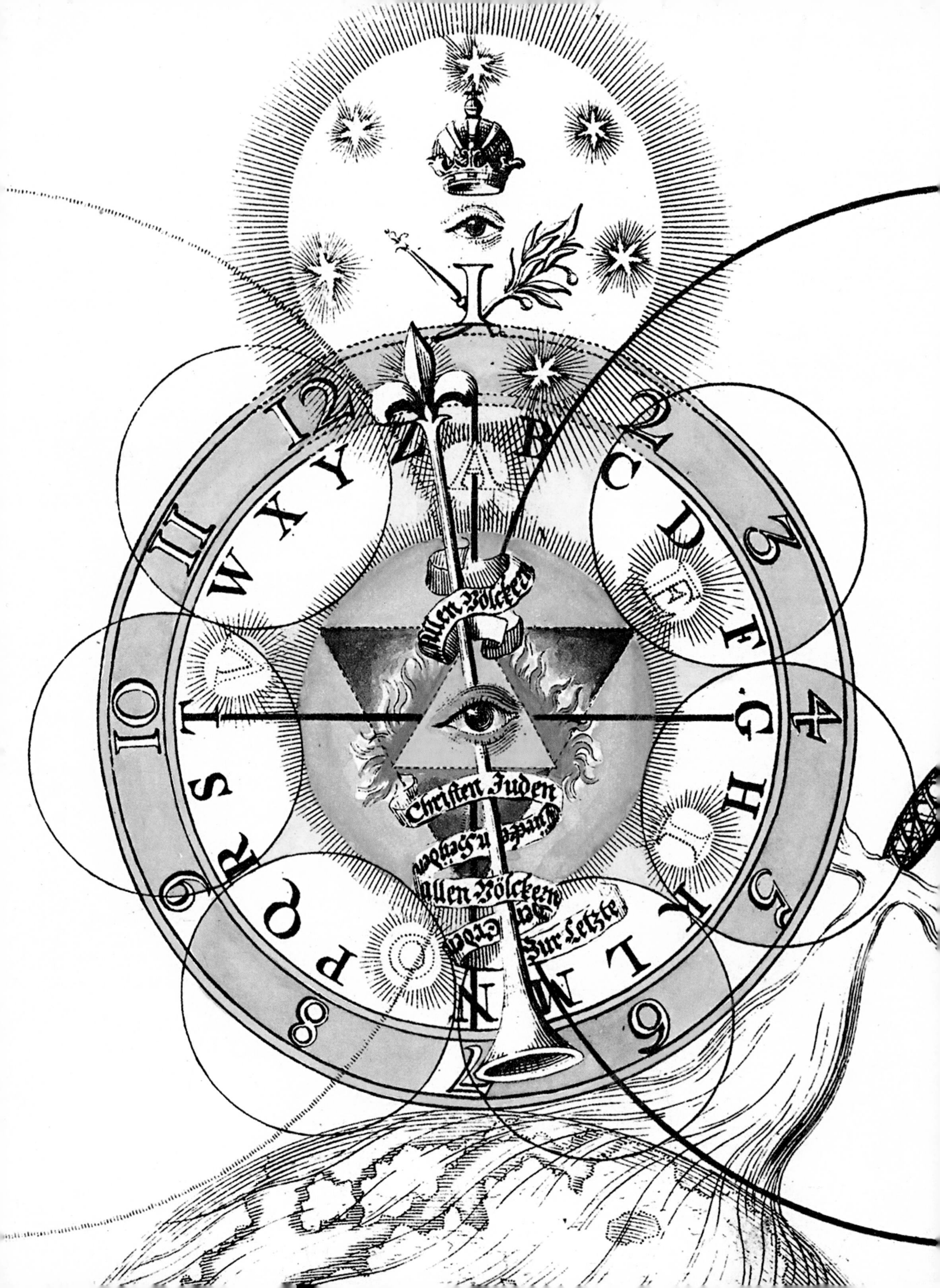

Allen Völckern
Christen Juden
Allen Völckern
Zur Letzte

The Rosicrucians

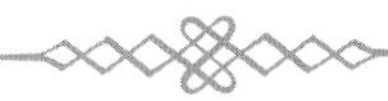

If you think you've read some wild stuff already, wait till you dig into this one. Here we have the quasi-Masonic "Brotherhood of the Rosy Cross," born in the early 15th century, and claimed by its adherents to have been vastly influential in spurring the Enlightenment and in various political revolutions (including the French and American), but that, in fact, never existed.

How's that again? Here goes: Three works published anonymously in Germany between 1614 and 1616 delineate the life of the Middle Ages knight Christian Rosenkreutz (German for "rose cross"). Rosenkreutz was a man who traveled widely in the Middle East, acquiring great wisdom. He returned home and formed a secret organization of eight fellow seekers in 1408. They were interested in philosophy; alchemy and magic; healing the sick; intellectual inquiry that might end all war; and, more generally, the hidden forces of all nature and the harnessing of natural power. Rosenkreutz died in 1484 and was buried in a vault. When the vault was opened in 1604, a parchment delineating the life and times of the Rosicrucian Brotherhood was found in the hand of Christian's uncorrupted corpse.

The tripartite Rosicrucian history—the so-called Rosicrucian Manifestos—followed a little more than a decade after the vault was opened. They created a great stir in popular and intellectual circles in post-Reformation Europe. Great thinkers were intrigued by this quest for bending nature to man's will and among the new Rosicrucians were several members, in good standing, of the Western intellectual elite.

But here's the thing: The Manifestos were, unbeknownst to their rapt readership, works of fiction. There was no Christian Rosenkreutz. There never had been a Brotherhood of the Rosy Cross. The myth gave rise to a veritable army of true believers.

Natural magic remains at the heart of modern Rosicrucianism, but in the last few centuries many things—self-improvement, Egyptology, the abolition of slavery in America, occultism, sex magic—have attached themselves to the movement. Today there remain many who say they are Rosicrucians. And, when you think about it, they *are*—as much as anyone has been, and far more than Christian Rosenkreutz ever was.

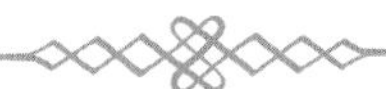

THE TITLE PAGE of a 1682 theosophical work by the vastly influential Jakob Boehme, in which we have an eye, a burning triangle, a clockface representing Time and alphabetic letters concentric to the dial representing Space. None other than the famous Quaker William Penn, when a young man in England, was fascinated by mysticism and the Rosicrucians, and once called Boehme "his master in the art and law of divine wisdom."

CHARLES WALKER/TOPFOTO/THE IMAGE WORKS

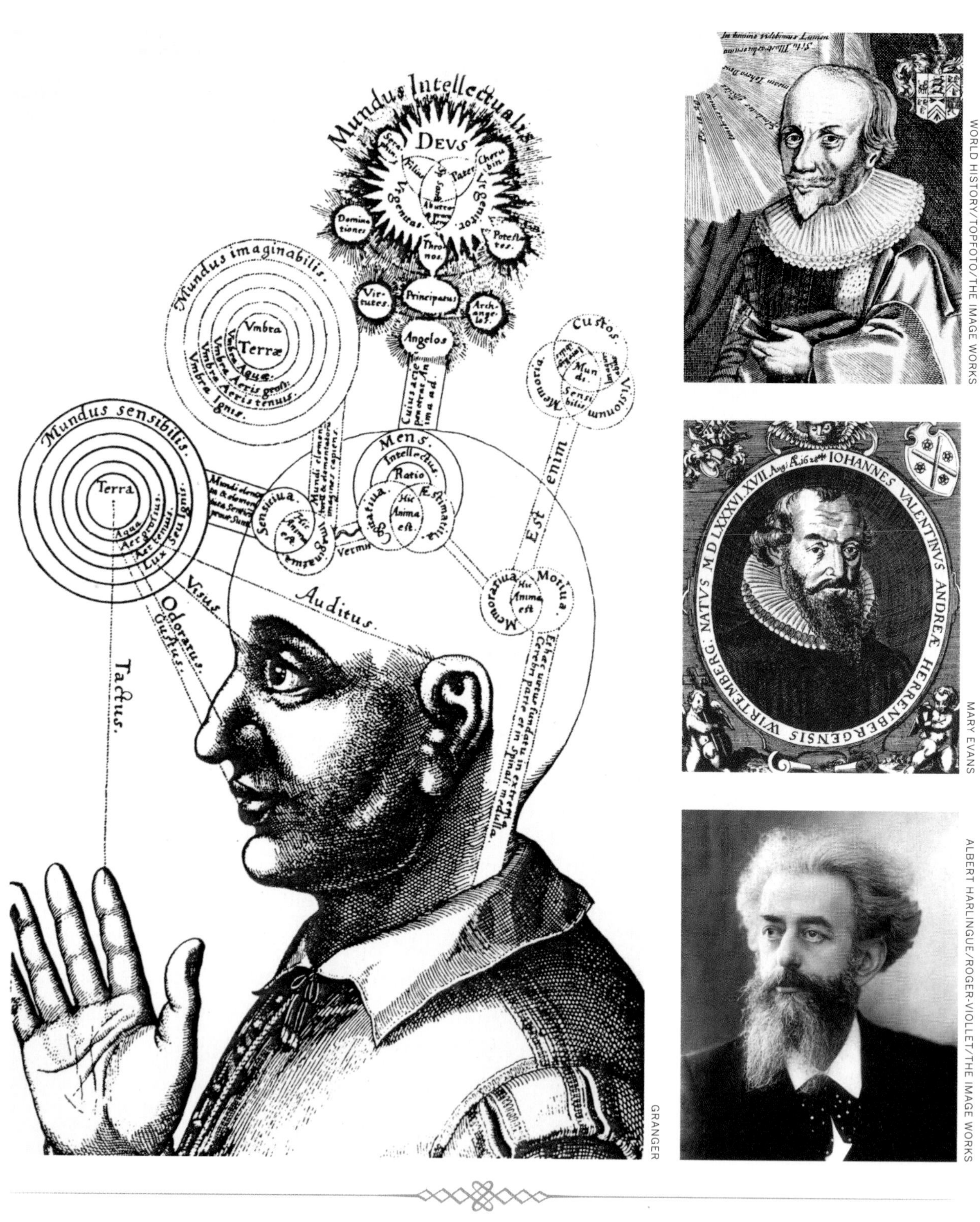

WORLD HISTORY/TOPFOTO/THE IMAGE WORKS

MARY EVANS

ALBERT HARLINGUE/ROGER-VIOLLET/THE IMAGE WORKS

GRANGER

ABOVE IS Robert Fludd's line engraving of human mental capabilities in terms of God and the universe. Opposite is an illustration from Fludd's *Utriusque Cosmi* that depicts his theory that the entire universe, from the planets and the elements to the letters of the alphabet, is a "divine monochord" tuned by the hand of God. At top, right, is Fludd himself, an Englishman born in 1574 who would become a renowned chemist, astrologer, mystic and supporter of all things Rosicrucian. In the center is Johann Valentin Andrea (1586–1654), a German theologian, writer, mystic and the probable founder of Rosicrucianism. It remains uncertain who wrote the first two Manifestos, but is generally accepted that the third,

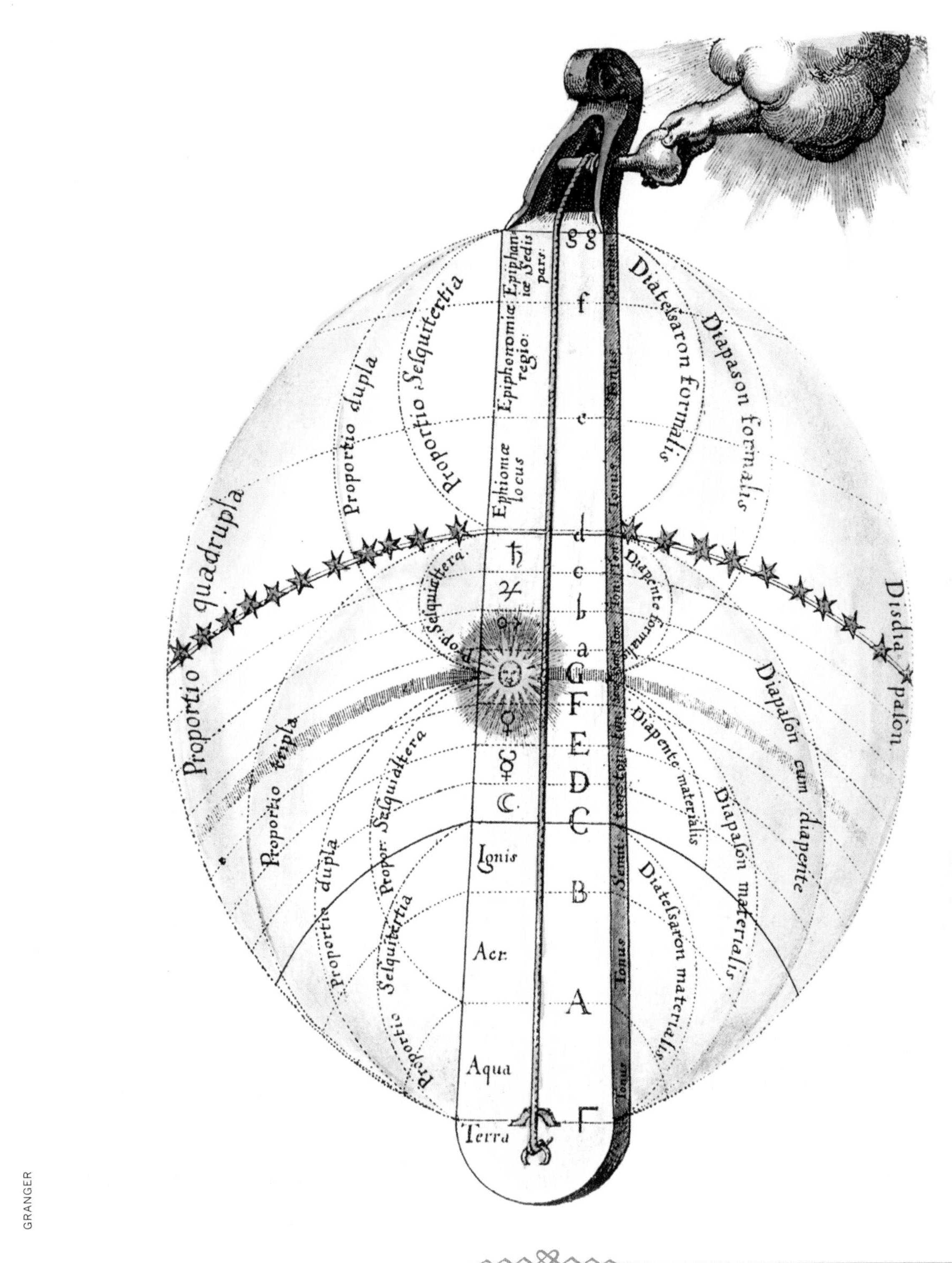

GRANGER

The Chemical Wedding of Christian Rosenkreutz, was the work of Andrea. He admitted as much, saying it was a "youthful literary trifle" he had meant as a satire on occultists. At bottom is Joséphin Péladan (1859–1918) a French writer who founded the Salon of the Rosicrucians in 1882. Other reputable—so to speak—neo-Rosicrucian societies have been formed over time in every country in the Western world, including the United States. By the way, Péladan's version of Rosicrucianism embraced elements of the Kabbalah, a form of Jewish mysticism practiced in the present day by, among others, Madonna, Lindsay Lohan and Ashton Kutcher.

The Illuminati

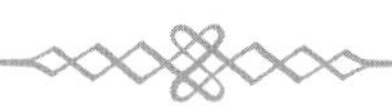

As we have clearly seen, the intermingling of symbols and raisons d'être among secret societies is manifold. Adam Weishaupt, a German philosopher who became a Freemason in 1774, was cognizant of these. And he thought he had an even bigger and better idea. Sure he would appropriate a few items—most prominent, the all-seeing eye, and also the aspirational pyramid—but his overarching goal would make those of the Masons or Rosicrucians look like small potatoes. He foresaw nothing less than a liberty-based New World Order. There are theories afloat today that secret Illuminati still have a plan to bend the world to their way of thinking.

To a greater degree than most if not all secret societies, the society of the Illuminati is about one man. Weishaupt began his boyhood education at a Jesuit school, and the Jesuit sense of discipline would influence him greatly. As would, obviously, the ages-old process of illumination, by which the mystical practitioner came to divine "the light" sent by a higher source. There were Illuminati in Spain in the early 1500s; Ignatius of Loyola, founder of the Jesuit order, was one. Cross-bred tribes of Illuminati/Rosicrucians were not uncommon. But it is Weishaupt who trademarked the idea.

He secretly founded the Ancient Illuminated Seers of Bavaria, on May 1, 1776, with four associates. They and their recruits infiltrated Masonic lodges in Europe and took control of some; the Illuminati grew to number perhaps 2,000. Their goal was to perfect human nature—Weishaupt felt that that was what Jesus Christ had been urging his followers to do—and thereby human society. The corrupt Catholic Church needed to be brought down. And the world would then be one big democratic republic.

The leader of this republicanism, though, was a dictator at heart and infighting came quickly. In 1784, the government of Bavaria, hearing of plans against the Church and the state, issued laws banning secret societies. The Illuminati were thoroughly suppressed by 1787. Weishaupt fled to Saxony, where he wrote defenses of his intentions and the Illuminati. He died in 1830.

MARY EVANS PICTURE LIBRARY

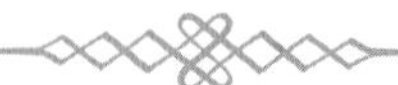

FORMING HIS ILLUMINATI even as the United States was forming, Weisthaupt (right) and his philosophy were regarded with respect by many of the world's great men, including Goethe (opposite) and several of our Founding Fathers. Weisthaupt was, said Thomas Jefferson, a man who believed "in the indefinite perfectibility of man. He thinks he may in time be rendered so perfect that he will be able to govern himself in every circumstance so as to injure none, to do all the good he can, to leave government no occasion to exercise their powers over him, & of course to render political government useless."

SEF/ART RESOURCE, NY

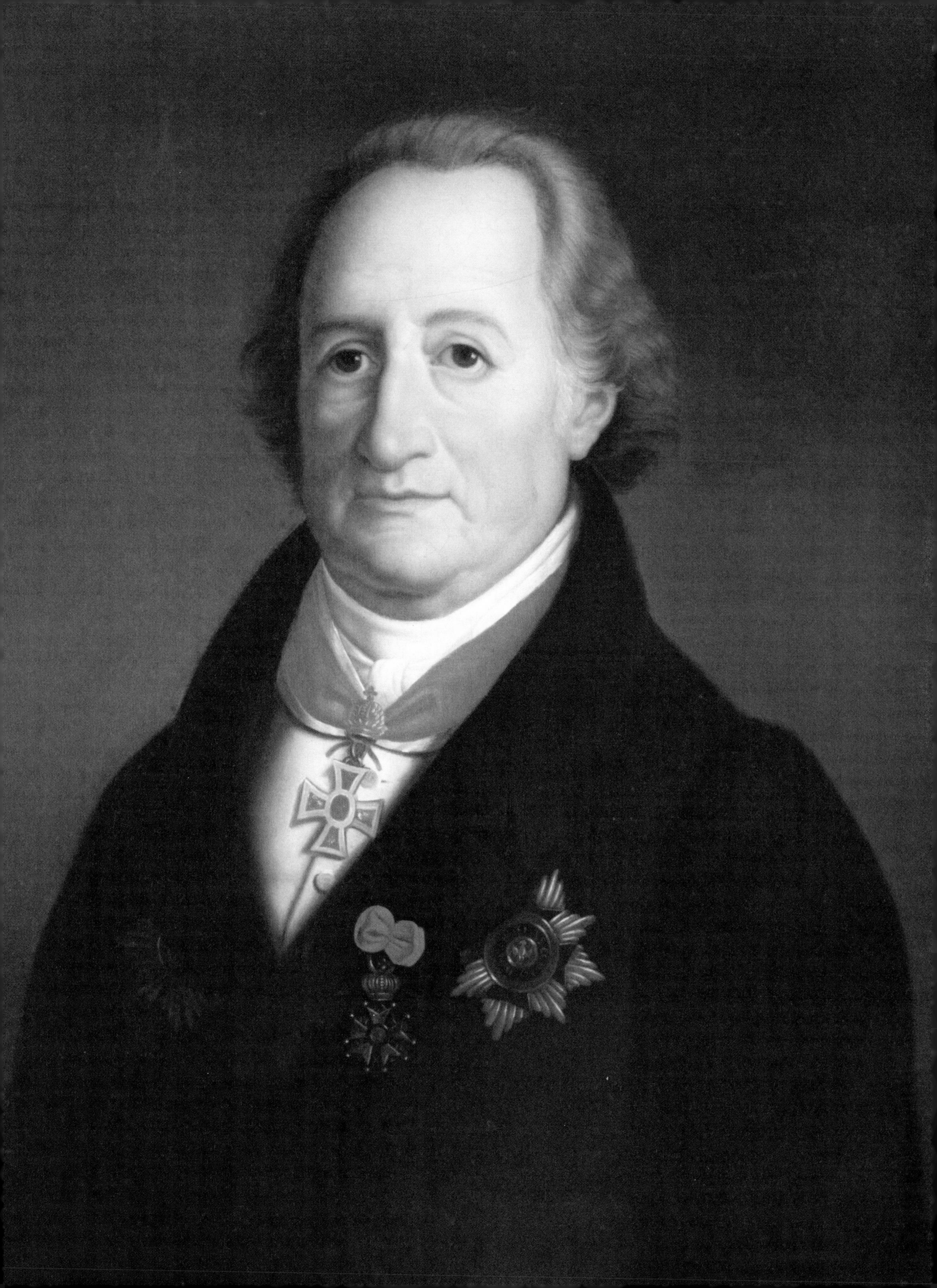

The Carbonari

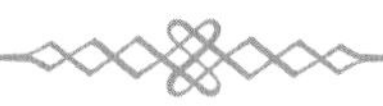

There is certainly a sameness to this European secret society of the early 1800s: It clearly borrowed many of its rituals, from initiation rites to secret handshakes to regional places of assembly, from the Freemasons. But it is useful to look at the differences the Carbonari represent. Theirs was an overtly political organization. Sure, they were for self-improvement and fraternity and all that. But they didn't want to just meet and have a nice time. Inspired by what they had seen in the French Revolution, they wanted to effect social change on a grand scale. Specifically, they sought a constitutional monarchy or, better yet, a republic in the Kingdom of Naples and the States of the Church: They wanted nothing less than a unified and democratic Italy. (In its post-Roman period, the country had fragmented into various city-states.) In 1814, the Carbonari (it means "charcoal burners," and they took many expressions from that trade, though they were made up largely of middle-class men and intellectuals) decided that force was justified to obtain a constitution for the Kingdom of Naples, and that armed rebellion and assassination were acceptable paths. In 1820, they entered the fray militarily. Things were going well for the Carbonari side, but then Austria, which ruled a part of northern Italy, sent in troops to support the regime of King Ferdinand I of Naples, and the revolt was put down. Any hope of a Neapolitan constitution was suppressed, at least for the time being.

Was that the end of the Carbonari? Not quite. Yes, in the Kingdom of Naples the society lost influence and saw its organization greatly harmed. But it continued to agitate there and elsewhere, and inspired brethren Carbonari to spring up in Spain and especially in France, where the *Charbonnerie* took part in the July Revolution of 1830.

More significantly, the Carbonari had greatly influenced the early careers of two men, Giuseppe Mazzini and Giuseppe Garibaldi, who would never give up the cause and were leaders of the ultimately successful Italian unification movement of the 1800s. After Mazzini, who had been imprisoned for his revolutionary activities, was released from jail in 1831, many of his former associates in the Carbonari joined him in his new "Young Italy" movement. Garibaldi, too, joined him then. One of the titanic figures of the century, Garibaldi spent 12 years in exile in South America before returning to rejoin the fight to unite Italy. It can be said: The Carbonari spirit rode with him into battle.

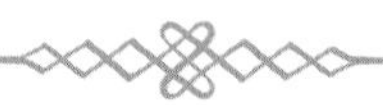

GARIBALDI POSES in 1865 in La Maddalena Archipelago National Park on the Italian island of Caprera, off the coast of Sardinia. As a general, he has won the war for Italian unification, and he and his longtime associate Giuseppe Mazzini are now seen as two of Italy's "fathers of the fatherland."

HULTON-DEUTSCH/CORBIS

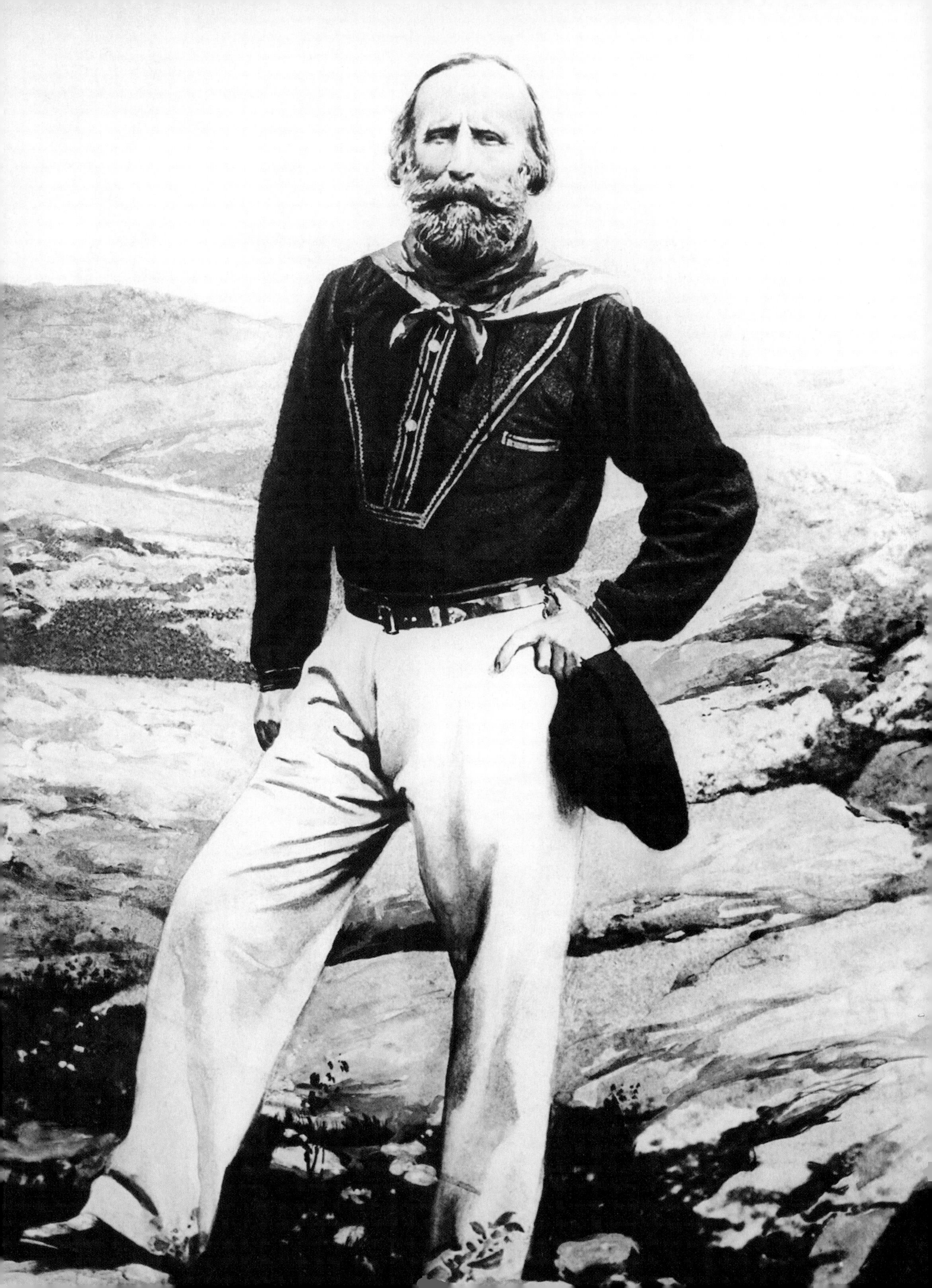

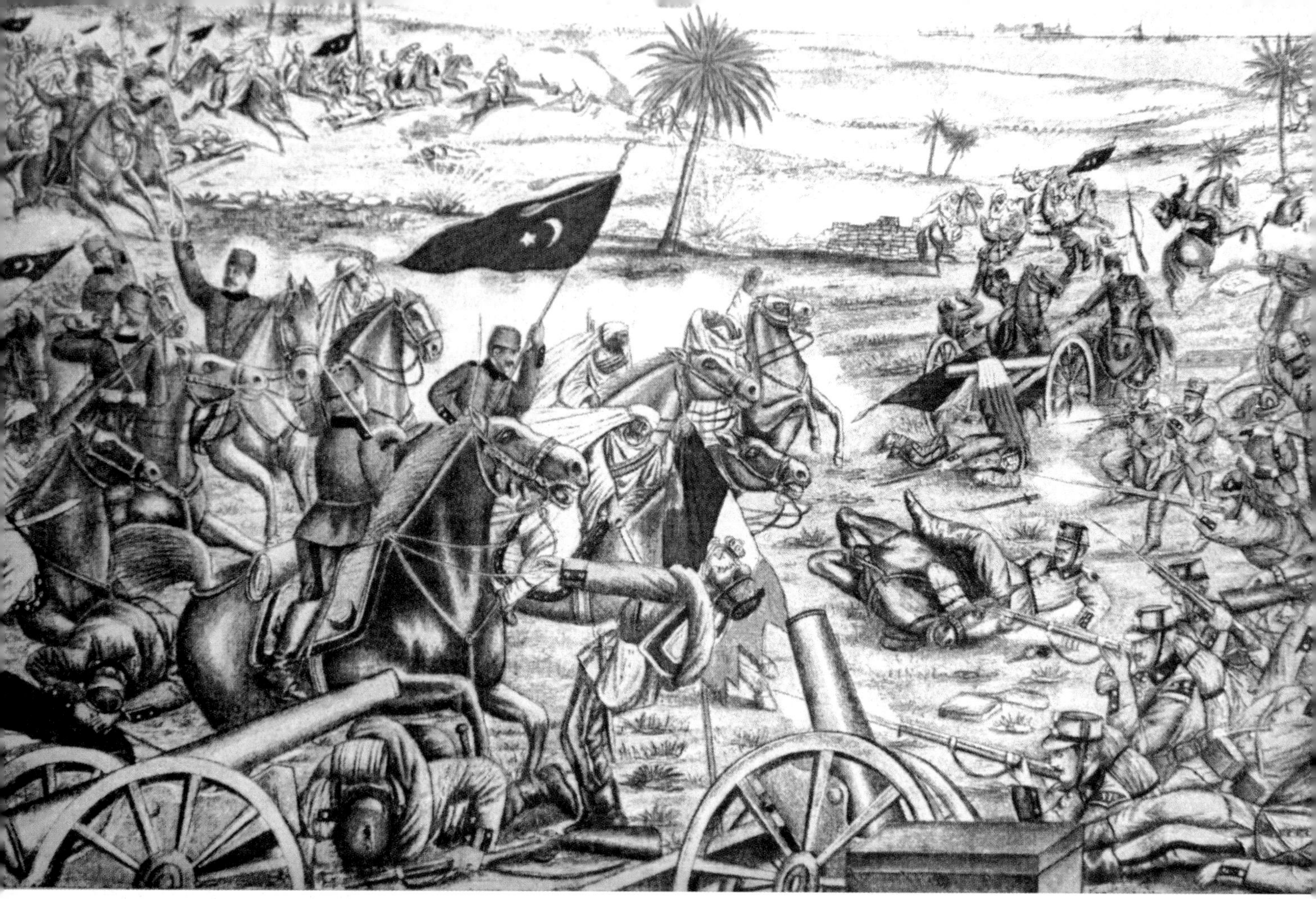

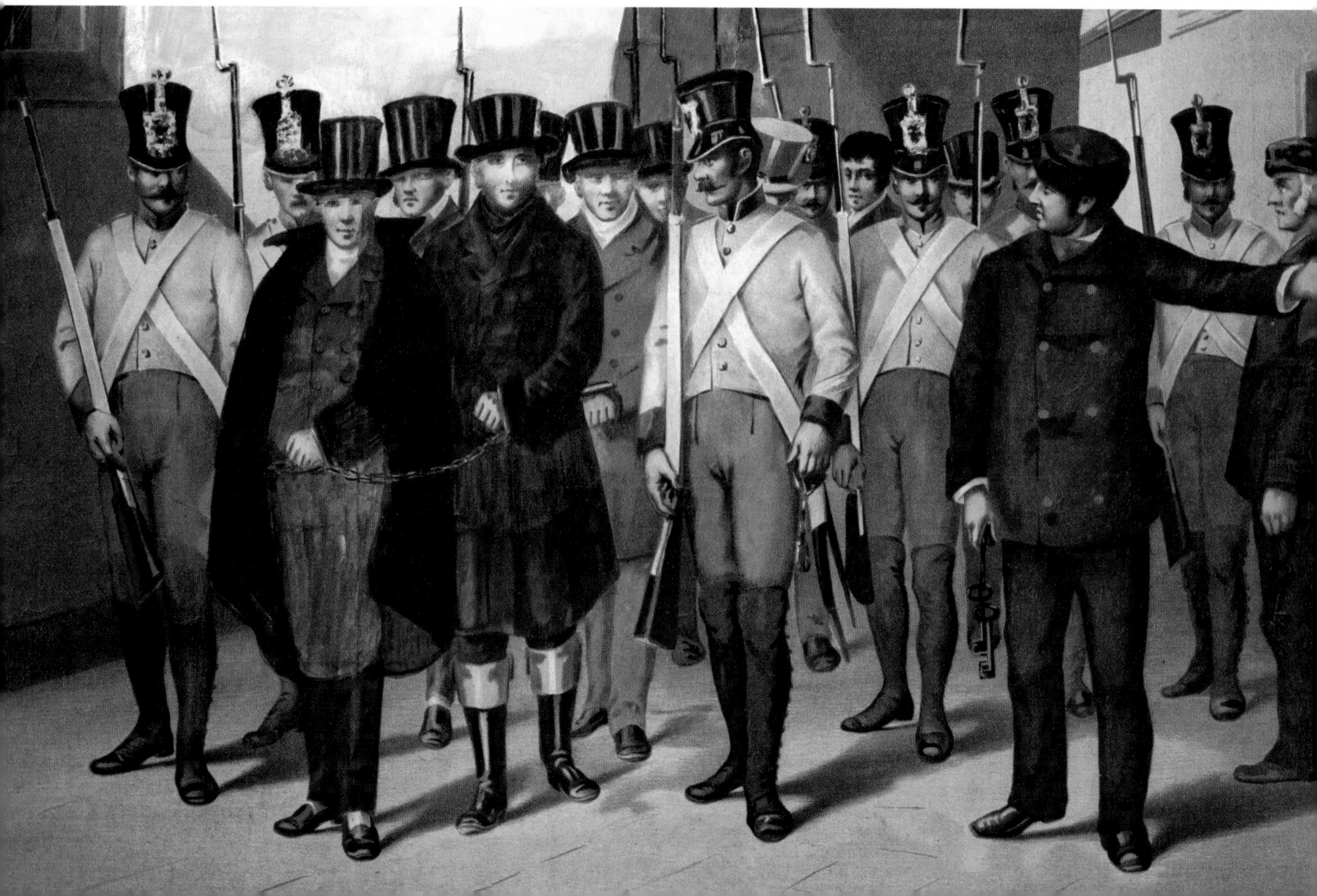

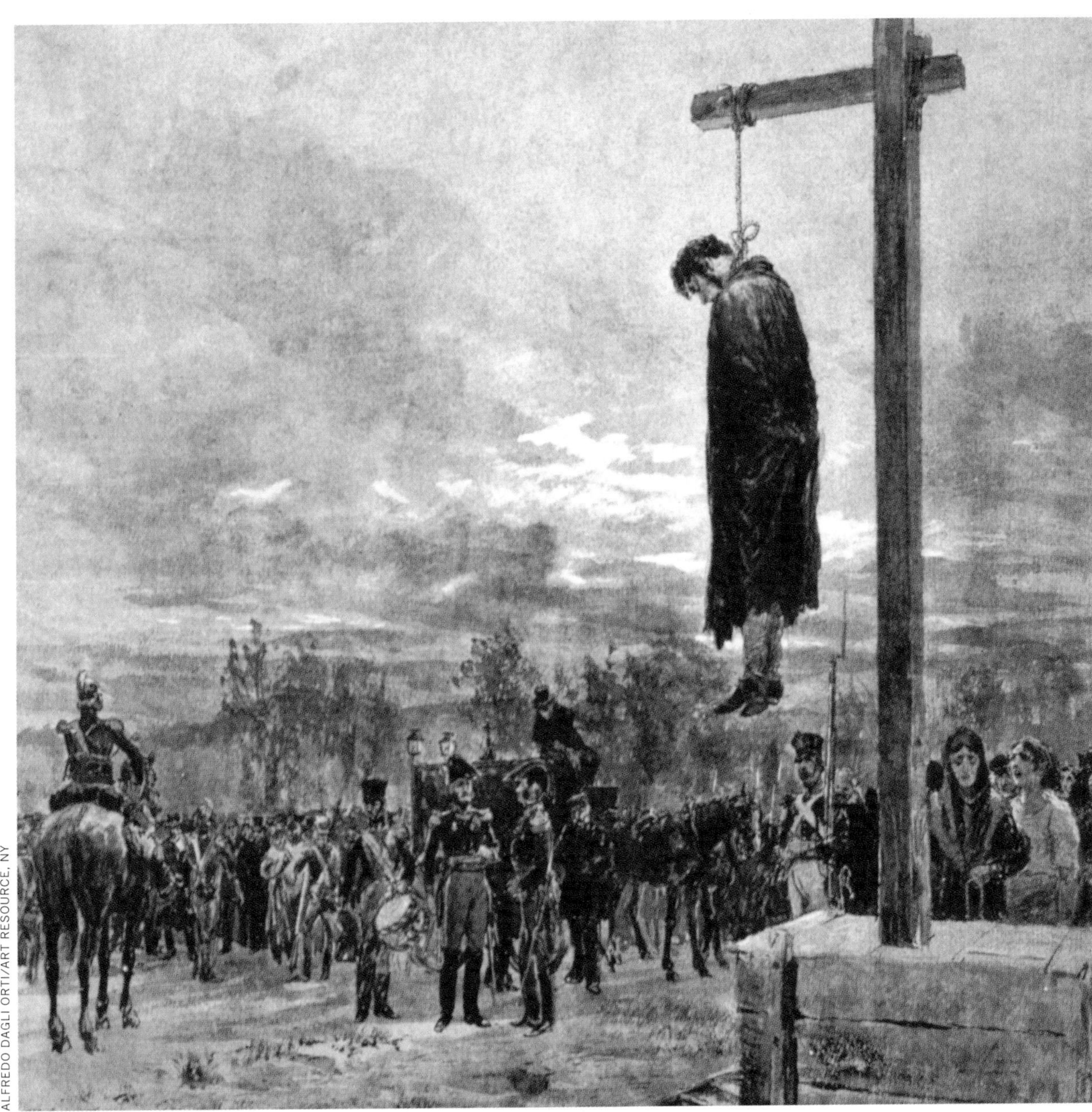

ALFREDO DAGLI ORTI/ART RESOURCE, NY

THE CARBONARI wanted the fight, and they got it. On the opposite page, bottom: A color print showing several of the group's members, having been rounded up. At top and above: Garibaldi's revenge, in two scenes depicting the action of September 7, 1860, as he and his army make their entrance into Naples. The English historian A.J.P. Taylor has said that Garibaldi, who was also an active Freemason and who always fought with the people in mind, was "the only wholly admirable figure in modern history." Abraham Lincoln was certainly an admirer, and at the outbreak of the American Civil War offered Garibaldi a major general's commission in the Union Army. Garibaldi politely demurred for two reasons: He thought he could only be useful as commander-in-chief of all forces, and, as the Italian historian Arrigo Petacco writes, "Garibaldi was ready to accept Lincoln's 1862 offer but on one condition: that the war's objective be declared as the abolition of slavery. But at that stage Lincoln was unwilling to make such a statement lest he worsen an agricultural crisis." When Lincoln did in fact issue the Emancipation Proclamation in 1863, Garibaldi wrote to the President: "You will pass to posterity with the name of the Emancipator—more enviable than any crown or any treasure."

BETTMANN/CORBIS

ALFREDO DAGLI ORTI/ART RESOURCE, NY

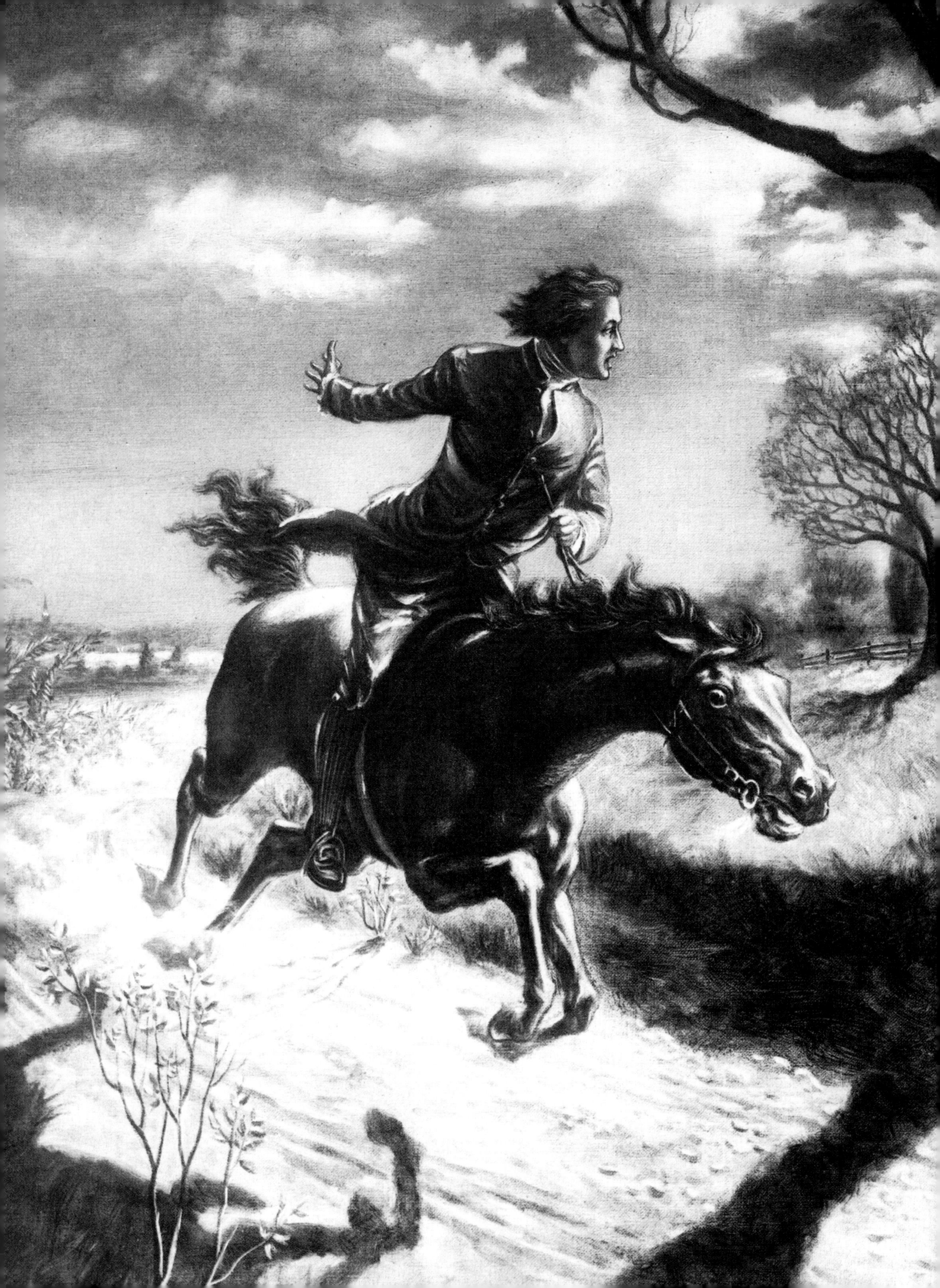

Chapter 2

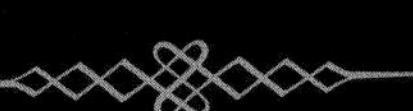

ALL-AMERICAN

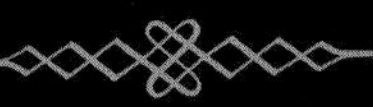

IN APRIL OF 1775, Paul Revere, having been summoned by his Masonic lodge Grand Master for a special mission, is hoofing it northwest to Lexington, Massachusetts, to let his fellow colonials know that the British are coming. The talented silversmith is a member in good standing of the underground, politically oriented Sons of Liberty—a Boston-based revolutionary group much like the later Carbonari, but more effective and with more quickly achieved results than their Italian counterparts. They, as much as anyone, ignited the American Revolution.

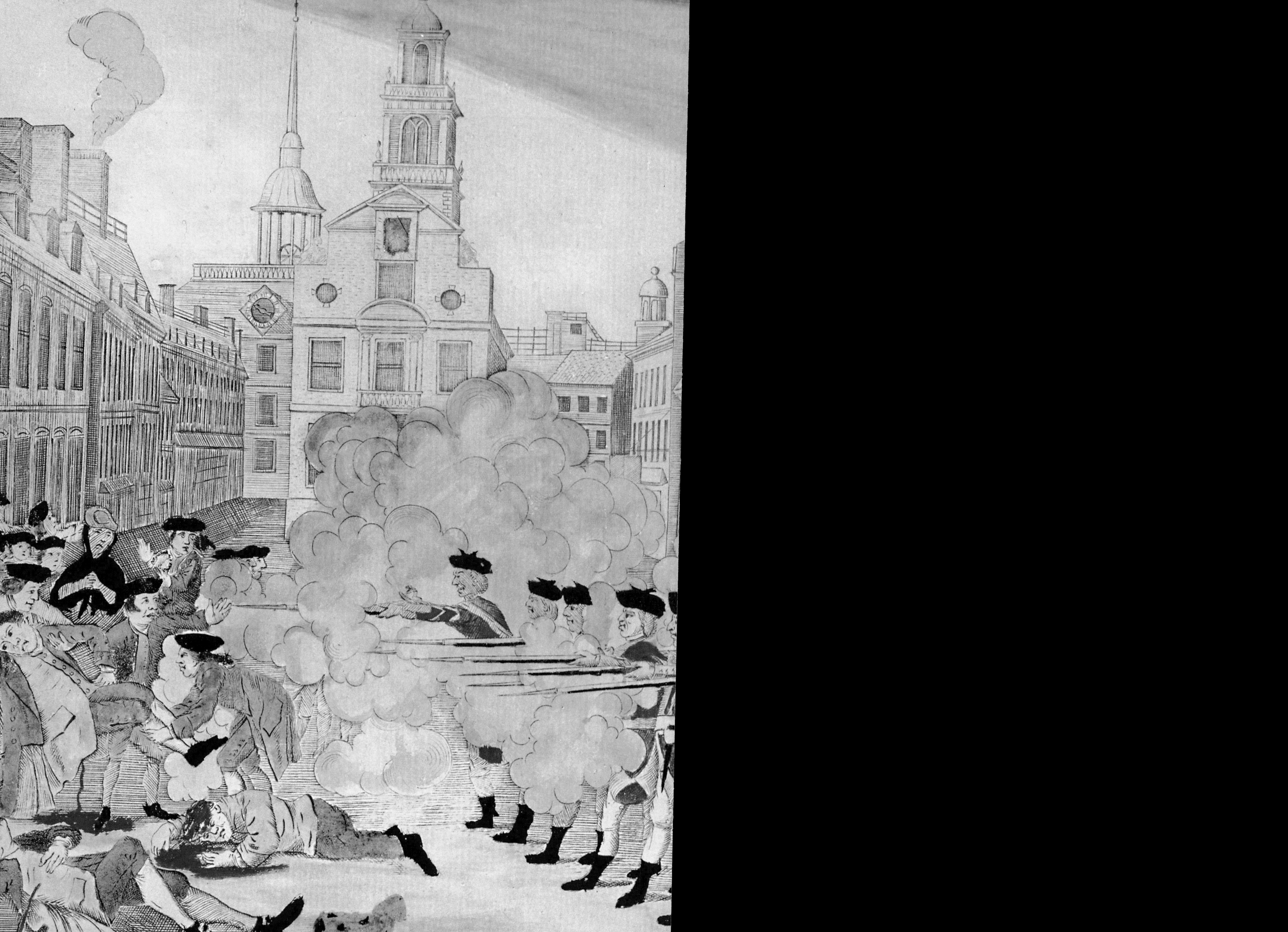

Freedom Fighters in the Shadows

It is too much to say the founding of the United States followed on from the spread of idealistic Freemasonry on the east coast of the continent. But there sure were a lot of Masons involved, and once it got down to brass tacks, several Masons from the local lodges assumed leadership roles.

This was the Age of Enlightenment, and bold goals regarding such principles as fair representation and democracy were things to be actively chased. Rationalism, humanism, an individual's rights, self-improvement: These Masonic principles were worth fighting for, and perhaps could be the basis of a grand new experiment. That, of course, would be daring in the extreme. But Massachusetts in the second half of the 18th century was full of daring men.

Political radicals among the colonials would gather at the Green Dragon Tavern in Boston's North End. So would St. Andrew's Lodge Freemasons. Some simply hung around for both meetings. Paul Revere was a Mason and also one of the so-called (and very secretive) Sons of Liberty. So was John Hancock. So was the essential Dr. Joseph Warren, a lodge Grand Master and a hero of the June 17, 1775, Battle of Bunker Hill, where he died.

Around 10 o'clock on the evening of April 18, 1775, Revere later remembered, Warren "sent in great haste for me, and begged that I would immediately set off for Lexington." His mission, with William Dawes, was to warn of the British advance on Lexington and Concord. On the next morning, the Shot Heard Round the World was fired. Did Revere think his assignment had come from his political comrade-in-arms, or his Grand Master?

The term *Sons of Liberty* has been appropriated over the centuries. In 1864, the Knights of the Golden Circle reorganized as the Order of the Sons of Liberty and opposed the U.S. government's disallowance of the South's right to leave the Union. Today, the Tea Party movement aligns itself with the Sons of Liberty's 1773 escapade against taxation without representation. One must ask: What would Warren think?

The Sons of Liberty would not be America's last secret movement to fight for individual rights; we will soon meet, as well, the Molly Maguires.

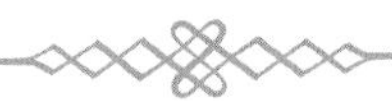

PRIOR TO the Shot Heard Round the World, there were a few famous incidents that forwarded the inexorable march to revolution. There was the Boston Tea Party, as noted, which was focused on the fact that the colonies had no representation in the British Parliament yet were burdened with underwriting the British program through taxation. And on March 5, 1770, there was the "Bloody Massacre"—now known as the Boston Massacre. Inflammatory illustrations such as this one by Paul Revere show Redcoats mowing down unarmed innocents. In fact, the five people killed were part of a hostile mob.

ART RESOURCE, NY

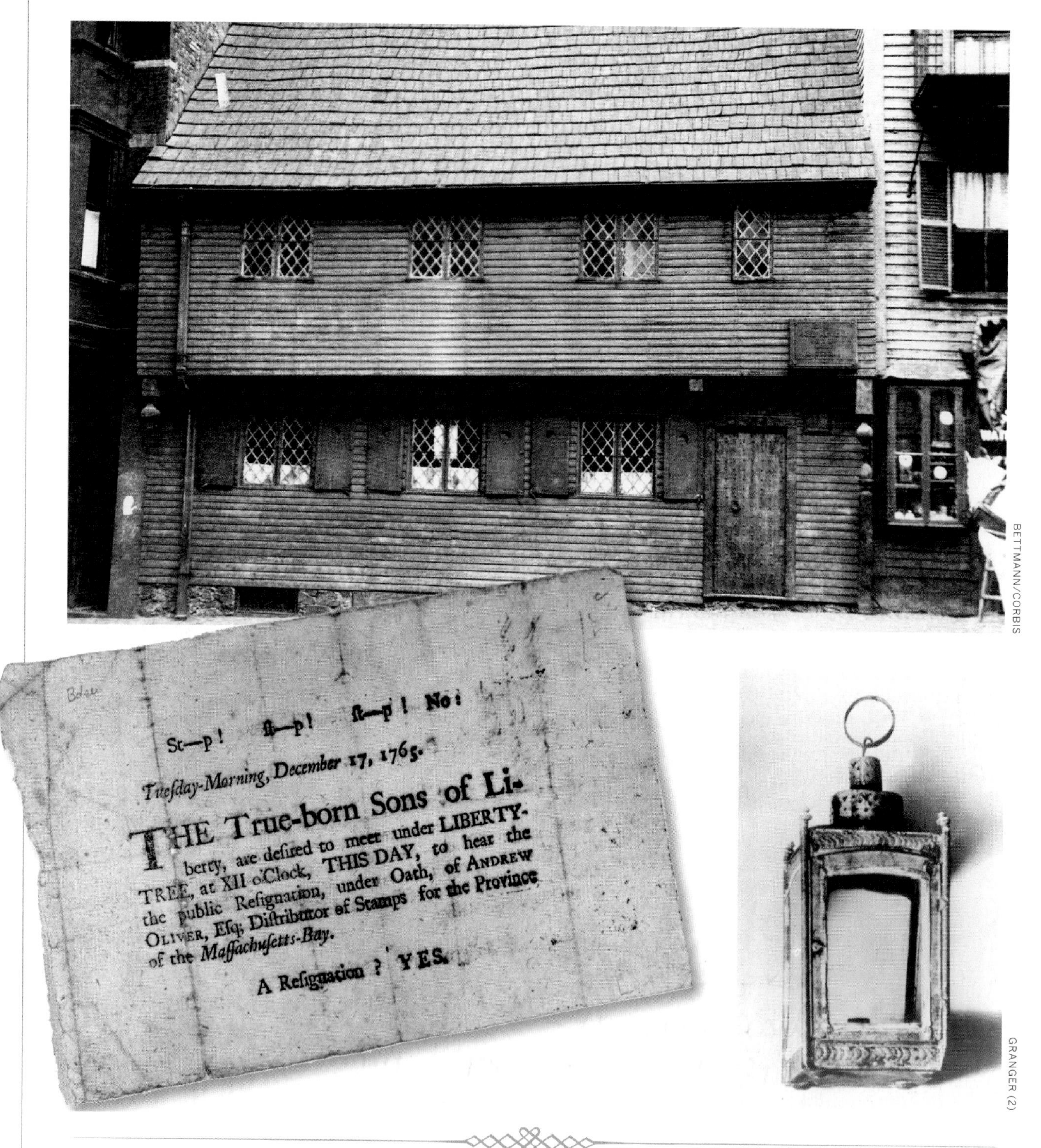

St—p! ſt—p! ſt—p! No:

Tueſday-Morning, December 17, 1765.

THE True-born Sons of Liberty, are deſired to meet under LIBERTY-TREE, at XII o'Clock, THIS DAY, to hear the public Reſignation, under Oath, of ANDREW OLIVER, Eſq; Diſtributor of Stamps for the Province of the *Maſſachuſetts-Bay.*

A Reſignation ? YES.

BETTMANN/CORBIS

GRANGER (2)

THE BROADSIDE ABOVE, which was circulated to like-thinkers, dates to December 1765, and illustrates that the Sons of Liberty operated for a full decade before the incidents at Lexington and Concord. Also on the page: Paul Revere's house and one of the two lanterns he had arranged to be hung in the belfry of Boston's Old North Church to signal the patriots as to which way the British would travel on April 19, 1775. Seeing the lights, the patriots went off to warn fellow colonials, and Revere and Dawes dashed to warn John Hancock and Samuel Adams, who were in Lexington. Opposite: The Old South Meeting House, built in 1729 at the corner of Washington and Milk streets, which, then still a church, was the site of Adams's 1773 meeting that evolved, down in the harbor, into the Sons of Liberty's Boston Tea Party.

CORBIS

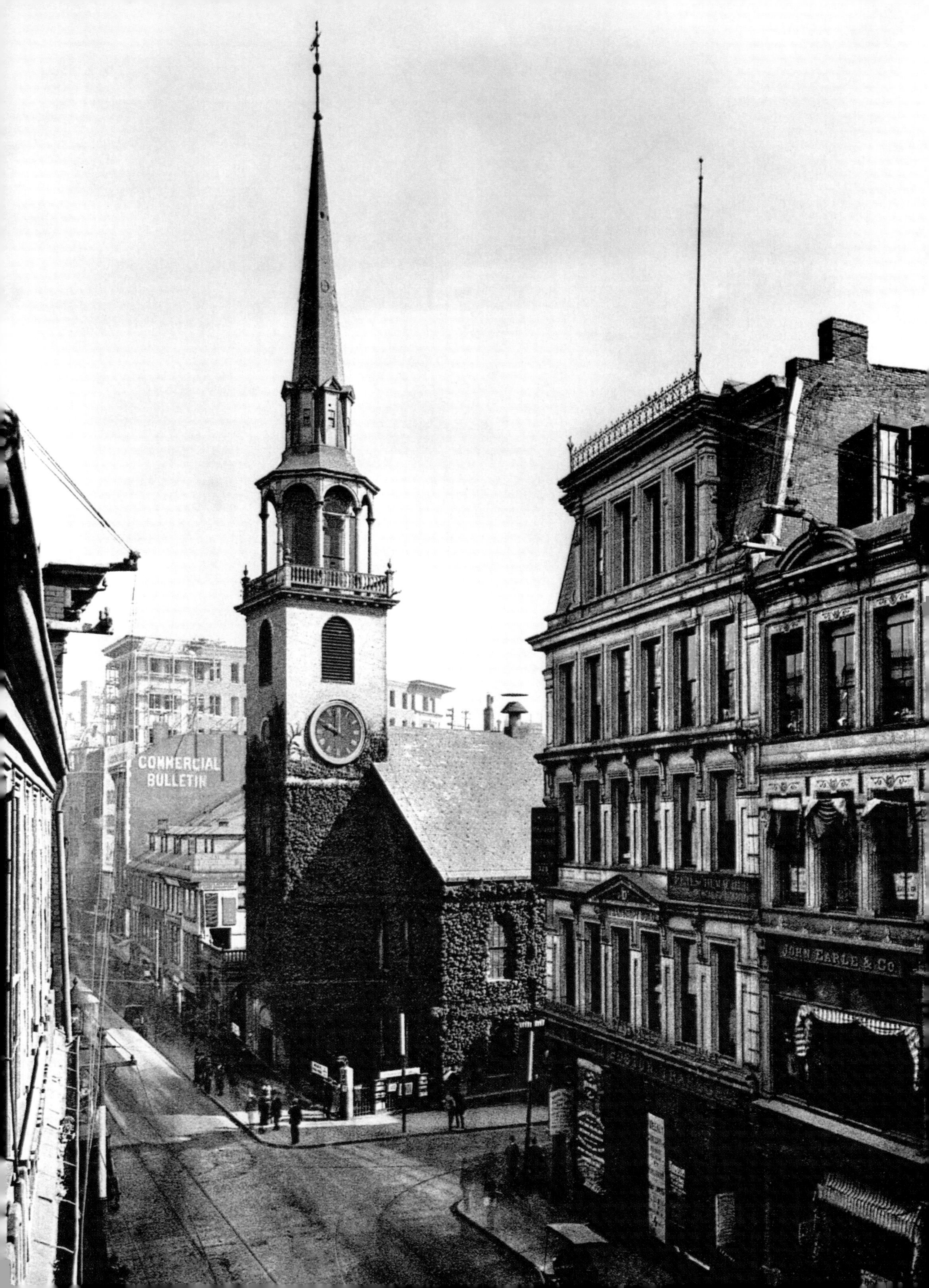
COMMERCIAL
BULLETIN
JOHN EARLE & CO.

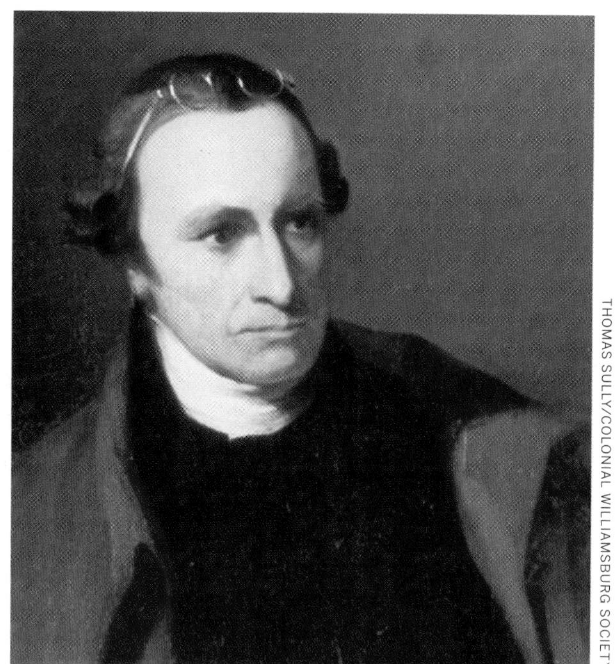

THOMAS SULLY/COLONIAL WILLIAMSBURG SOCIETY

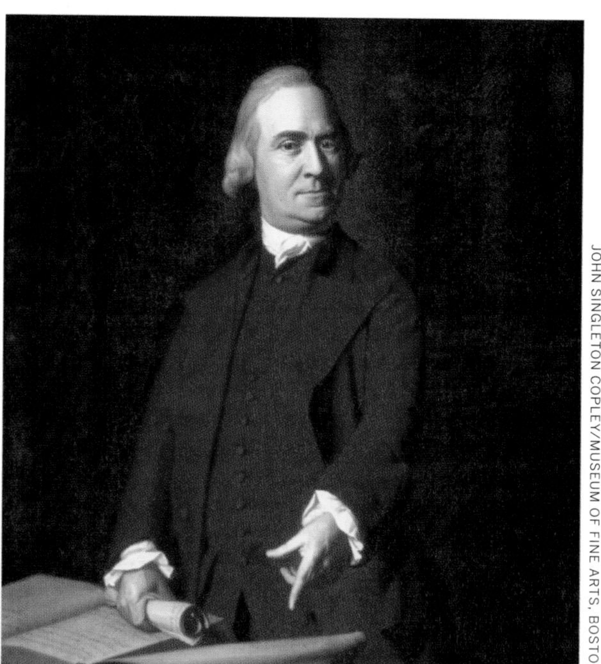

JOHN SINGLETON COPLEY/MUSEUM OF FINE ARTS, BOSTON

IN THE LEAD-UP to what would become the Revolutionary War, coordination was key, and the fellowship principles of such institutions as Masonry built a bridge of trust among the American rebels. At left, above, is Patrick Henry, a Virginia orator, soldier and politician (he would become the first governor of his state and serve five terms) best remembered for his "give me liberty or give me death" speech. He, Samuel Adams (above, right) and Thomas Paine were perhaps the most inspirational exponents of American independence in the 1760s and '70s. At one point, revolutionary leaders in Massachusetts implored those in other colonies to help create committees of correspondence to unify their stance against the British, and in March 1773, Henry, whose official Masonry is unproved but whose sympathies were clear, made it happen in Virginia. After the colonies had banded, the First Continental Congress was formed in 1774. Henry was an elected delegate, as were Mason and fellow Virginian George Washington, two more Mason sympathizers from Massachusetts (the Adamses Samuel and John) and many others. Opposite are two illustrations depicting activities of the Molly Maguires. At top, the membership holds a clandestine meeting during a strike in the coalfields of Pennsylvania in 1874. At bottom, three years later, 11 Molly Maguires are executed in Pottsville, Pennsylvania. The Irish-American Mollies are illustrative of another kind of political secret society: one focused on labor reforms rather than governmental revolution. Their progenitor organizations originated in Ireland in the 18th century, when the country was rife with secret societies: the Peep o'Day Boys, the Whiteboys and the Defenders. Ireland's agrarian rebels struck a chord with workers in America—and, in fact, through emigration, their rebellion was sometimes exported firsthand—and eventually the hub of Molly activity was the anthracite fields in several counties of Pennsylvania's coal region. There is little doubt that the Mollies endorsed and initiated not only labor strikes but violent tactics in pressing their case against their bosses during the 19th century "Land Wars." And there is little doubt that the bosses pressed back, just as harshly or more so, against the Mollies. By 1873 one of these mine owners was said by a confidant to be "fully impressed with the necessity of lessening the overgrown power of the 'Labor Union' and of absolutely exterminating, if possible, the Molly Maguires." This would be achieved, after loss of life on both sides, by the hangings of 1877–1878. The fairness of the trials and who was most in the wrong continue to be debated. For our purposes, the Mollies stand as an interesting case in point: a society that felt it had to take to the caves to form its plots, before emerging to fiercely press its grievances. As we know, in modern times in the U.S. we have seen some fringe groups do the same, with far less justification than had the Molly Maguires.

GRANGER (2)

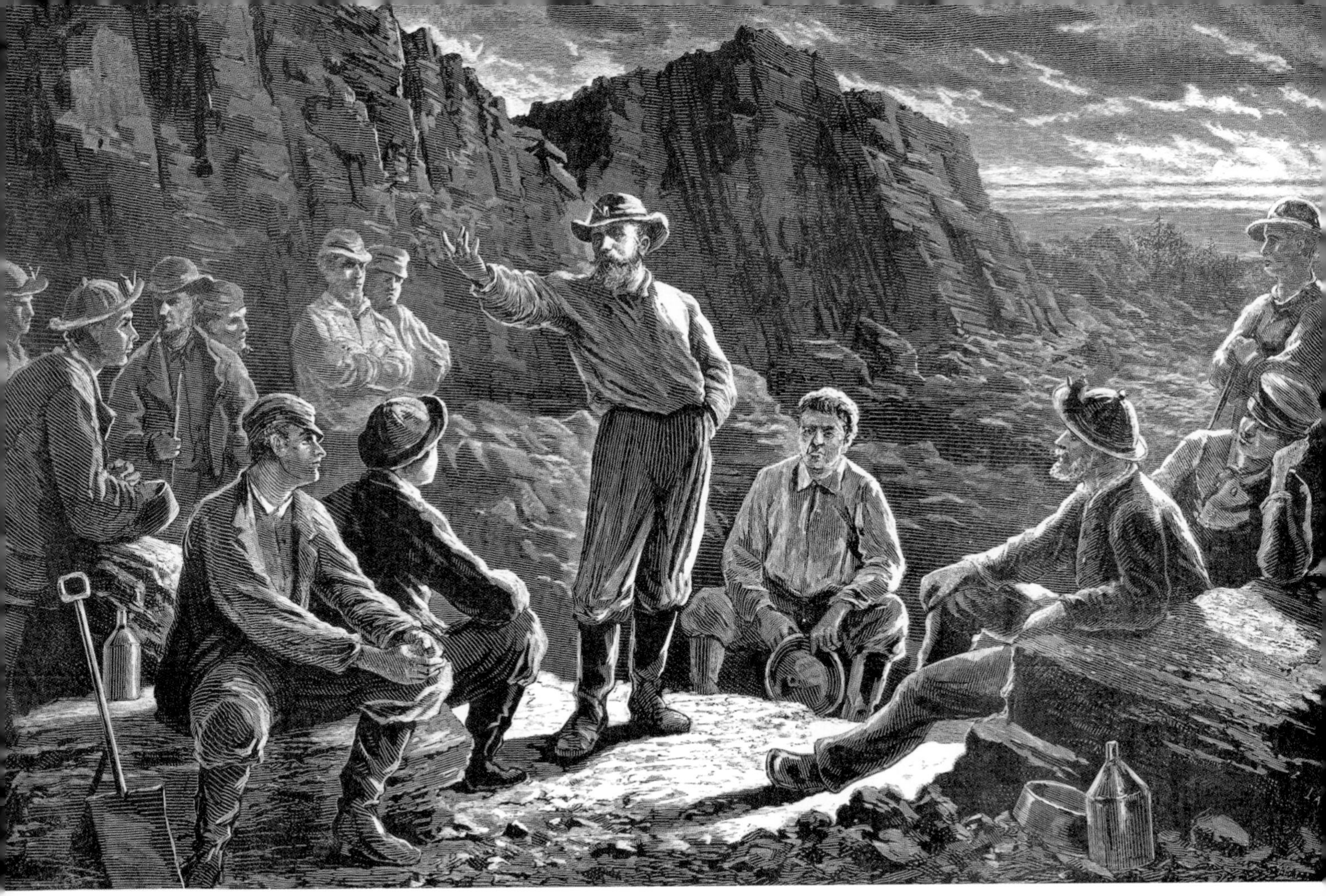

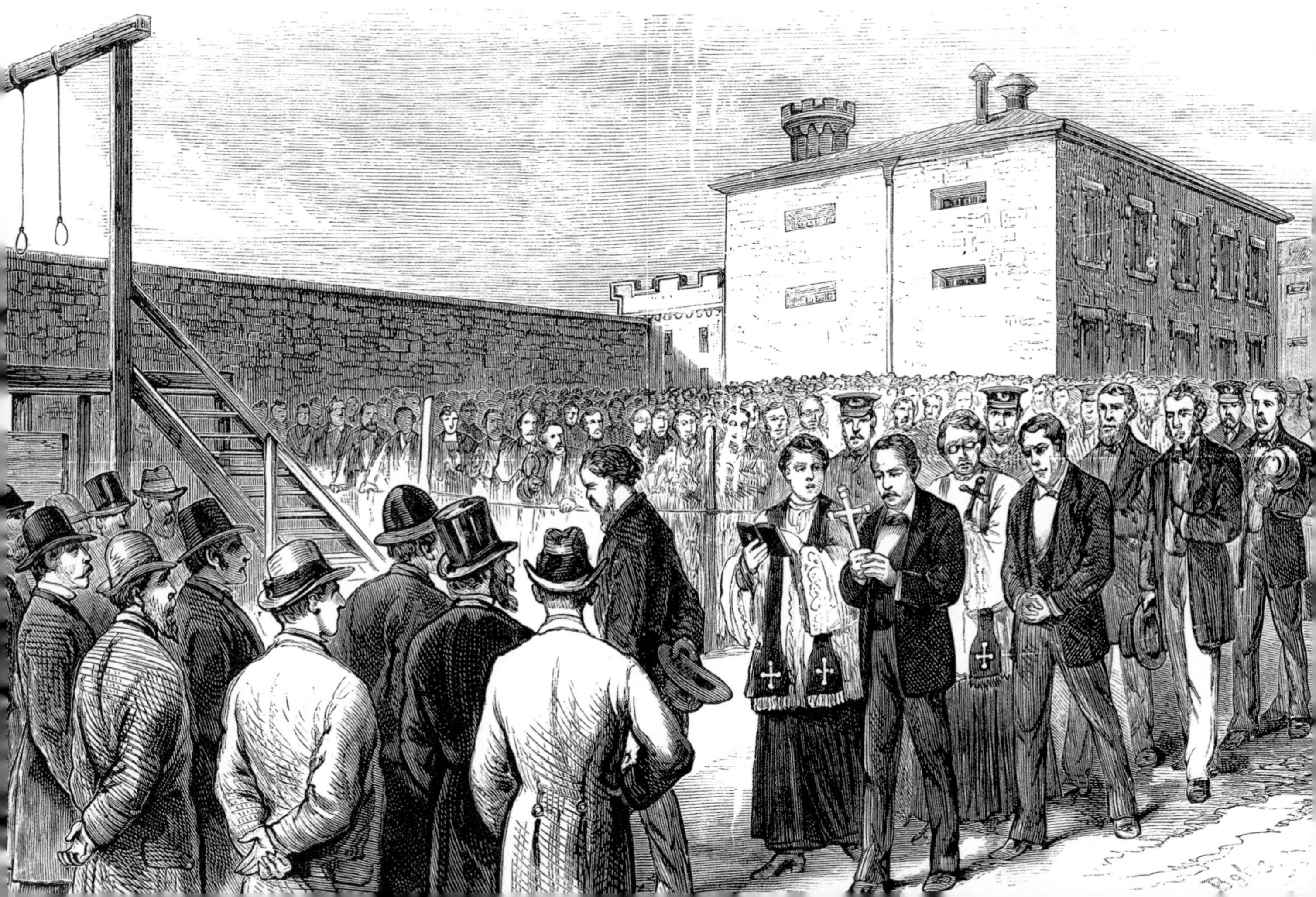

OUR MASON IN CHIEF

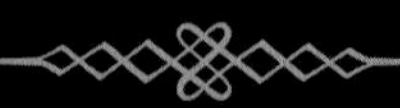

IN A COLOR LITHOGRAPH from 1899, we see George Washington, proud Mason, holding a scroll and trowel, with portraits of fellow members of the Craft, his friend and fellow general in the Revolutionary War the Marquis de Lafayette (who would name his son after Washington) and the later U.S. President Andrew Jackson, as well as biblical scenes. By the way, the *G* at top does not stand for "George." It is thought that when it first appeared in Masonic symbolism, it stood for "Geometry," dominant among sciences. The following is from the Regius Manuscript (or "A Poem of Moral Duties"): "On this manner, through good wit of Geometry—Began first the Craft of Masonry." In later interpretations the *G* represented "God," and even "God: Grand Geometrician of the Universe."

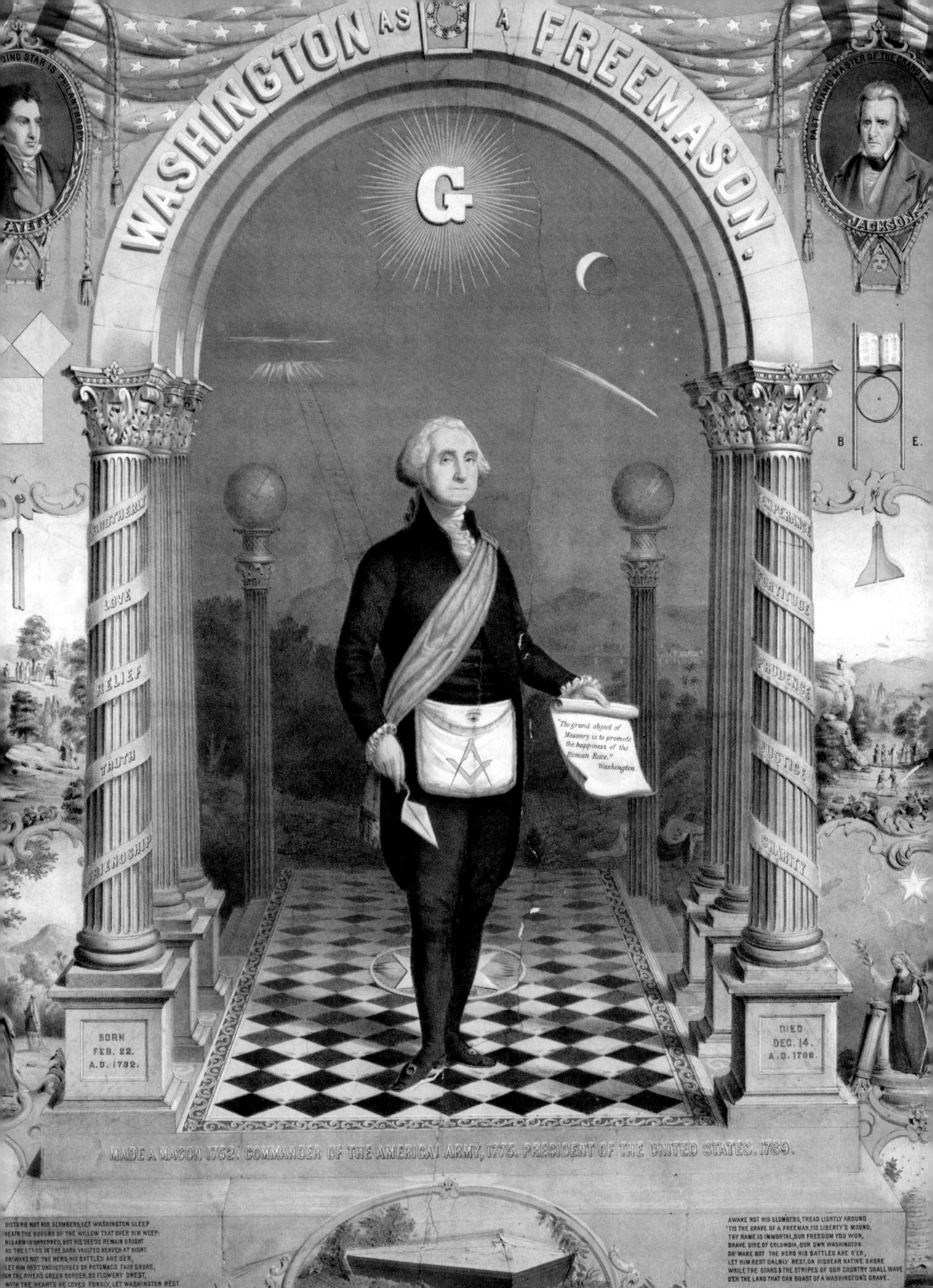
WASHINGTON AS A FREEMASON.
G
BROTHERLY LOVE
RELIEF
TRUTH
FRIENDSHIP
TEMPERANCE
FORTITUDE
PRUDENCE
JUSTICE
CHARITY
JACKSON
B
E.
"The grand object of Masonry is to promote the happiness of the Human Race." Washington
BORN FEB. 22. A.D. 1732.
DIED DEC. 14. A.D. 1799.
MADE A MASON 1752. COMMANDER OF THE AMERICAN ARMY, 1775. PRESIDENT OF THE UNITED STATES. 1789.
DISTURB NOT HIS SLUMBERS, LET WASHINGTON SLEEP
NEATH THE BOUGHS OF THE WILLOW THAT OVER HIM WEEP:
HIS ARM IS UNNERVED, BUT HIS DEEDS REMAIN BRIGHT
AS THE STARS IN THE DARK VAULTED HEAVEN AT NIGHT.
OH! WAKE NOT THE HERO, HIS BATTLES ARE O'ER,
LET HIM REST UNDISTURBED ON POTOMACS FAIR SHORE,
ON THE RIVER'S GREEN BORDER, SO FLOWERY DREST,
WITH THE HEARTS HE LOVED FONDLY, LET WASHINGTON REST.
AWAKE NOT HIS SLUMBERS, TREAD LIGHTLY AROUND
'TIS THE GRAVE OF A FREEMAN, 'TIS LIBERTY'S MOUND,
THY NAME IS IMMORTAL, OUR FREEDOM YOU WON,
BRAVE SIRE OF COLUMBIA, OUR OWN WASHINGTON.
OH! WAKE NOT THE HERO HIS BATTLES ARE O'ER,
LET HIM REST CALMLY REST, ON HIS DEAR NATIVE SHORE
WHILE THE STARS & THE STRIPES OF OUR COUNTRY SHALL WAVE
O'ER THE LAND THAT CAN BOAST OF A WASHINGTON'S GRAVE.

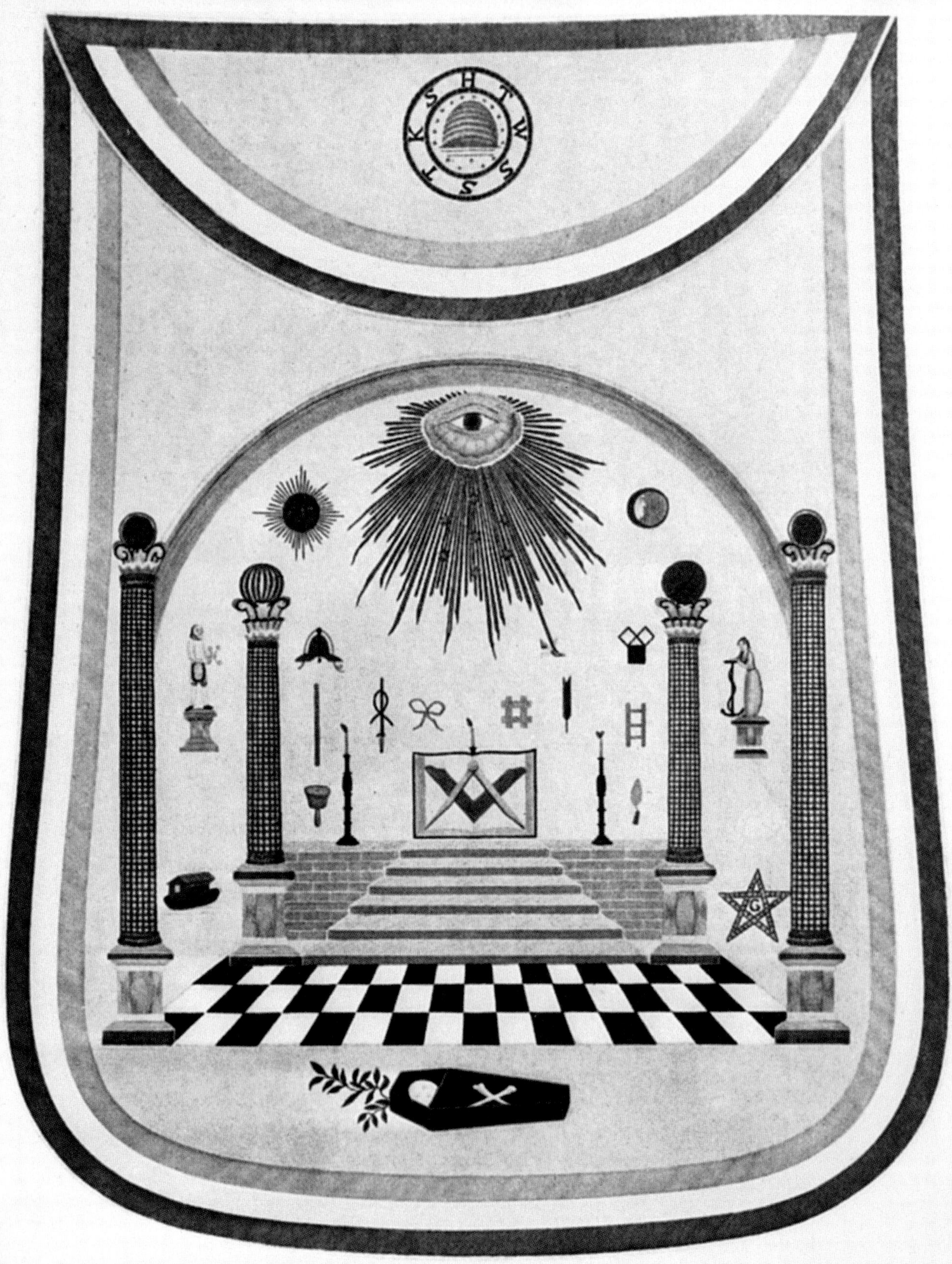

WASHINGTON'S MASONIC APRON.

EMBROIDERED BY MADAM LAFAYETTE; PRESENTED AUGUST, 1784, BY

BRO. GEN. LAFAYETTE TO BRO. GEN. WASHINGTON;

PRESENTED OCTOBER 26, 1816, BY THE LEGATEES OF BRO. WASHINGTON TO THE

WASHINGTON BENEVOLENT SOCIETY OF PENNSYLVANIA;

PRESENTED JULY 3, 1829, BY THE WASHINGTON BENEVOLENT SOCIETY TO THE

R. W. GRAND LODGE, F. & A. M. OF PENNSYLVANIA.

Founders, Leaders, Craftsmen

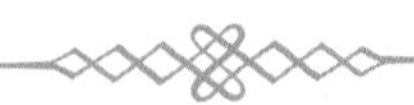

It is interesting to note how many of our nation's early heroes were Masons. Of the 56 signatories of the Declaration of Independence, nine were Freemasons. Perhaps 13 Masons signed the Constitution. Of the 74 generals in the Continental Army, 33 were Masons—and George Washington made sure that those at his right hand, making decisions that counted, were of the Craft.

A corollary of this is that while these founders were God-fearing men, many, though they may have been raised in the Anglican Church, were not specifically, as adults, Christian. Many were intrigued by what we now know, in a blanketed form, as Unitarianism. Through their writings, we can conclude that an influential block within the Founding Fathers were deists or theists: the former believing in natural religions based on human reason rather than revelation, with an emphasis on personal morality; the latter, in a universe created by a god who is present yet transcendental. Neither deists nor theists consider Jesus divine, as much as they might admire him and his philosophy.

So maybe it isn't so surprising that so many of the Founding Fathers were Masons, since rationalism and moralism and humanism are at the heart of Freemasonry, as they are at the heart of both the Constitution and the Declaration of Independence (and represent the core of Freemasonry's problems with Rome; up until the Vatican II reforms of the 1960s, a Catholic could be excommunicated for joining the Masons, and it remains a grave sin). Also: Such thinking would lead in a straight line to the separation of church and state, and to a set of laws underpinning what is right and just.

George Washington was not only a Mason, he was a thoroughgoing (even devout) Mason. He was 20 in 1752 when he was admitted into the Craft, and his qualities were soon recognized. Later, General Washington used Freemasonry as a way to bind his soldiers, and lodge meetings served as support when the going got tough. Even as the snow fell at Valley Forge, Pennsylvania, meetings were held, and fellow Mason the Marquis de Lafayette joined his dear friend there during those dire days. What did Washington value most in Freemasonry? Perhaps its sense of fellowship, loyalty and service. "[T]he virtues that ennoble mankind are taught, nourished and fostered in the halls of the Freemasons," wrote our first Mason in Chief. "They encourage domestic life and serve as a standard for the highest duties of State."

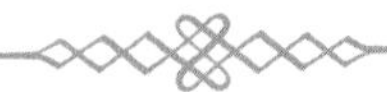

GEORGE WASHINGTON'S Masonic apron, replete with symbols, embroidered by Lafayette's wife. The letters *KSHTWSST* at top indicate the Masonic degrees into which the President-to-be had been admitted.

GRANGER

E.L. CRANDALL/NATIONAL GEOGRAPHIC/CORBIS

ABOVE IS, of course, the Washington Monument in our nation's capital. It is topped by a pyramid, and it's interesting to know that when funds couldn't be scared up for this physical tribute before the Civil War, the late President's brother Masons passed the hat. When the monument was finally finished after the war, there was great Masonic fanfare at the dedication. On the opposite page is the George Washington Masonic Memorial in Alexandria, Virginia, a little more than a stone's throw from the monument. Washington was never shy about his Masonic standing during his lifetime—he was quite proud of it, in fact—and all these years later, his Mason-ness remains on flagrant display.

RICHARD T. NOWITZ/CORBIS

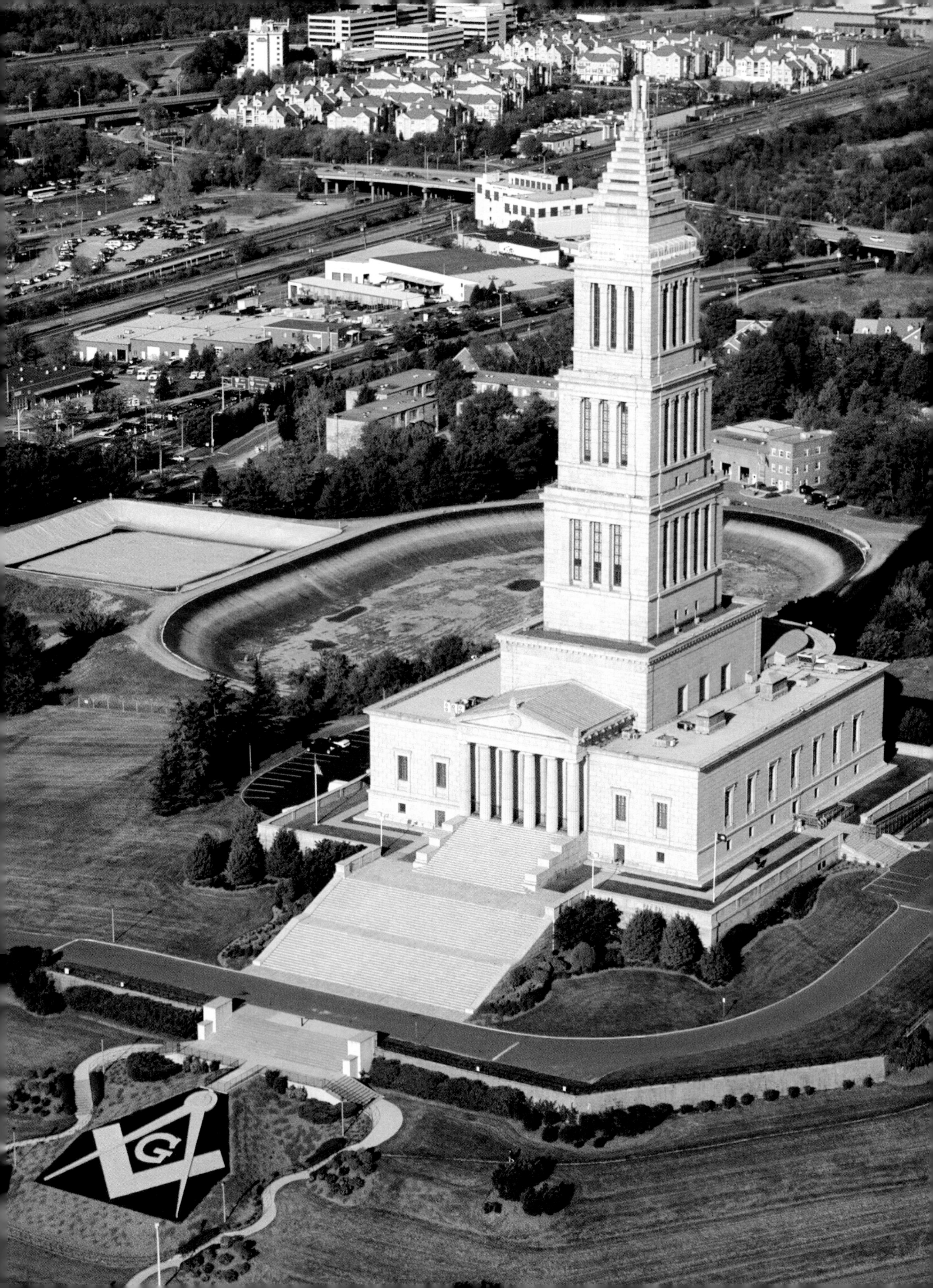
G

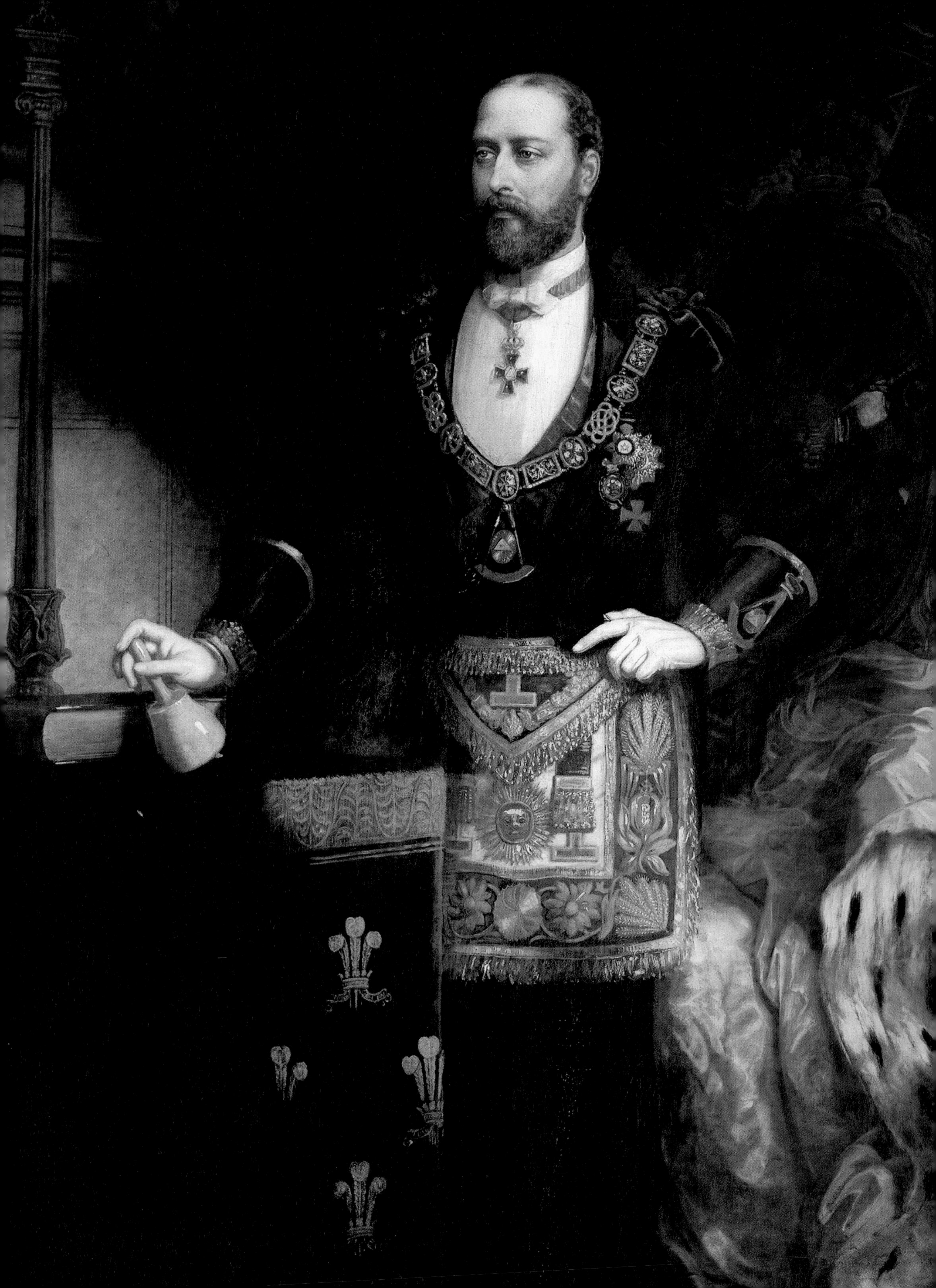

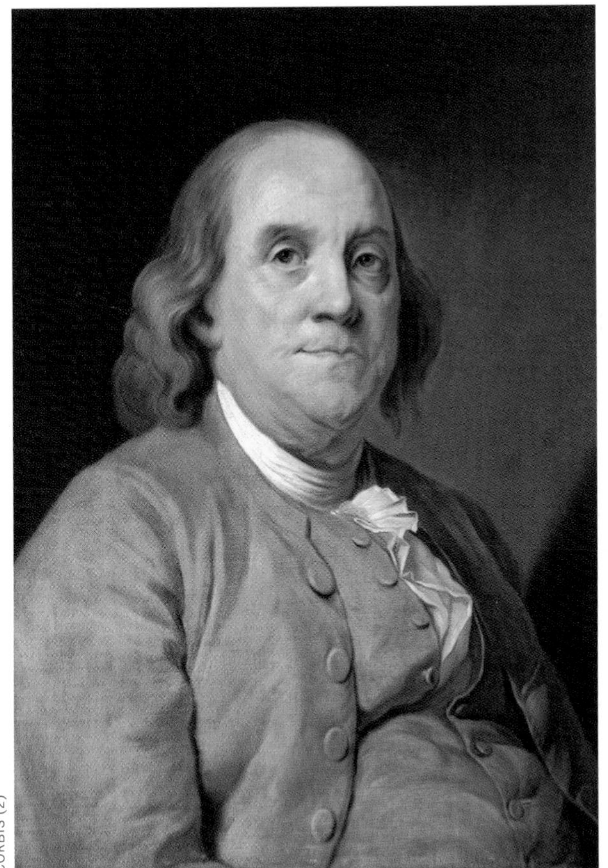

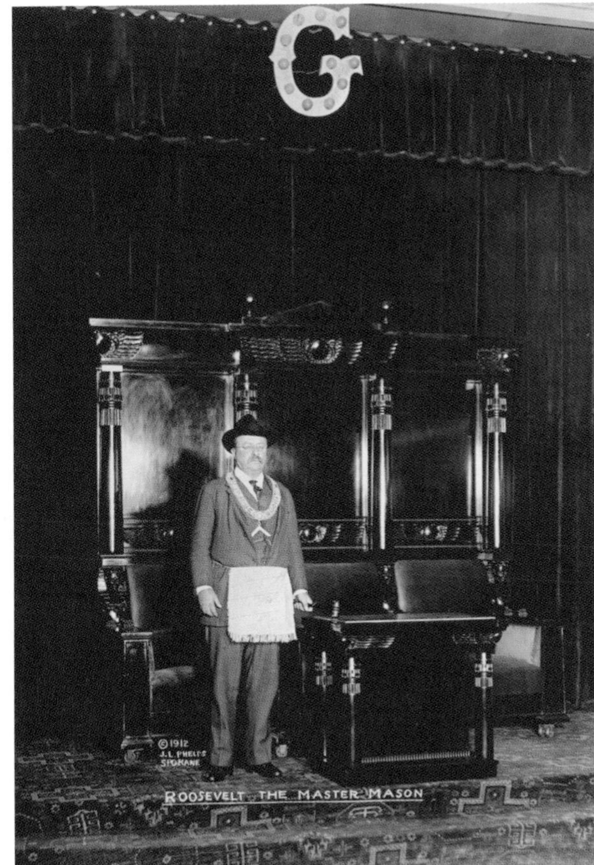

CORBIS (2)

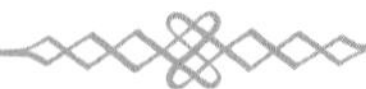

WHETHER MASONIC VALUES enhanced leadership skills or whether natural leaders were courted by Masons to enhance the lodge must be debated on a case-by-case basis, but the fact remains: Many men of social and political eminence were Masons, particularly in days gone by. They weren't all Americans, as the earlier example of the Marquis de Lafayette illustrates. Opposite is Great Britain's Prince Edward, who would later become King Edward VII; he was a Mason, as were his grandsons, the kings Edward VIII and George VI of *The King's Speech* fame. (Winston Churchill, too, was a Mason.) Edward VII was a most serious Freemason throughout his life: a Grand Master in 1874 and a public supporter of the Craft in England and during foreign sojourns throughout the Empire. He was forever laying foundation stones of public buildings, dockyards and churches, with his fellow Masons ritualistically celebrating. It was said that he was one of the world's biggest financial supporters of Masonry, and in England the Grand Lodge grew from 637 local lodges in 1814 to 2,850 in 1901—the year Edward VII resigned his Grand Mastership upon becoming king. Across the English Channel in France, Freemasonry was also attractive to the elite; Voltaire was a Mason. A lover of all things French was Mason Benjamin Franklin (above, left), and during an official visit to Paris to seek support for the American Revolution in 1778, he was invited to join a lodge there. He did so, and it was through his Freemasonic contacts that he met not only Lafayette but John Paul Jones. The Continental Navy captain Jones christened his "I have not yet begun to fight" ship the *Bonhomme Richard* in tribute to Franklin's best-selling *Poor Richard's Almanack.* Above, right: Theodore Roosevelt joined a New York Freemasons' lodge in 1901. When he was sworn in as President of the United States that same year after the assassination of William McKinley, he became our ninth Masonic chief executive. Later, his fifth cousin Franklin Delano Roosevelt also became a Mason and also became President. On the pages immediately following, FDR is at center, front row, during a gathering of Masons in New York City on November 23, 1935. Behind him are his two sons, James and Franklin. The wee man standing fifth from the left is none other than the "Little Flower" himself, New York mayor Fiorello LaGuardia.

COURTESY THE UNITED GRAND LODGE OF ENGLAND, LONDON

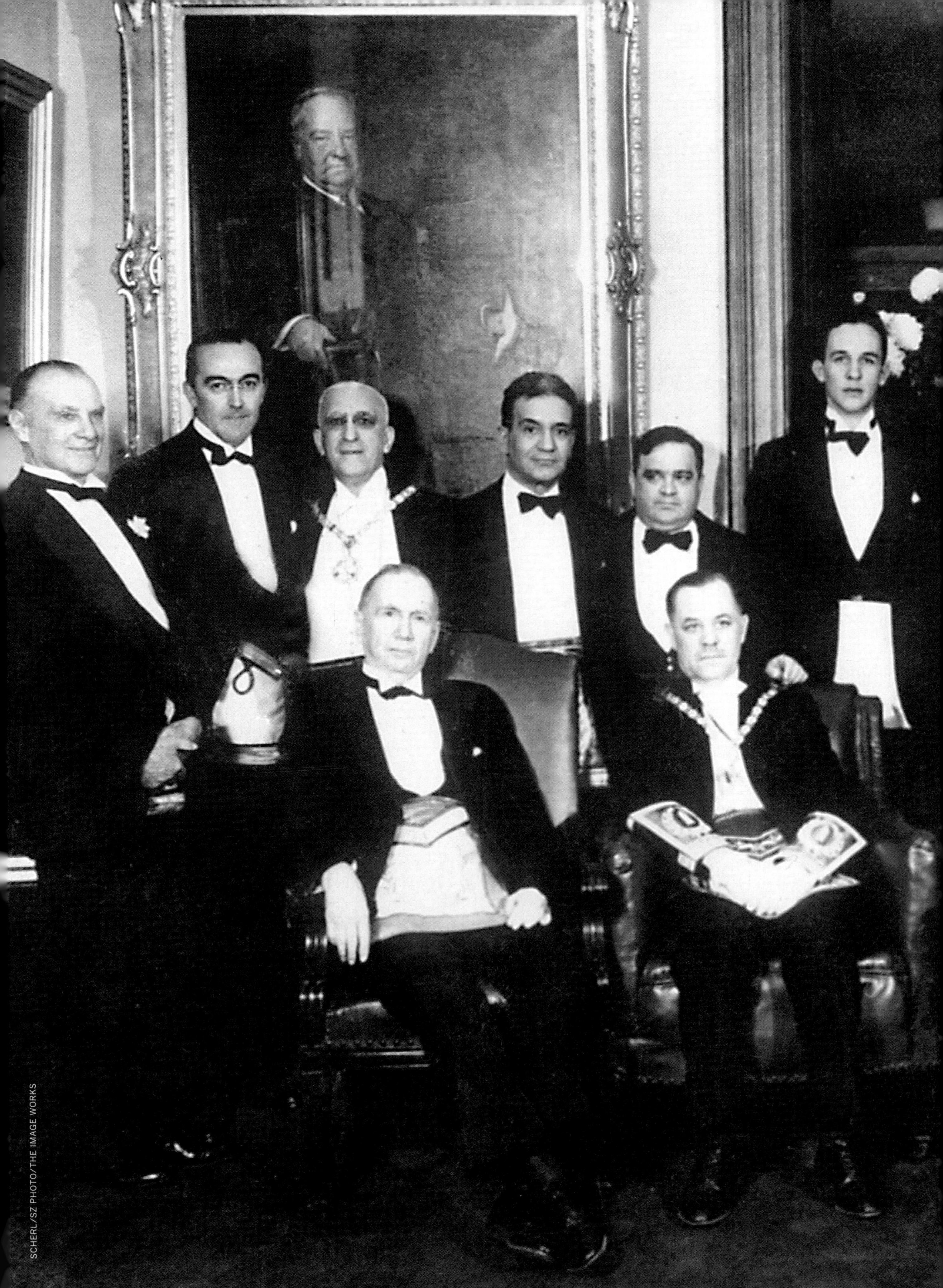

SCHERL/SZ PHOTO/THE IMAGE WORKS

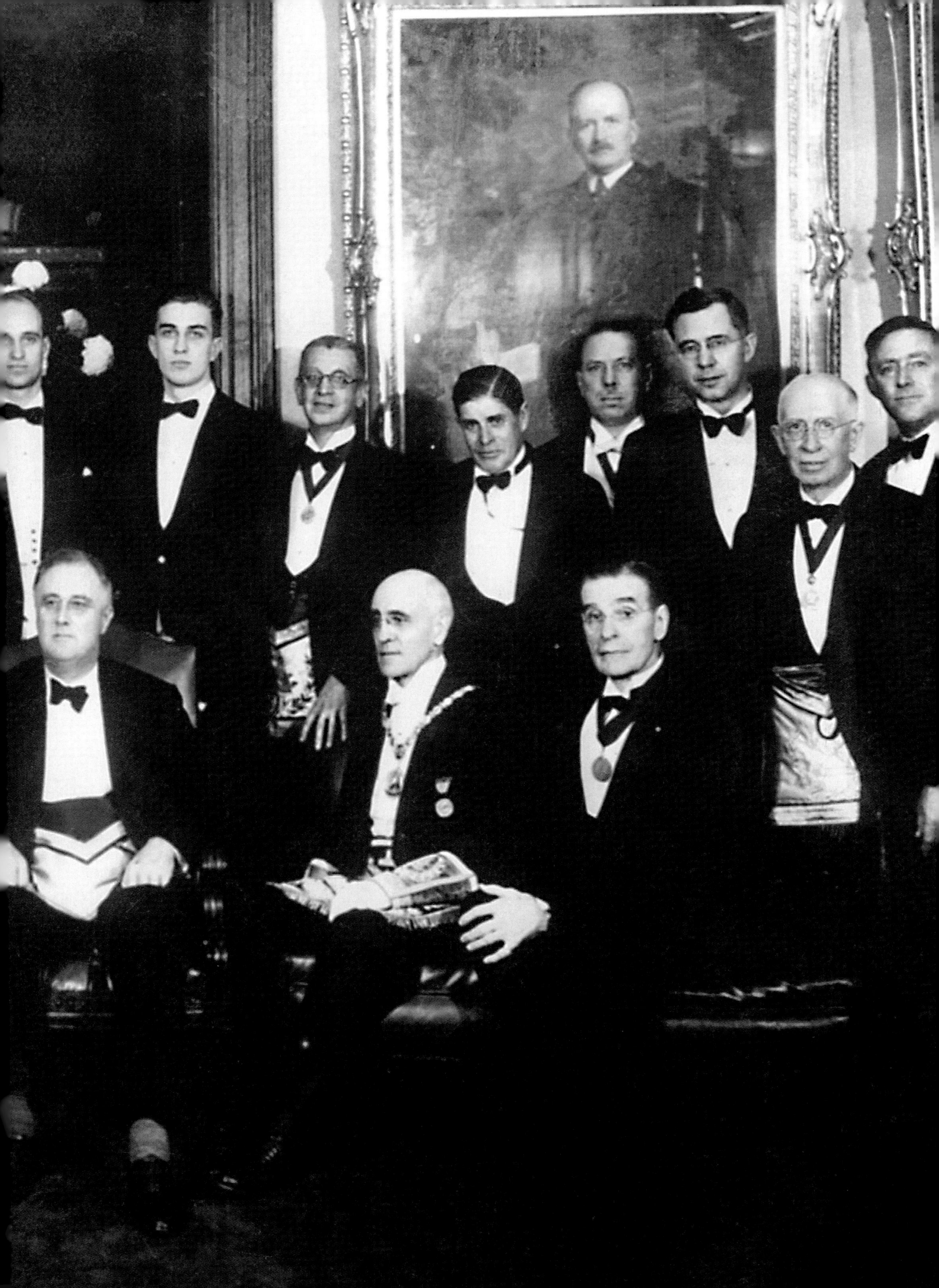

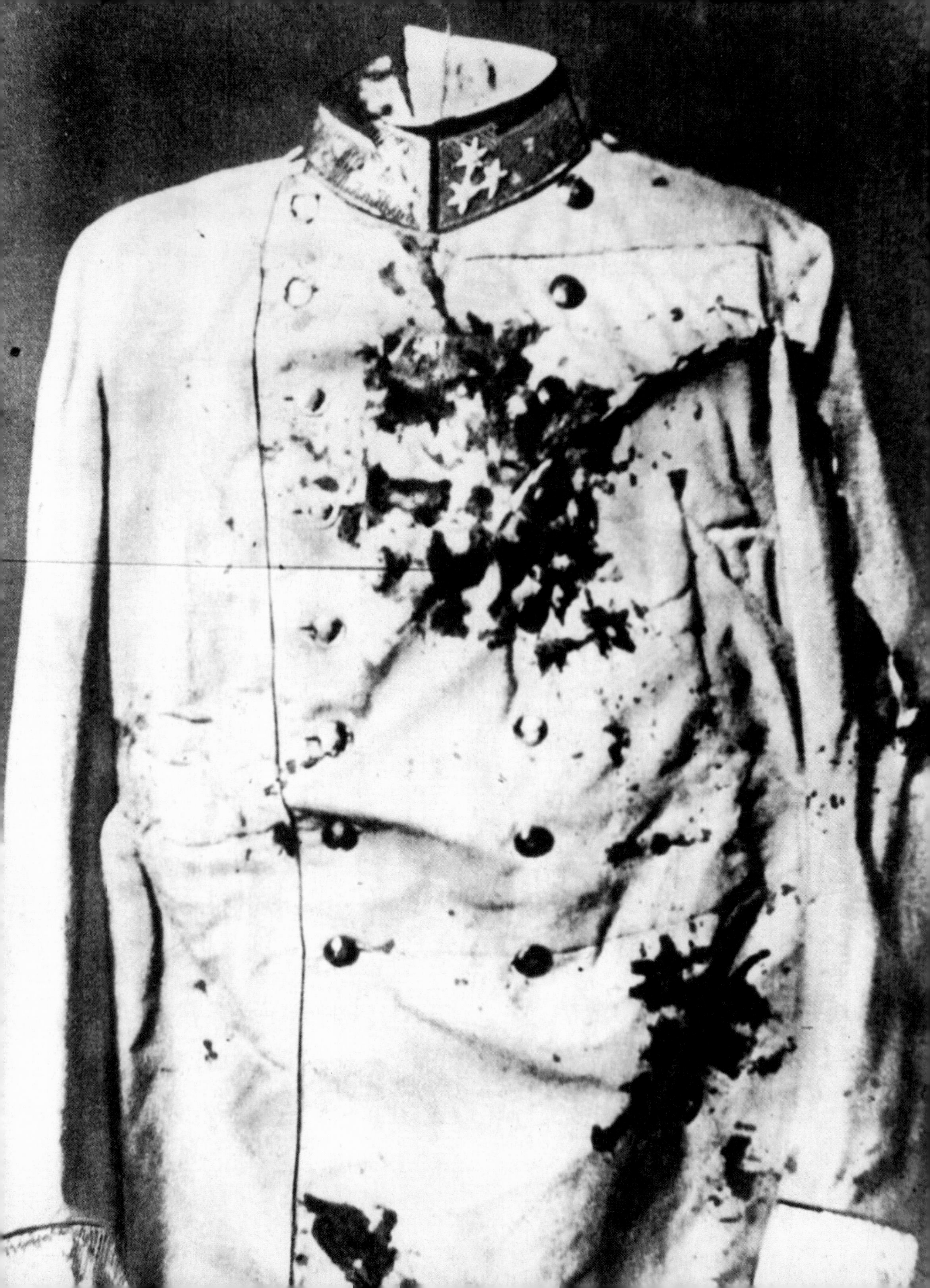

Chapter 4

NEFARIOUS

PERHAPS NO DEED in secret society history, even if we consider the Boston Tea Party, so affected world events as that of the Black Hand on June 28, 1914, when it caused the assassination of the Austrian archduke Franz Ferdinand in Sarajevo, the capital city of Bosnia and Herzegovina (Ferdinand's bloodied coat is pictured). That brazen act committed in the light of day led to the dark night that was World War I, one of the most devastating conflicts ever visited upon our planet. What was the Black Hand? And what was the Thule Society? What was and is the Ku Klux Klan? What were all of these villainous secret societies? Read on.

At Bottom, Thugs

The headline here could apply to many groups in this chapter, but here it is a specific appellation. The 13th century Thuggee of India gave us this term: *thugs*. Thanks so much. Really appreciated.

Thugs were, as long ago as the 1200s, gangs who roamed from town to town, looting and pillaging, often in disguise. Naturally, they didn't announce themselves—which gave them a leg up—before they struck. They were pioneers in organized crime, and in the use of the notion "secret society" for anti-societal purposes.

Smuggling and drug-trafficking rings are as old as the hills in Asia and Africa, and extant criminal organizations in Italy and Japan trace their histories back several centuries. The Mafia came together as a secret society in Sicily in the late 1800s, formed from rogue groups who had fought to protect the land from foreign invaders, such as Normans and Arabs.

On this page, our book takes a turn. Heretofore we have been talking about optimists and altruists. The Knights Templar could behave in reprehensible fashion, slaughtering their foes even after they had conquered them, but they felt they were acting in the name of God. Others, from the Masons to the Sons of Liberty to the Carbonari, saw a higher purpose. Now, here, we come to secret societies that organized as they did because they sought to evade the law.

Consider the Thugs (or, as said, Thuggee): They claimed to be a religious organization honoring Kali, the goddess of chaos and destruction, as they plagued India for centuries. Their most well-honed methodology was to insinuate themselves among travelers, strangle their victims, mutilate the bodies, steal any valuables and disappear into the night. The distance between this behavior and that of the Freemasons is wide—yet both the Thugs and the Masons are (or were) secret societies and share an outsider's stance. What they do not share, in our estimation, is a sense of honor.

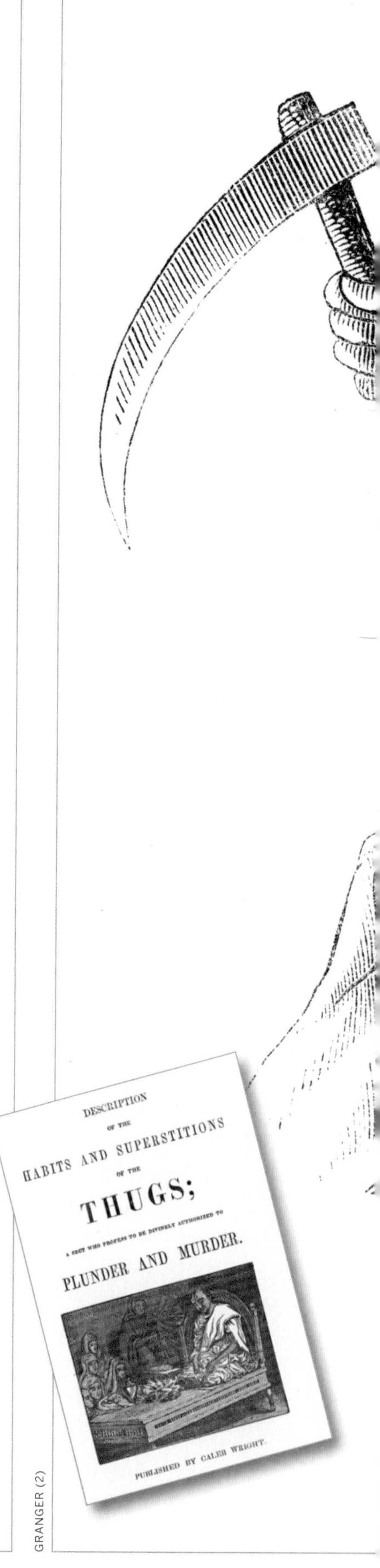

DESCRIPTION
OF THE
HABITS AND SUPERSTITIONS
OF THE
THUGS;
A SECT WHO PROFESS TO BE DIVINELY AUTHORIZED TO
PLUNDER AND MURDER.

PUBLISHED BY CALEB WRIGHT.

GRANGER (2)

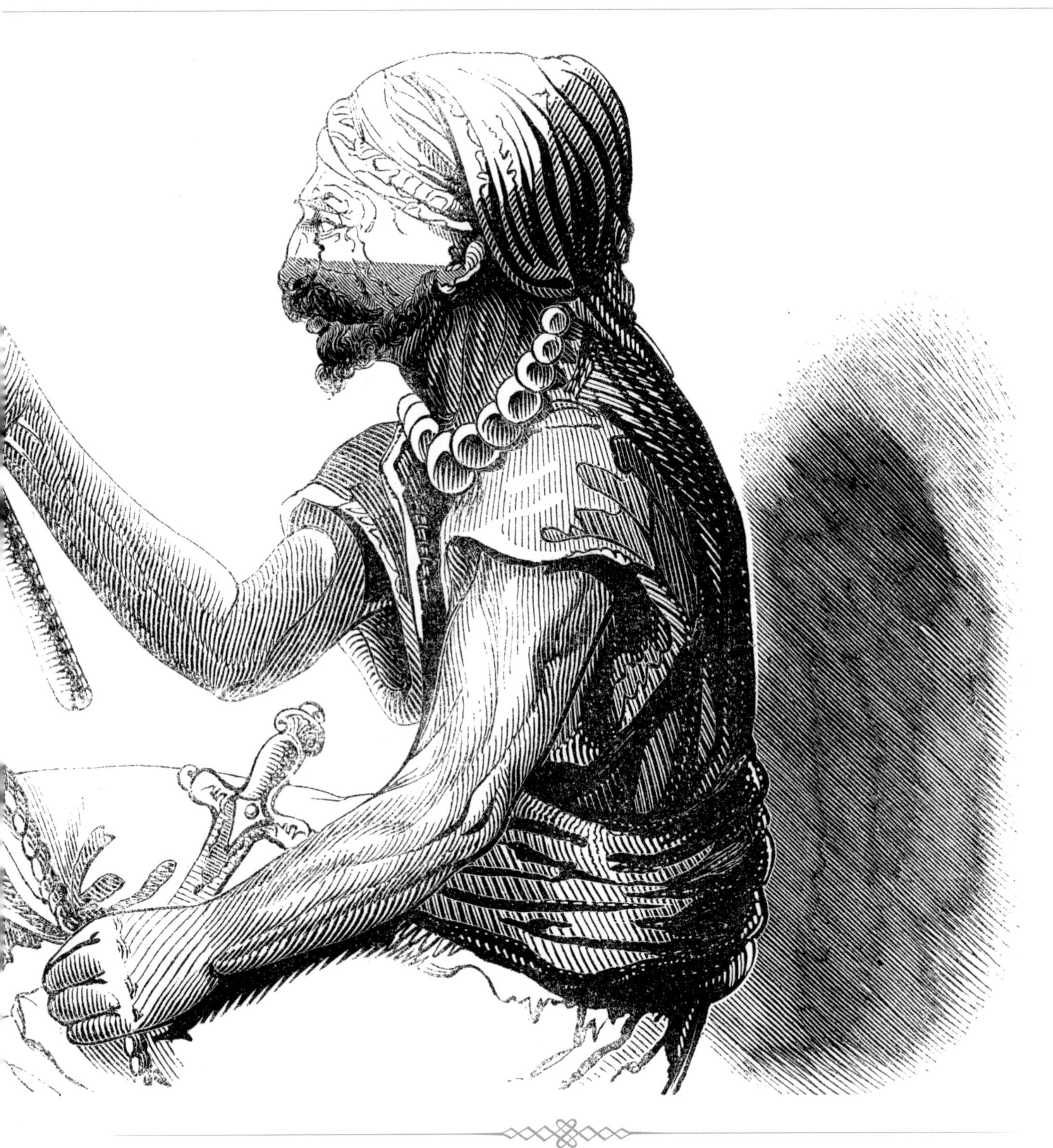

THIS INDIAN THUG has disguised himself as a traveler's escort by painting the upper half of his face white. Estimates of how many people the Thugs killed in six centuries before being suppressed range from 50,000 to perhaps 2 million. One of their gang leaders, Behram, holds the distinction of being, perhaps, the world's most prolific serial killer, with 931 murders to his credit between 1790 and 1830 (he said he personally was responsible for "only" about 200 of those deaths, and the rest should be laid to his gang members). Behram was promised immunity for ratting on his Thuggee brethren, but was nevertheless hanged in 1840; and that points to what finally quashed the Thugs: With the coming of British rule in India in the 19th century, they were outmatched and were no longer to be tolerated.

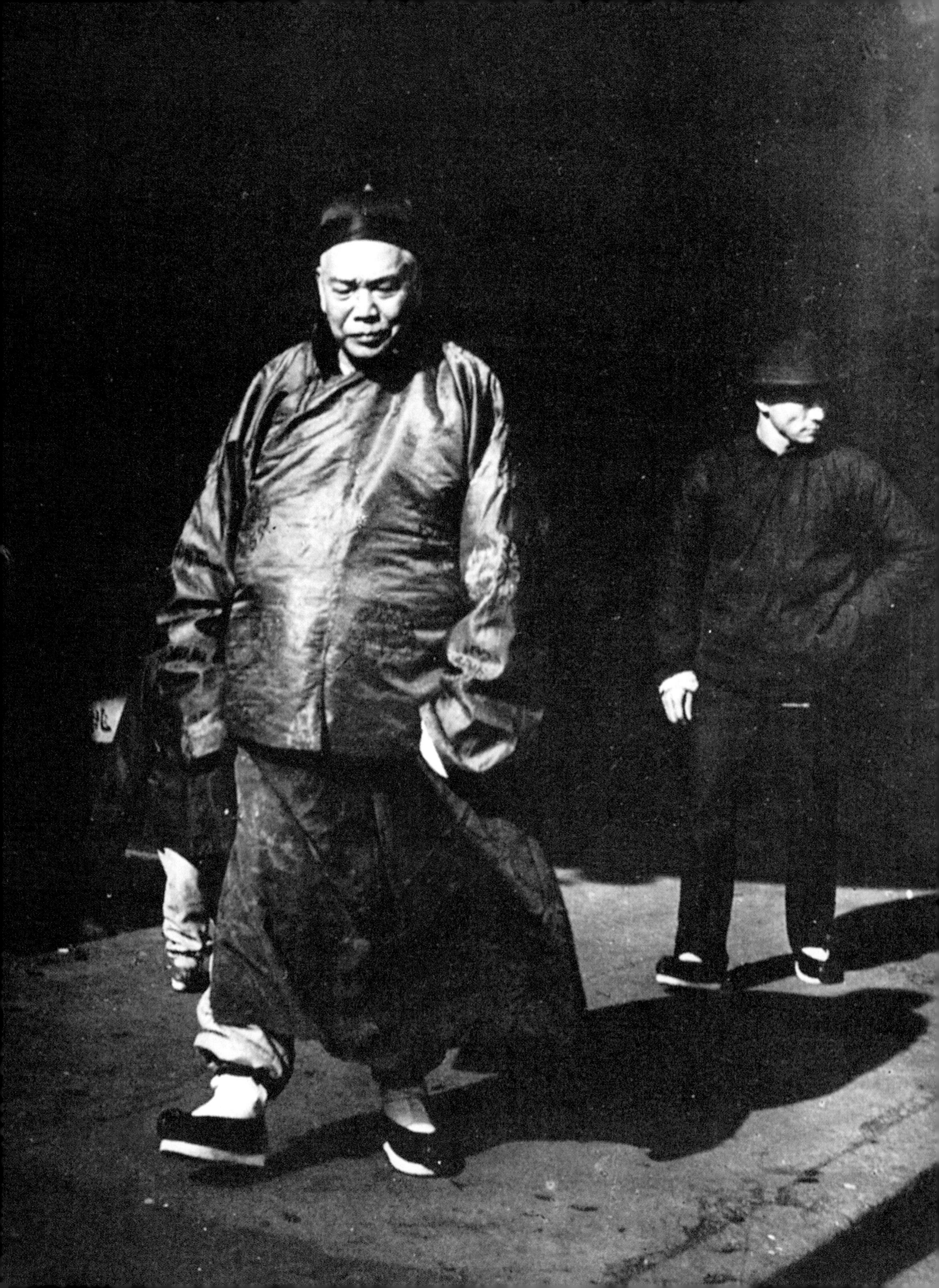

The Tongs

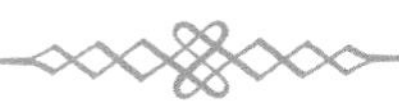

In the present day in many Chinatowns an informed sleuth can find halls designated for, or used by, this Tong association or that one—criminal gangs operating much like their counterparts in the Mafia or other organized-crime organizations. This was not always so with the Tongs, whose beginnings were honorable, and certainly it is unfortunate where this story has led.

Let's start by thinking of the mid-19th century Tongs as Masons rather than mafiosi. *Tong* means "hall or gathering place": This was about lodges of Chinese immigrants arriving, scared, in North America. When they landed in California and other points in the West and set to work for peanuts, they became the instant enemies of labor unions; some persevered, and others moved east into urban centers. Here formed the Tongs. The Tong movement's precedents were back home in other secret societies, particularly the Triads, headquartered in Hong Kong. The Triads featured initiation ceremonies similar to those adopted by the Tongs, and the Tongs respected the same deities as did the Triads. The Triads were formed with the aim of overthrowing the Qing Dynasty. The Tongs saw themselves, at first, as secretive, community-oriented, semipolitical and progressive.

But before long, these secret brotherhoods in America were focused on criminal activity—gambling, prostitution, extortion—and on vying with rival Tong factions for turf and treasure. There were Tong wars on the West Coast and on the East.

It can be claimed that the history of the Tongs is a redemptive one. As might be expected, the lawless Tongs ran up against the establishment on regular occasion. In recent years, the pro-community Tongs have reasserted their presence, and today members of the Chinese Consolidated Benevolent Associations support many urban Chinatown organizations in such efforts as adult education and immigrant counseling. Have the Tongs come full cycle? No. They have become diffused. There are Chinese gangs fighting in the cities today, and there are also civic-minded groups doing good.

It may be hard to say what a Tong is today; the name has been so twisted and turned. But to apprehend what has gone on in America for more than a century and a half: a Chinese Masonry, and a Chinese Mafia.

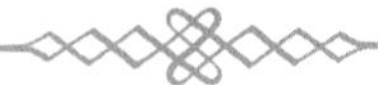

CIRCA 1900, a Tong official is followed closely by his bodyguard in San Francisco's Chinatown. His enemies would have been law enforcement officers, certainly, but also rival Tongs. Many of the Tong wars of the late 1800s and early 1900s concerned control of the prostitution trade.

ARNOLD GENTHE/GRANGER

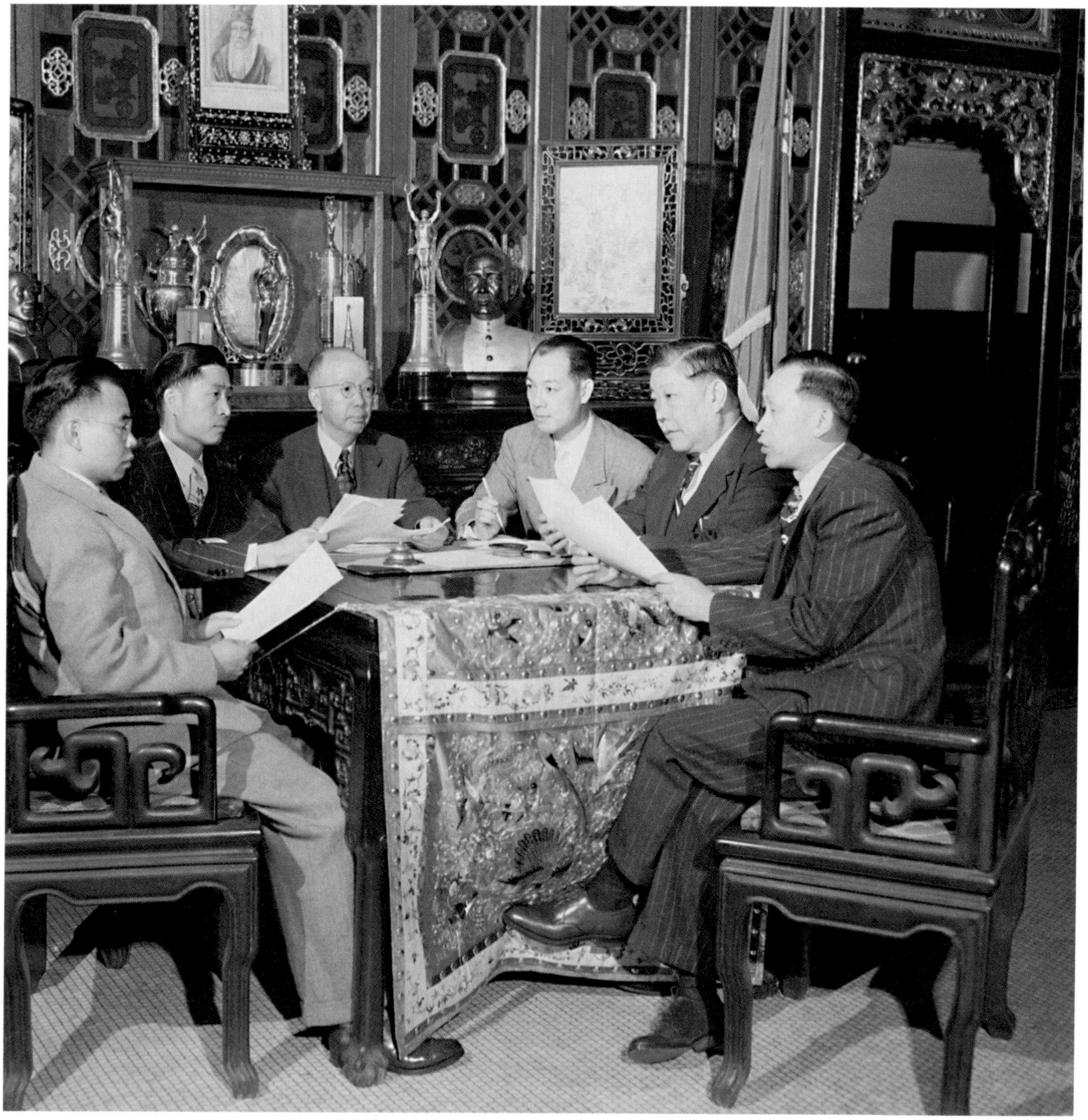

ABOVE is a scene from June 19, 1946, that is not unlike a gathering of the Corleone family and rivals. It is perhaps best to simply quote the original caption of this photograph, and let the reader judge for him- or herself: "Above is the Board of Chairmen of the Chinese Six Companies as they meet at their headquarters in [San Francisco's] Chinatown. The Six Companies are an association of six major Tongs, banded together for solidarity, having a membership of about 75,000 Chinese in North and South America. Chairmen meet monthly to settle differences arising between Tongs, keeping alive an ancient tradition of old China." Not all differences could be settled. Opposite is a *Naked City* scene outside a poolroom on Pell Street in New York City's Chinatown in 1930, after seven Chinese have been wounded in a Tong war. Violence begat violence that year, and press accounts of an August attack, which featured a "fusillade" of bullets, illustrated just how gangsterish the Tongs had become: "The ambush was cunningly contrived by five or more gunmen who showed no fear of police stationed in the district since the recent series of [T]ong shootings."

BETTMANN/CORBIS (2)

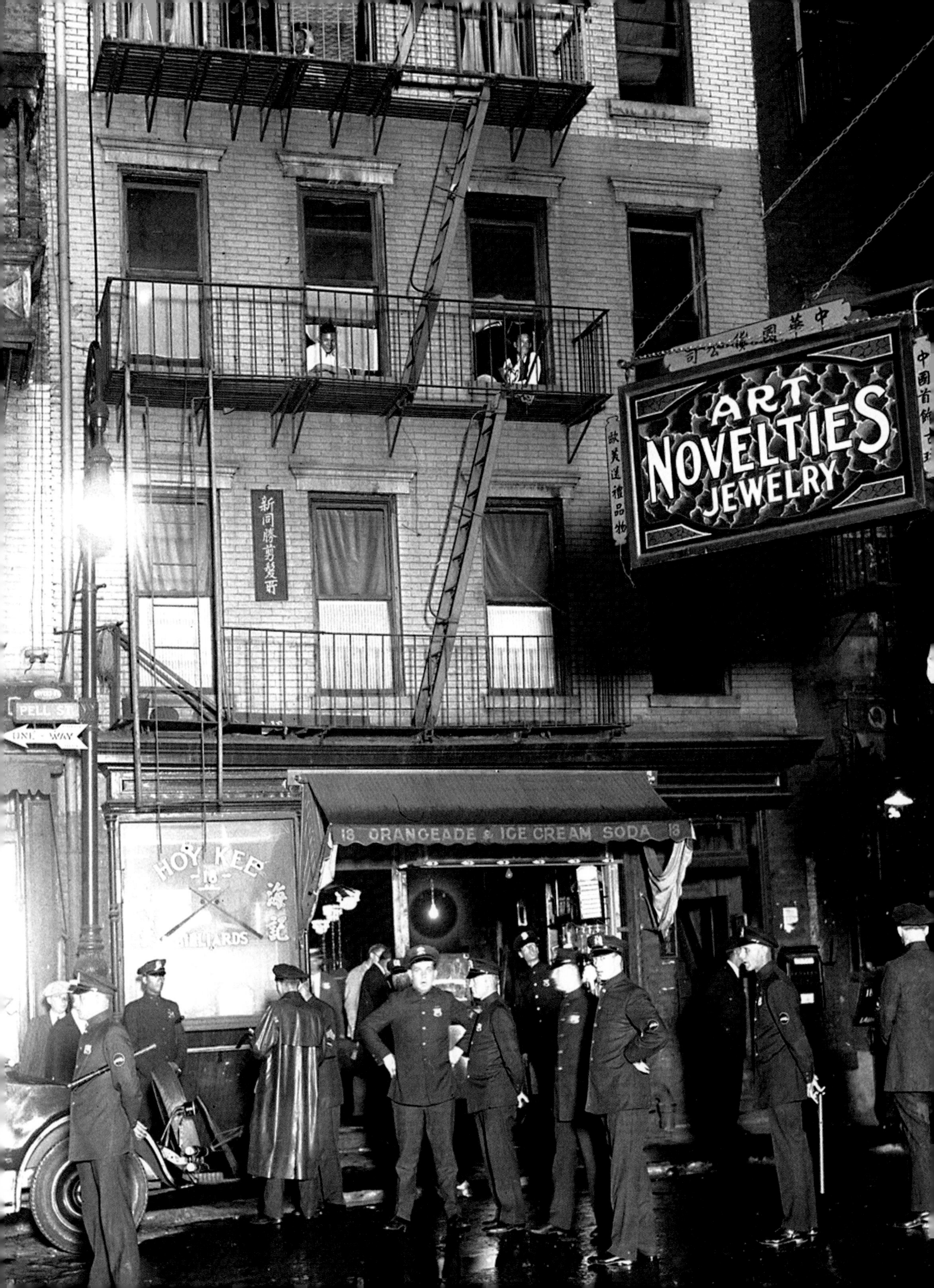
ART NOVELTIES JEWELRY
18 ORANGEADE & ICE CREAM SODA 18
HOY KEE
18
海記
PELL ST
ONE WAY

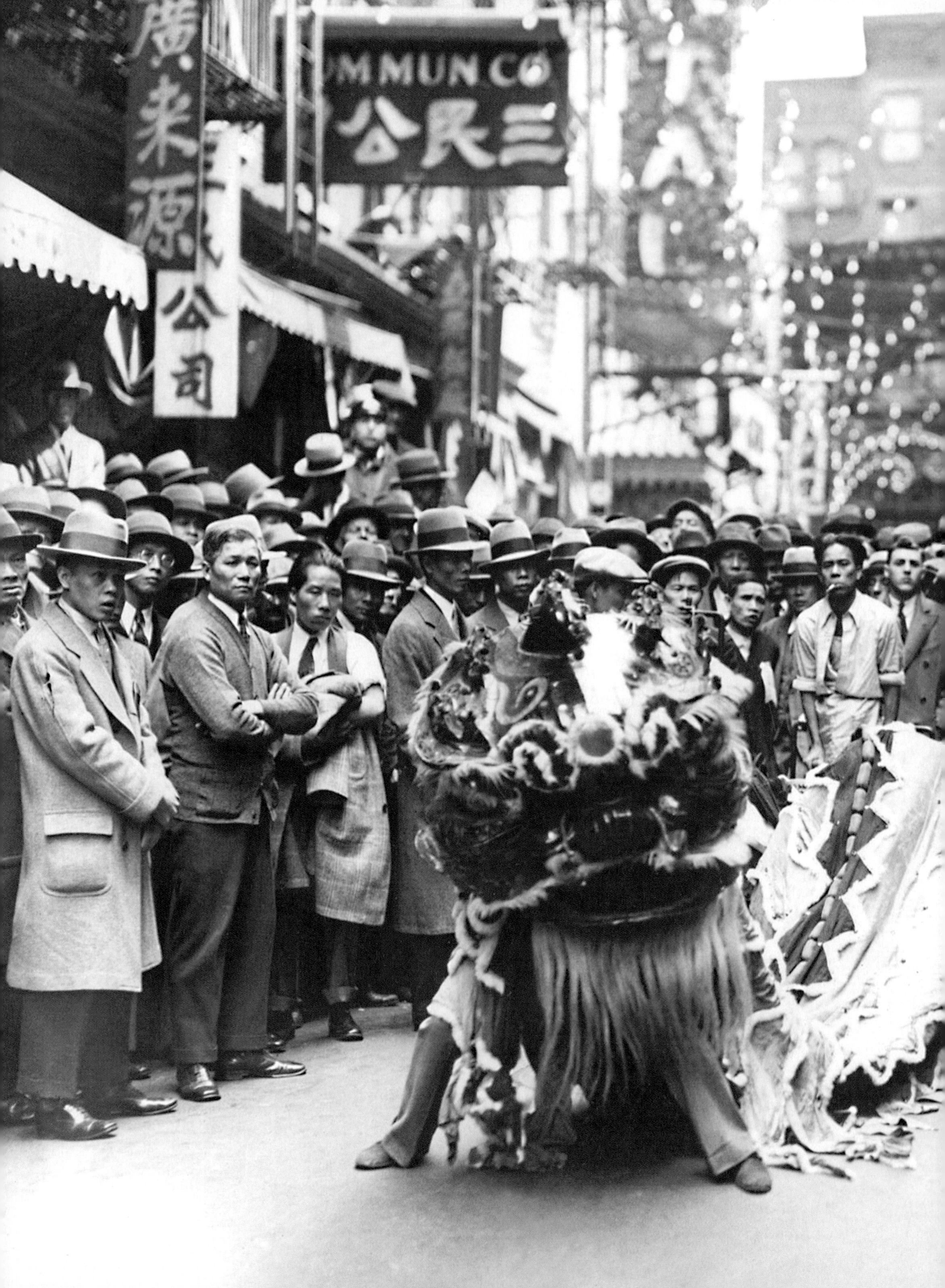

廣来源
UM MUN CO
三民公
公司

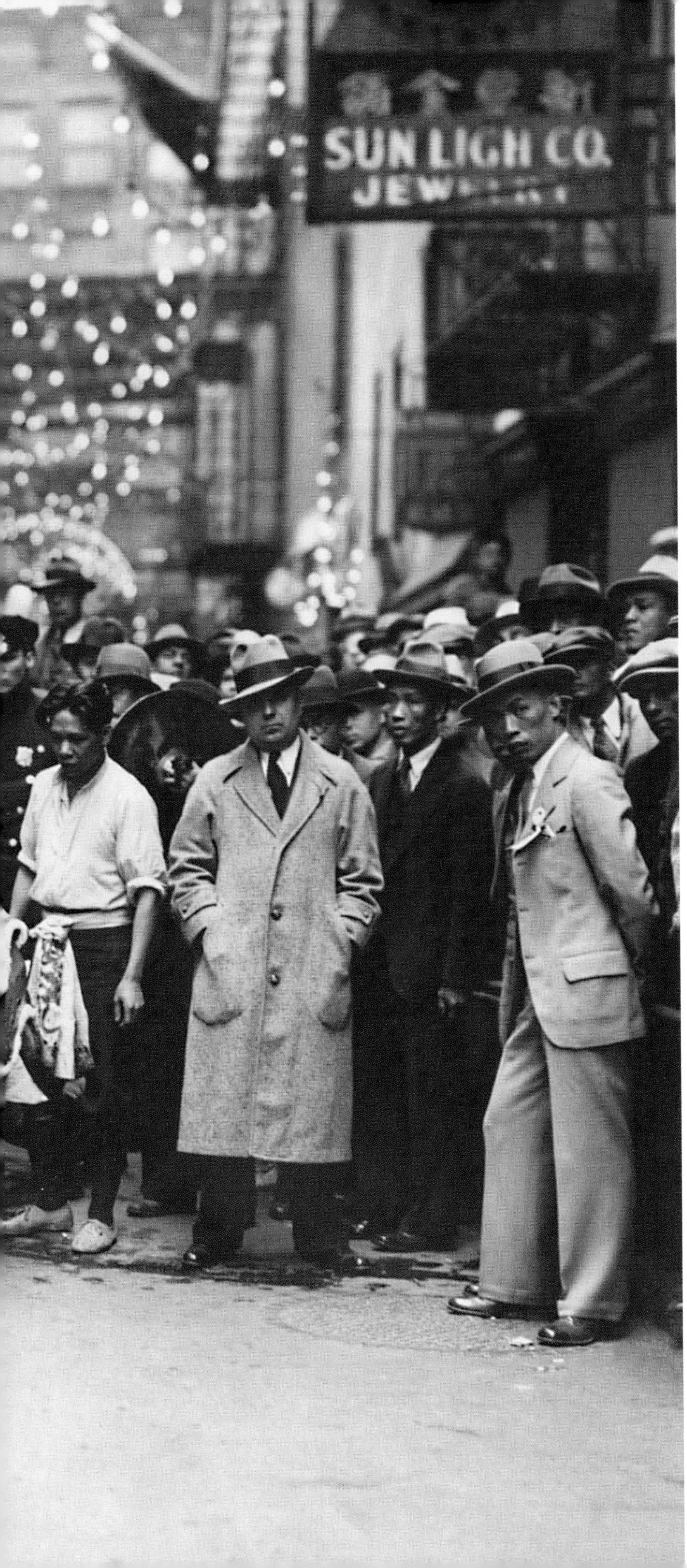

CLEVELAND STATE UNIVERSITY LIBRARY/EVERETT

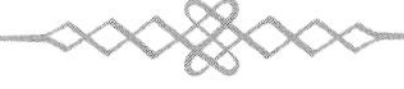

IF ONE CAN LOOK past the crummy aspects of organized crime, there is a lot of fun in this April 27, 1931, photograph taken—again on Pell Street—in New York City's Chinatown. On this day, the rival Hip Sing and On Leong gangs open their conventions and deign to pose (sort of) with a dragon in front of the Hip Sing headquarters. Please note not only the dour, even pained expressions of the On Leongs and Hip Sings looking on, but the American Mobster sartorial fashion that has been adopted by both groups. Ah, the Melting Pot. As said earlier, the secretive Tongs reached back to the Triads in Hong Kong for inspiration. Today, *Triad* remains an overarching term for Chinese criminal organizations constituting one of the world's largest outlaw outfits. With branches in Vietnam, Macau, Taiwan, China and also in countries with significant Chinese populations such as Malaysia, Singapore, the United States, Canada, Australia and the United Kingdom, the Triads have a worldwide membership of perhaps 2½ million members. The benevolent members of the American Tong movement do what they can to clear the group's name, but they face formidable obstacles.

The Thule Society

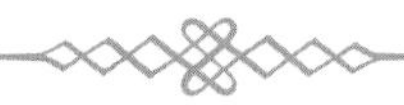

The man you see here is the Nazi Rudolf Hess. The ultimate Nazi, Adolf Hitler, never attended a Thule Society meeting. Nevertheless, this association, which was organized in backrooms around the same time as the German heartbreak of World War I, codified many of the ideas and principles that would mark the Third Reich. Hitler certainly didn't disdain the Thule Society. It just wasn't his cup of tea. Hard to believe, perhaps, but this particular movement had a little too much weirdness even for Hitler.

The Thule Society was born as a study group looking into German antiquity, and was headed by Walter Nauhaus, a World War I veteran who had become a keeper of pedigrees for the "Order of Teutons," a Berlin-based secret society founded in 1912. In 1917, Nauhaus moved to Munich, and was contacted, in 1918, by Rudolf von Sebottendorf, an occultist who had been elected head of the Germanenorden Walvater of the Holy Grail, a society established in 1916 by Hermann Pohl. The more esoteric elements of the group's concentration were soon overshadowed by a shift in emphasis to political, nationalistic and anti-Semitic concerns.

Thule is a Greek word referring to a far northern land (sometimes seen as Iceland or Greenland). In the influential American writer Ignatius Donnelly's speculations about Plato's Atlantis, Thule was the long-lost home of an Aryan race. He referenced swastika symbols in describing his Thule, and von Sebottendorf and company adopted them and wrote up their rules in accordance with Donnelly's teachings. Followers in the "Germanic Order," which in 1918 took the formal name the Thule Society, took a blood oath. An initiate swore "to the best of his knowledge and belief that no Jewish or colored blood flows in either his or in his wife's veins, and that among their ancestors are no members of the colored races." As Hitler biographer Ian Kershaw puts it, Thule's "membership list . . . reads like a *Who's Who* of early Nazi sympathizers and leading figures in Munich," including Hess and the notorious Hans Frank. Other prominent Nazis were, if not members, guests of the society. The Thule Society was hot for a while, but was destined to be eclipsed by Nazism and was dissolved around 1925. Von Sebottendorf wrote in his 1933 book, *Before Hitler Came:* "It was Thule people to whom Hitler first came, and it was Thule people who first united themselves with Hitler." He was proud of the claim.

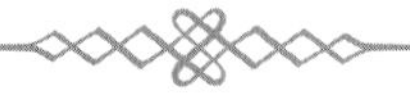

RUDOLF HESS IN 1938—after his association with the Thule Society, but evermore steeped in its ideals.

WOLFF VON GUDENBERG/ULLSTEIN BILD/GRANGER

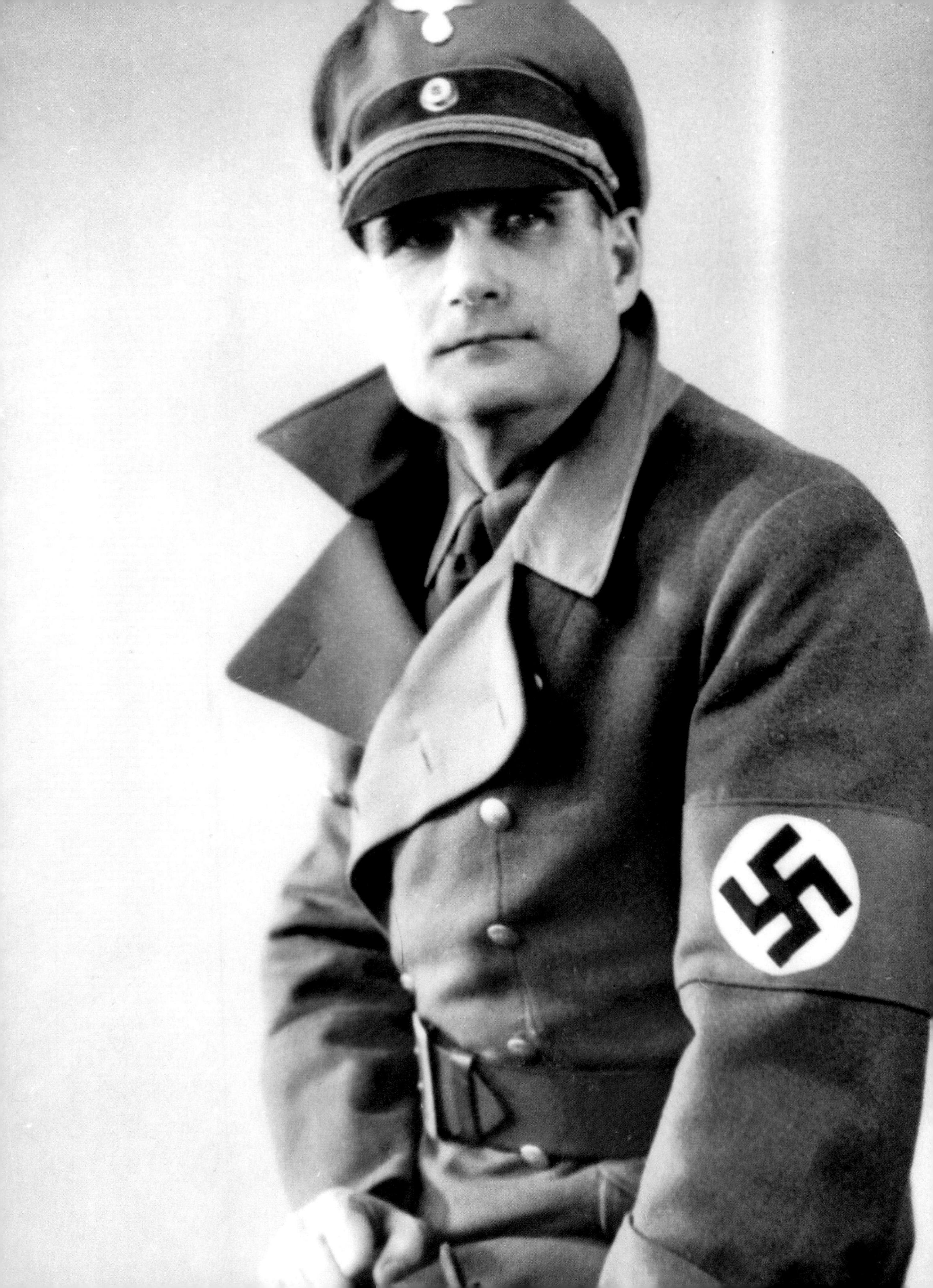

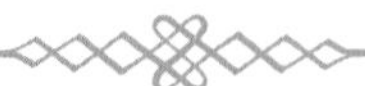

DURING ITS SHORT history, the Thule Society moved from being esoteric to being political and actively engaged. Postwar, in Bavaria, Thulers were in opposition to the Communist Red Army. They engaged in sabotage, and at one point killed Red Army prisoners. In reprisal, Thule members were among several of the Munich elite rounded up by the Reds in April of 1919. On the night of the 30th, seven were massacred in the Luitpold-Gymnasium, either shot (the bullet holes, above) or bludgeoned to death. Right: The Society's emblem, with swastika, dagger and oak leaves. Opposite: Hans Frank, a Hitler favorite and former Thuler, the Nazi regime's chief jurist and overlord of the German-occupied Polish territories early in World War II. He was responsible for the murder of millions of Polish Jews. In 1945, Frank was tried at Nuremberg and then executed. Wrote journalist Howard K. Smith: "Hans Frank was next in the parade of death. He was the only one of the condemned to enter the chamber with a smile on his countenance. Although nervous and swallowing frequently, this man, who was converted to Roman Catholicism after his arrest, gave the appearance of being relieved at the prospect of atoning for his evil deeds." Rudolf Hess, too, was tried at Nuremberg. He received a life sentence and died in Spandau Prison in 1987.

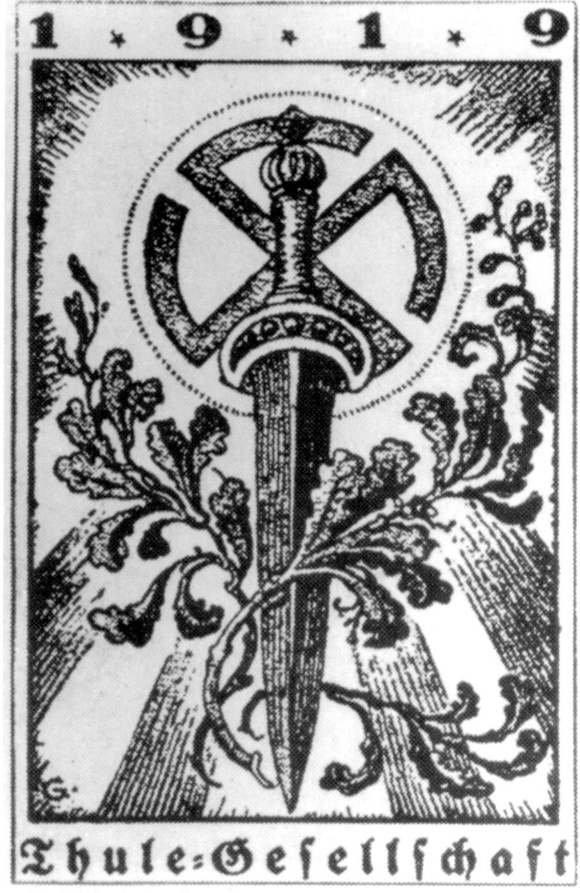

MARY EVANS PICTURE LIBRARY (2)

BETTMANN/CORBIS

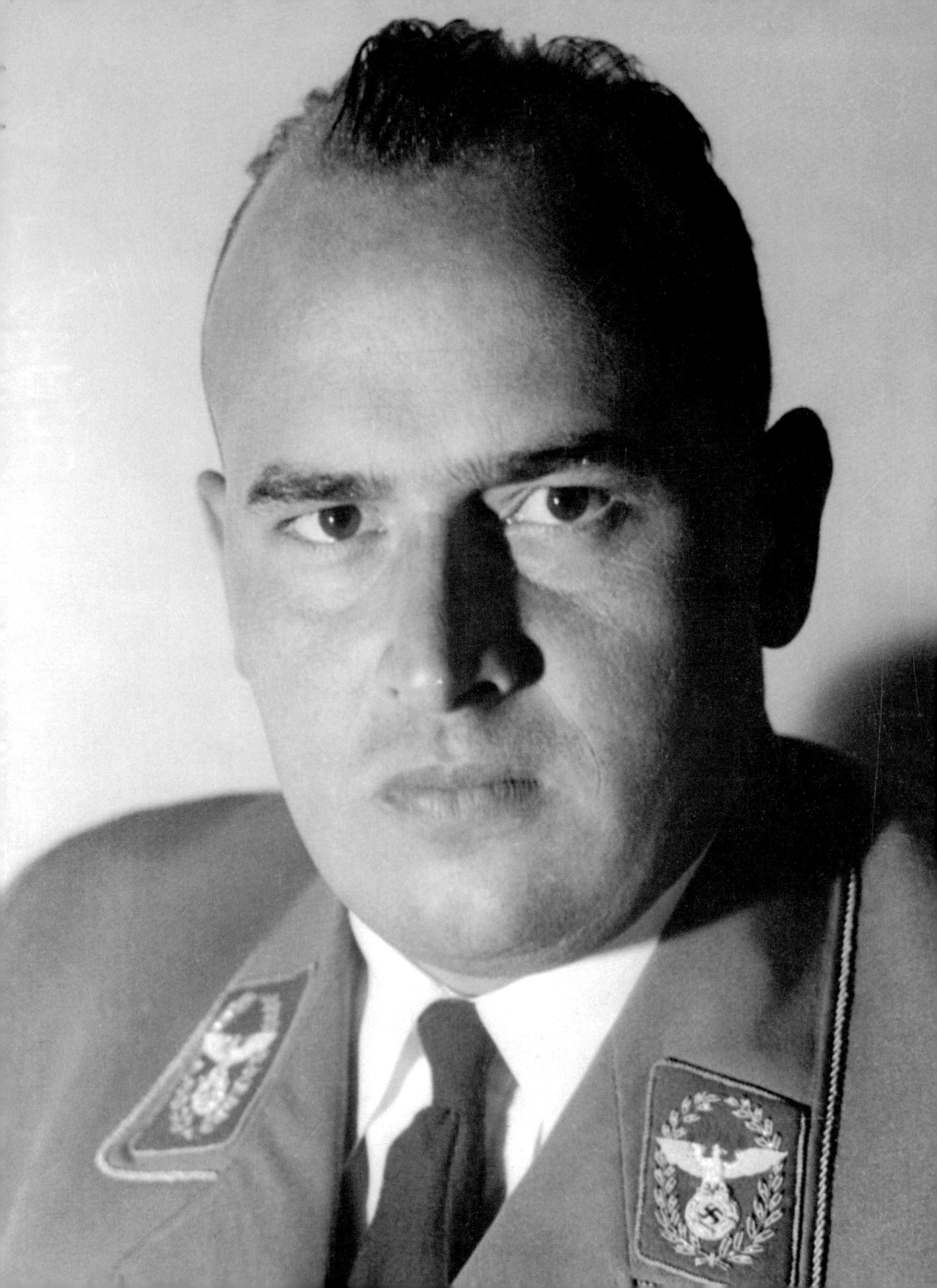

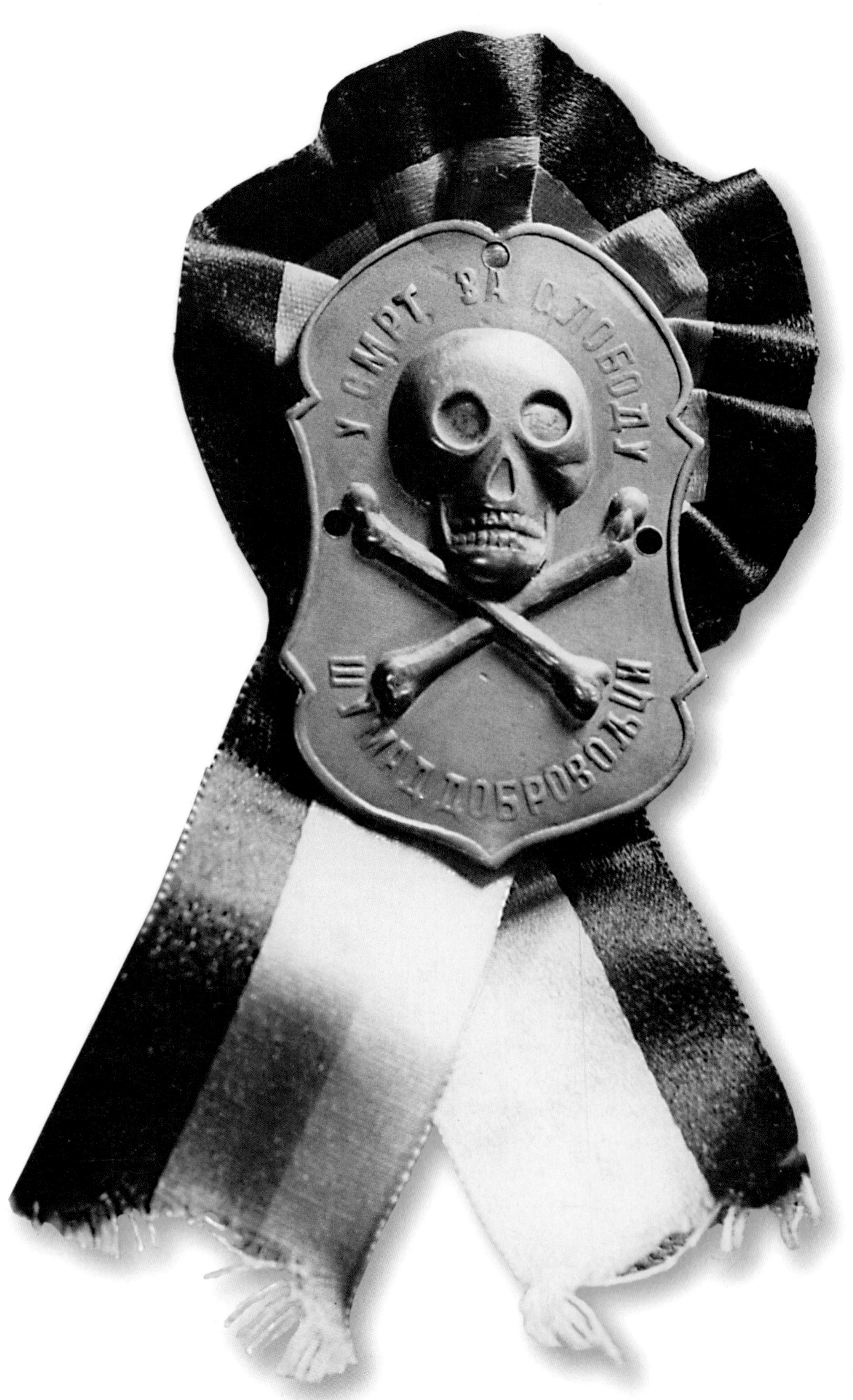
У СМРТ, ЗА СЛОБОДУ
ДОБРОВОЉЦИ

The Black Hand

It was a tough call for us to place such organizations as the Black Hand and the Irish Republican Brotherhood (a precursor to the IRA) among the ranks of the nefarious, while celebrating the noble aspirations of the Carbonari and the Sons of Liberty earlier in our pages. Each group saw itself as liberationist. And yet . . . there were differences.

We'll get to the IRA, but as to the Black Hand: This was not a progenitor organization of the Mafia. It is true that as La Cosa Nostra was rising in the U.S. at the turn of the 20th century, it was often associated with the so-called "Black Hand" gangs in New York. "There is talk of this terrible society of delinquents called 'la Mano Nera,' here in America," wrote Adolfo Valeri in the newspaper *Stamperia del Bollettino della Sera* in 1905. "[A]nd in New York above all, one hears and one reads every day of terrible crimes."

But the name and the fear it inspired had been borrowed. There were self-proclaimed (hardly secret) Black Hand gangs everywhere in U.S. and European cities, but they were disorganized, unaffiliated.

Not in Italy, but further east, the well-organized society that would become *the* Black Hand was founded on October 8, 1908, as a secret military fraternity in the Kingdom of Serbia. It was dedicated to uniting Serbian populations in lands annexed by Austria-Hungary. The name "Black Hand" would be applied years after the society was formed, as would its formal name, which was even scarier: *Ujedinjenje ili Smrt* ("Unification or Death"). Satellite units were organized; spies were employed; assassins and guerilla fighters were trained; stealth attacks were carried out. Many of today's historians, seeking to define the Serbian Black Hand, call it a terrorist organization.

Whether it was or not, it was a successful organization, and by 1914 had as many as 2,500 members, former and current Serbian army officers among them. That year, it plotted its greatest hit: the assassination of Archduke Franz Ferdinand, heir apparent to the Austro-Hungarian throne. The killing, which is recounted on the following pages, was carried out on June 28, 1914. In the days following, Serbia was generally blamed by Austria-Hungary; other European nations took sides. Eventually, World War I would claim the lives of many millions of civilians and nearly 10 million soldiers; 21 million more soldiers would be wounded.

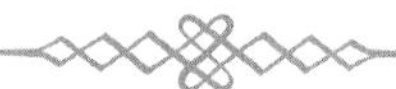

BADGE OF HONOR? Certainly a matter of perspective. The symbol of the Serbian Black Hand got its point across, and groups in Sicily and elsewhere saw value in appropriating the term and all that it conveyed.

SCHERL/SZ PHOTO

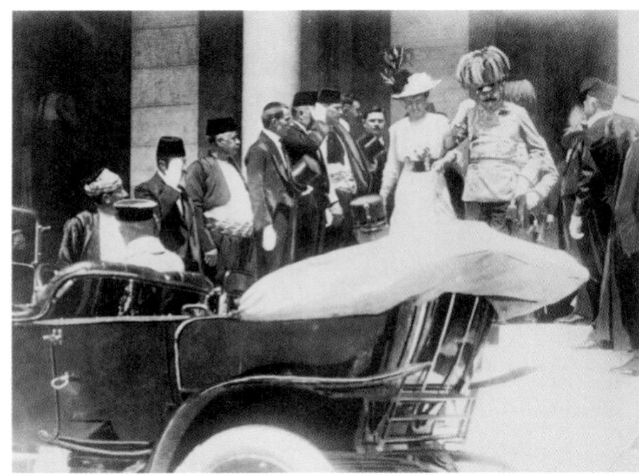

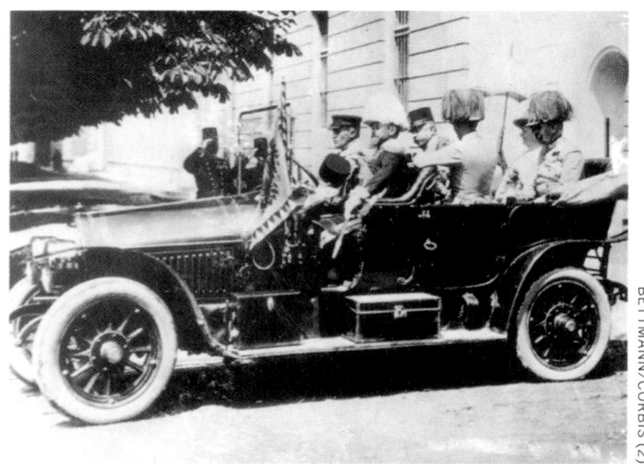

BETTMANN/CORBIS (2)

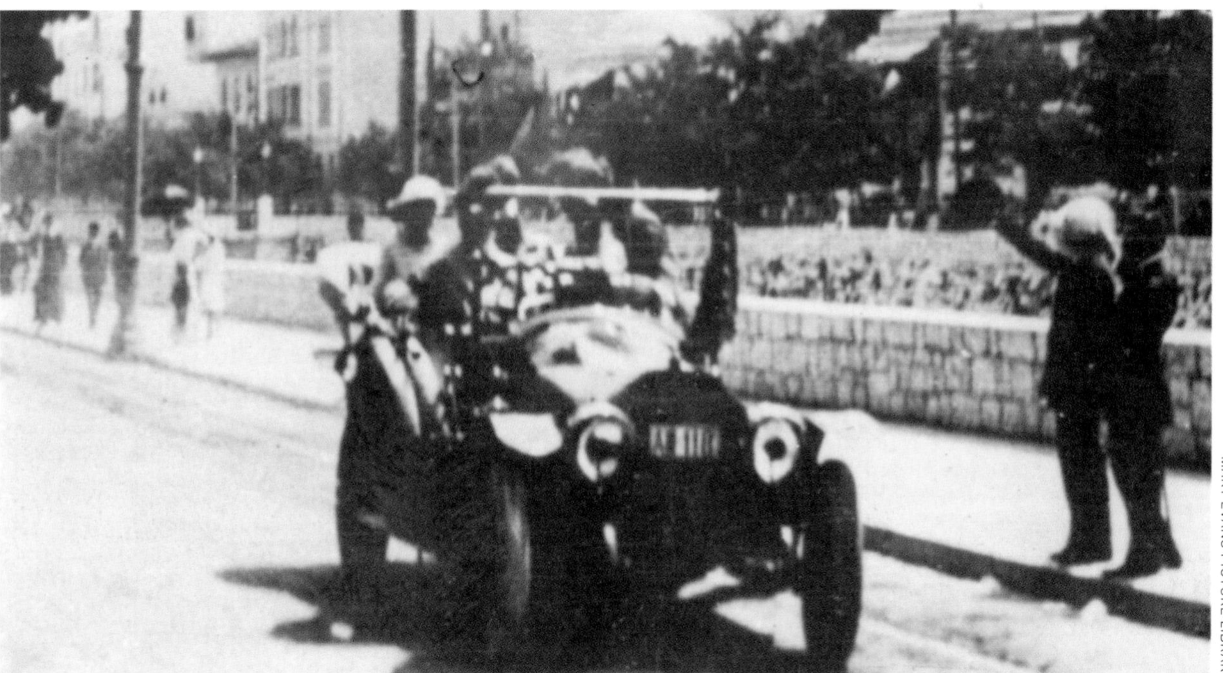

MARY EVANS PICTURE LIBRARY

RYKOFF COLLECTION/CORBIS

MUCH AS TERRORIST CELLS in our day recruit idealistic young people to serve the cause as suicide bombers, leaders of the Black Hand (but not the entire executive committee) recruited and trained three young Bosnian-Serbs, Gavrilo Princip, Nedeljko Cabrinovic and Trifko Grabez, to carry out the Ferdinand assassination. The masterminds, freelancing within their own clandestine organization, were probably content that the mission, if successful, would lead to war between Austria and Serbia. The boys might not have had a clue that the consequences could be that dire, or that they would lead to the massive destruction of World War I. Cabrinovic was unsuccessful in his attempt to kill Ferdinand, but on June 28, Princip, wielding a pistol, succeeded. In these dramatic photographs from the day, we see the archduke and his wife, Sophie, entering their car after leaving the Sarajevo Senate House in Bosnia and Herzegovina, and then the commotion as the schoolboy Princip is arrested (opposite, top). In the bottom photo, opposite: The chaotic aftermath. As had happened before in history and as has happened since (think of 9/11 and al-Qaeda), the Black Hand's triumphant moment signaled its downfall and demise. When the war grew terrible and the cause of Ferdinand's death became clearer, the future existence of the Black Hand was untenable. By the end of 1916, the prime minister of Serbia determined to destroy what was left of the Black Hand, and by the next year, through arrests, trials and even executions, he had done so.

MARY EVANS PICTURE LIBRARY

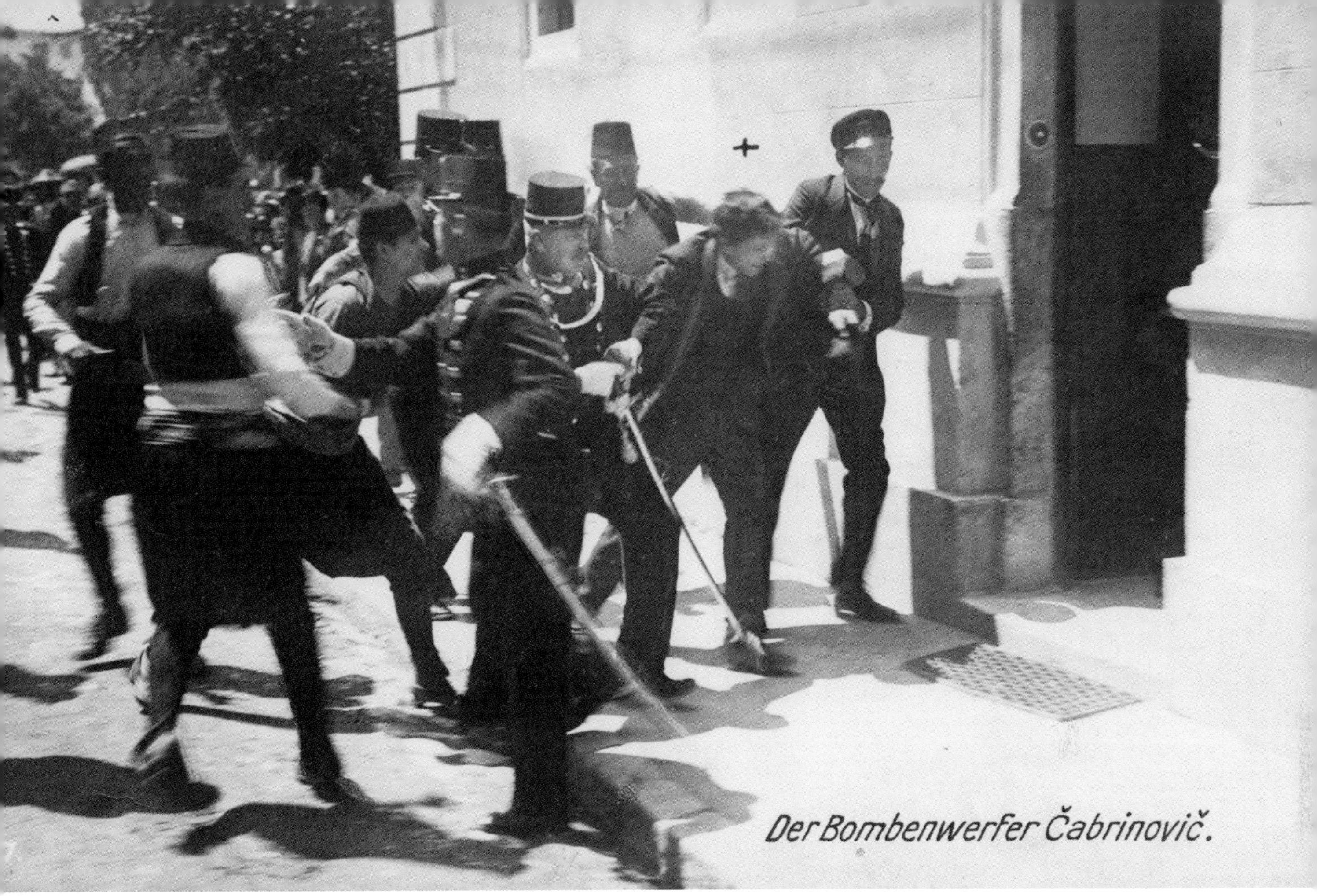

Der Bombenwerfer Čabrinovič.

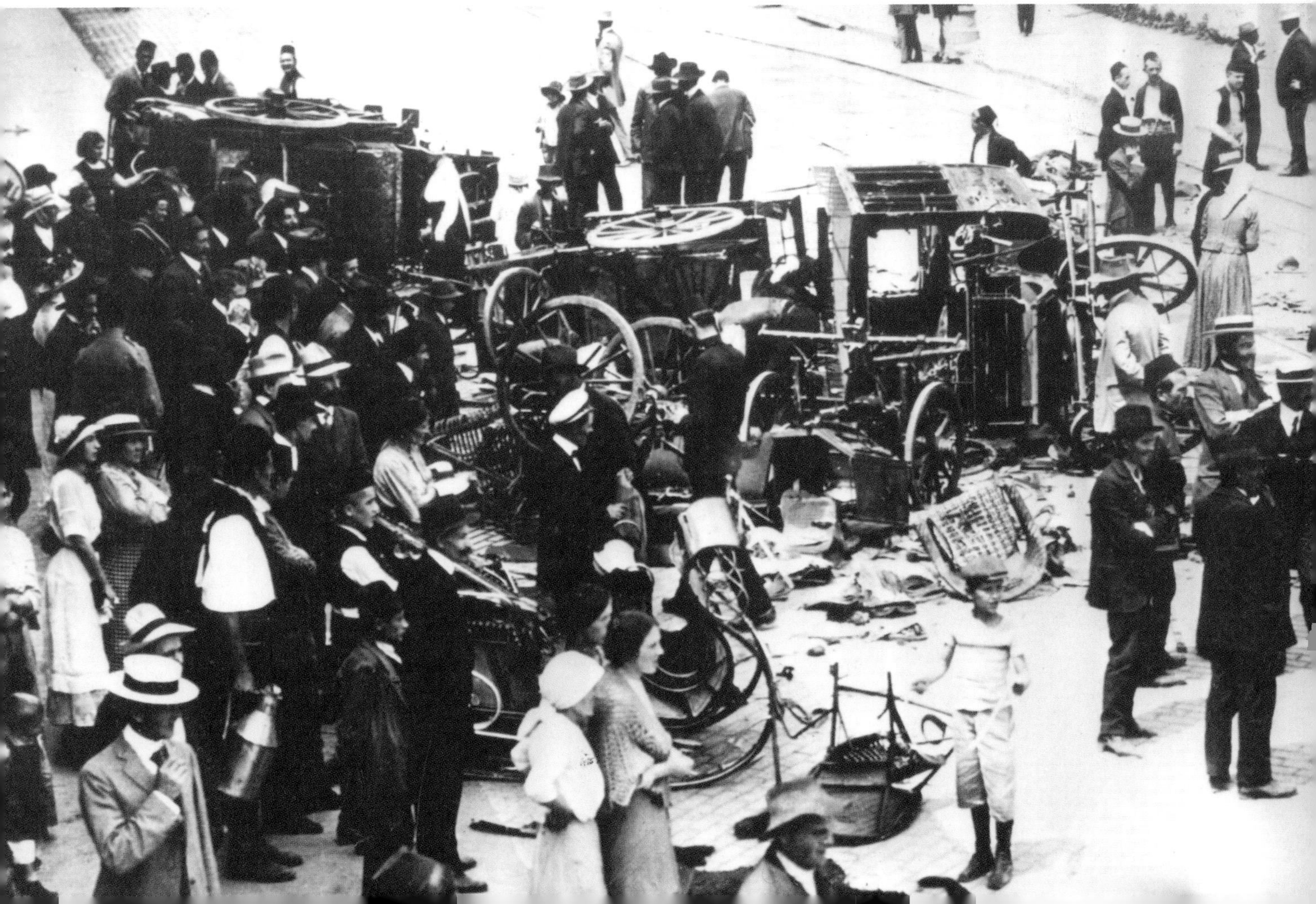

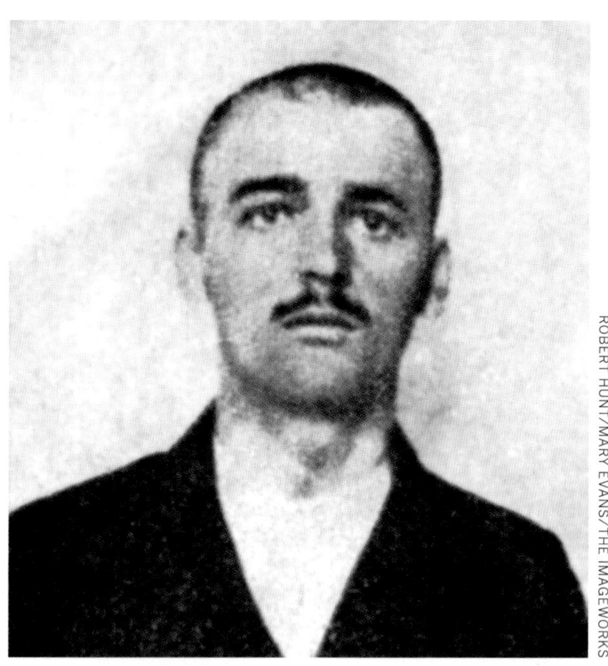

ROBERT HUNT/MARY EVANS/THE IMAGEWORKS

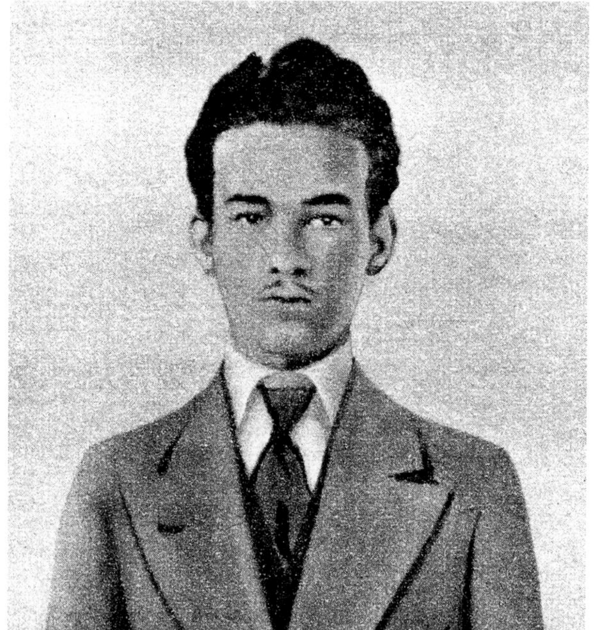

HULTON-DEUTSCH/CORBIS

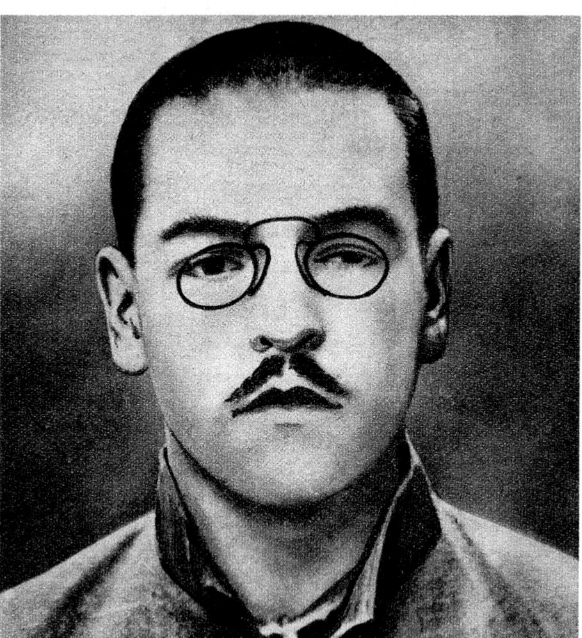

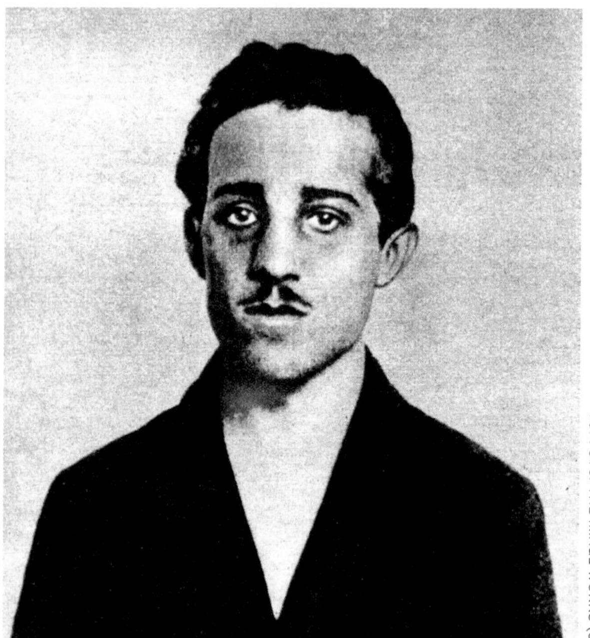

TOPFOTO/THE IMAGE WORKS (3)

BETTMANN/CORBIS

ON THE OPPOSITE PAGE, the archduke and his wife lie in state, and Princip and his collaborators are in the dock. On this page we have, upper left, Cabrinovic, a member of the Black Hand, who had earlier thrown a bomb toward Ferdinand but had mistimed his toss (he was sentenced to 20 years in prison, and died of tuberculosis in jail when he was only about 21); upper right, Dragan Kalembert, who was in charge of the firearms and ammunition; lower left, Ivo Kranchevich, who was positioned along the route to fire at the archduke if his colleagues missed; and Princip, who was convicted but was too young to be given the death penalty (he was not yet 20). He was politely defiant at his trial: "I am a Yugoslav nationalist, aiming for the unification of all Yugoslavs, and I do not care what form of state, but it must be free from Austria." He too contracted tuberculosis in squalid prison conditions and wasted away to 88 pounds before dying at age 23.

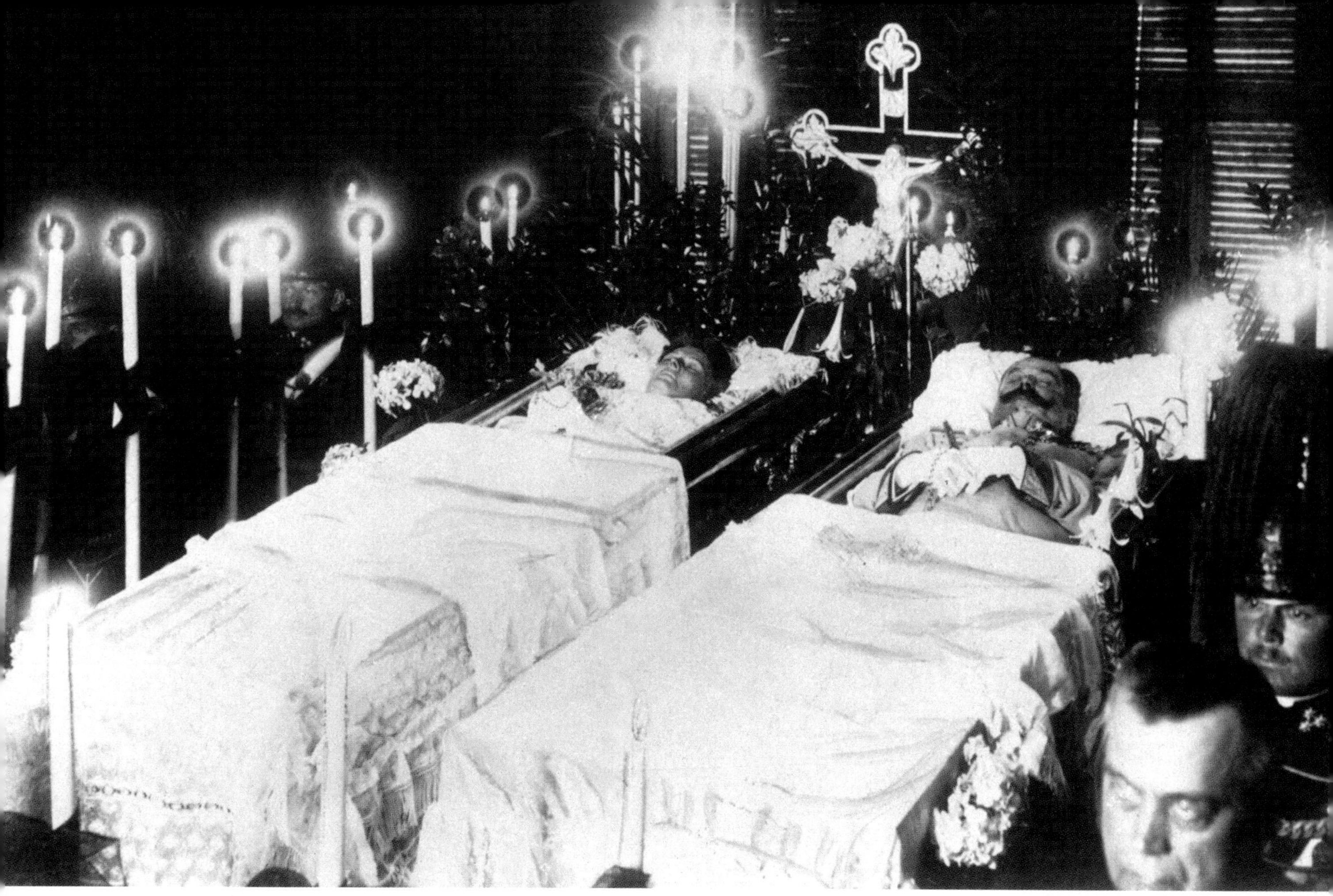

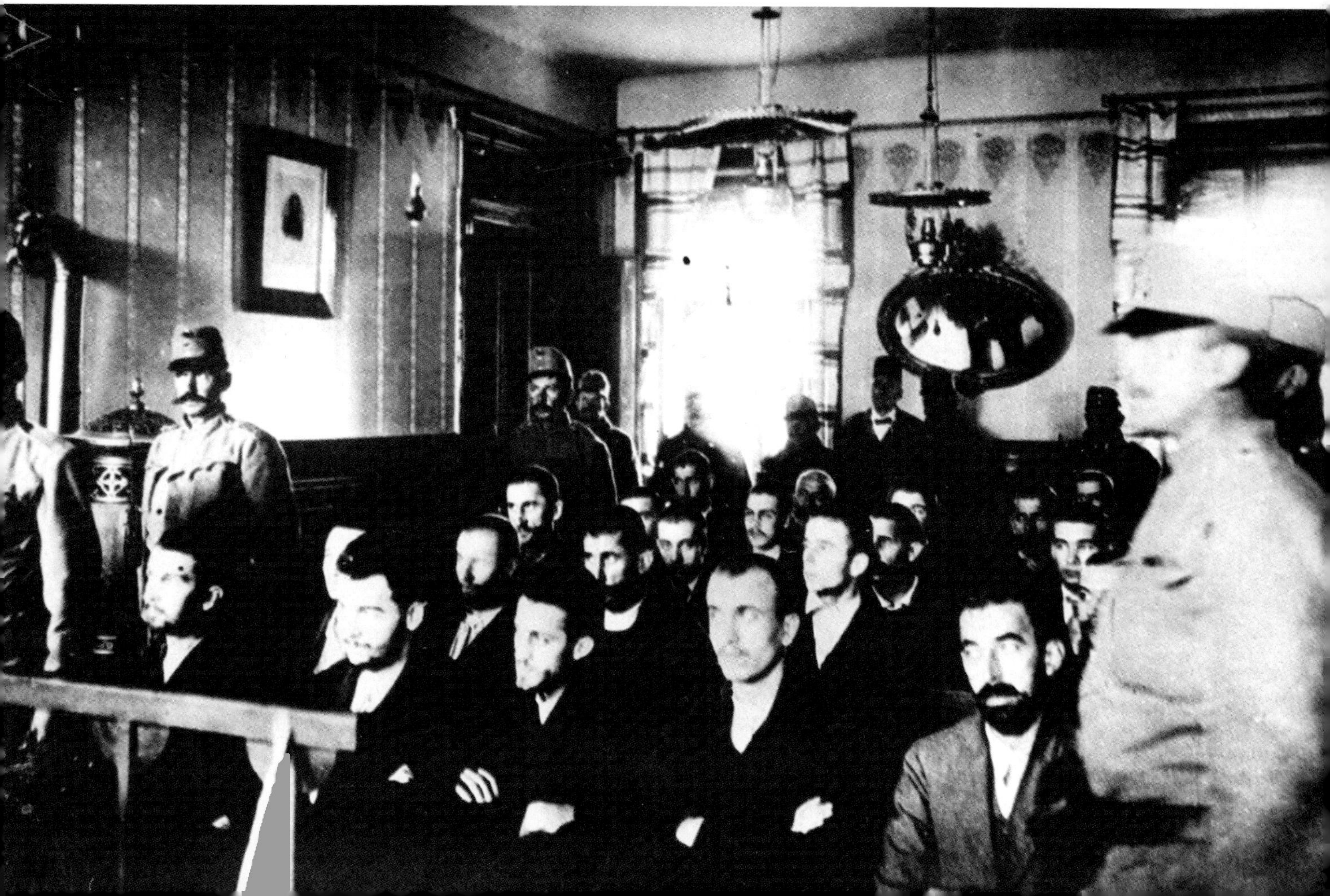

The Mafia

On the previous pages, we delineated what we consider the "official" and most historically important Black Hand organization and its effect on world history. But we also alluded to the fact that the term has floated from here to there.

Just what was the Italian version of the Black Hand? Neither a high-minded secret society nor an oracular curse, this Black Hand, as practiced by mafiosi in Sicily and on the mainland, and as exported to America during a flood of Italian immigration beginning in the 1890s, was a scummy extortion racket inflicted on its own people. The victims—from struggling fruit and vegetable sellers to the rich and famous—would receive a note, "Most Gentle Mr. Silvani: Hoping you will be so good as to send me $2,000 if your life is dear to you . . . ," stamped with *"La Mano Nera."* When opera star Enrico Caruso visited New York, he was threatened with a dosage of lye in his *vino,* and for years he forked over as much as a tenth of his salary to Black Handers. Uptown in Harlem's Little Italy, Ignatius "Lupo the Wolf" Lupo was a demonic exponent of the Italian Black Hand, killing more than 20 at his "Murder Stable" to keep his message clear, while netting thousands of dollars in the bargain.

Back in the old country, a more patrician practitioner of Black Hand–style extortion was Vito Cascio Ferro, as close to a Boss of Bosses as the Honored Society (which is to say, the Mafia) ever had. On the lam for kidnapping in 1899, he visited the U.S., and returned to Sicily with some new ideas, including the notion that he or a minion should be overlord of crime in America, and should seek to organize it after the Old World model.

It all worked out for the mob, as we know. Playing everything close to the vest, placing secrecy and loyalty at the apex of values, Masseria, Costello, Genovese, Gambino, Anastasia, Luciano, Maranzano, Bonanno, Mangano, Profaci, Gagliano, Valachi, Colombo and finally Gotti had nice lives in the United States—until they didn't.

The 20th century has been called the American Century. Vis à vis crime in America, it can also be seen as the Mafia Century. There is still organized crime in our country today, to be sure, but the era in which a nefarious secret society can have its way, day in and day out and nationwide, seems to be over.

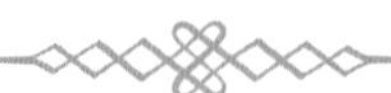

OPPOSITE: The Don of Dons, Ferro poses with his loving nephew (but, of course, a gun is at hand). On the pages following: Police check for bullet holes in the brick façade of the Bergin Hunt and Fish Club on 101st Avenue in Ozone Park, Queens, New York, in 1987, after reports of a possible hit attempt on Gambino crime boss John Gotti at his "rumored" headquarters.

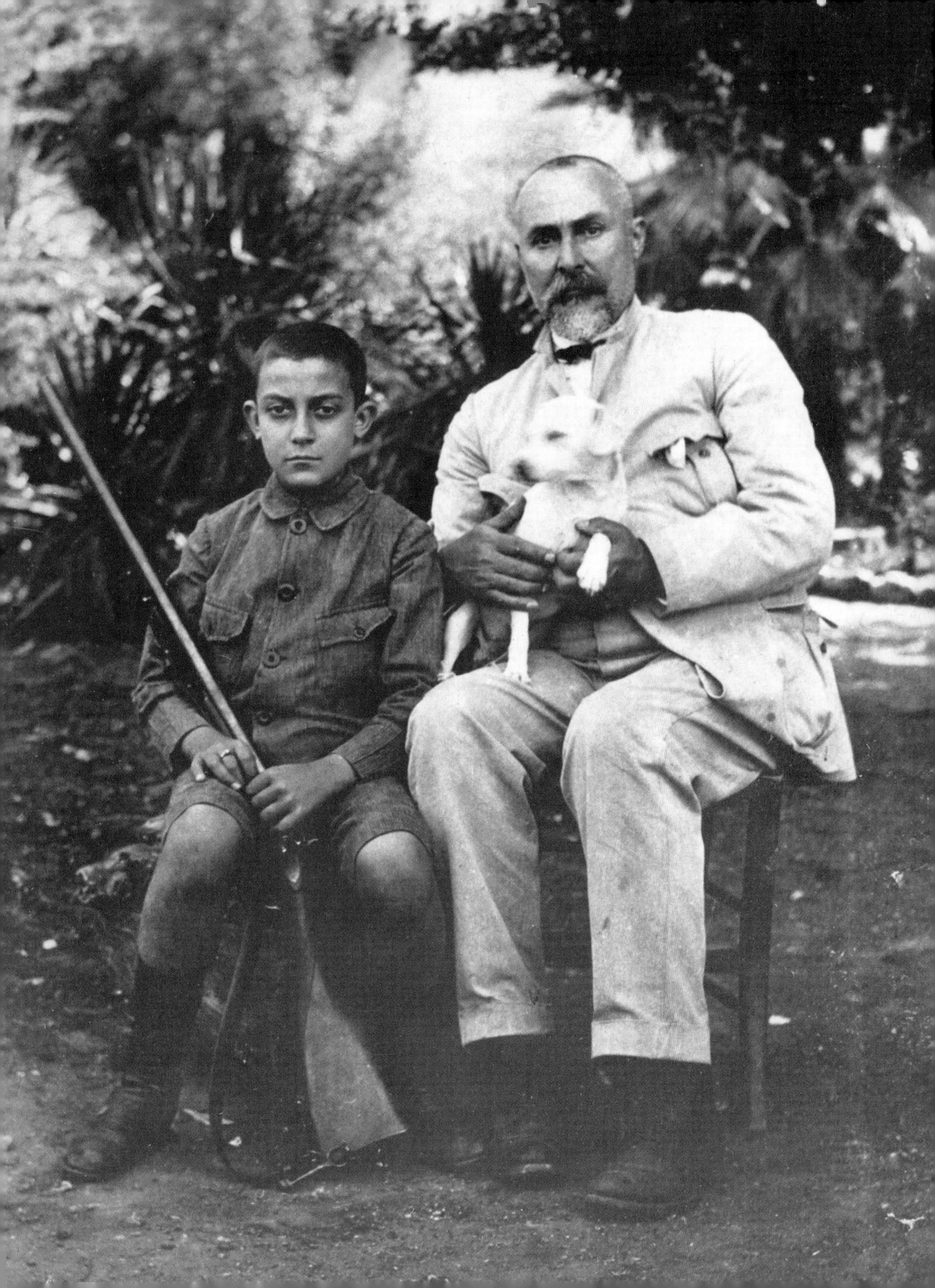

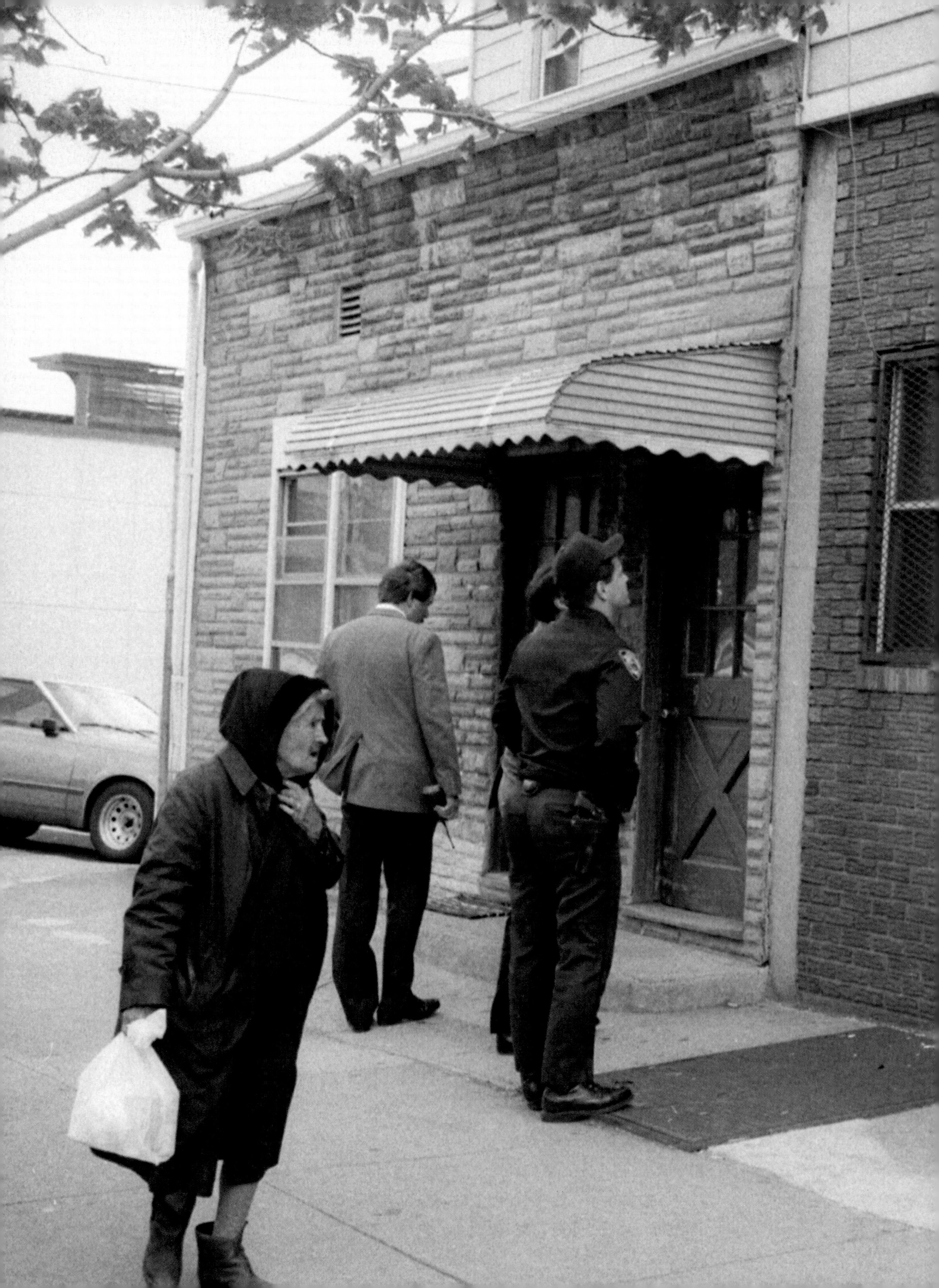

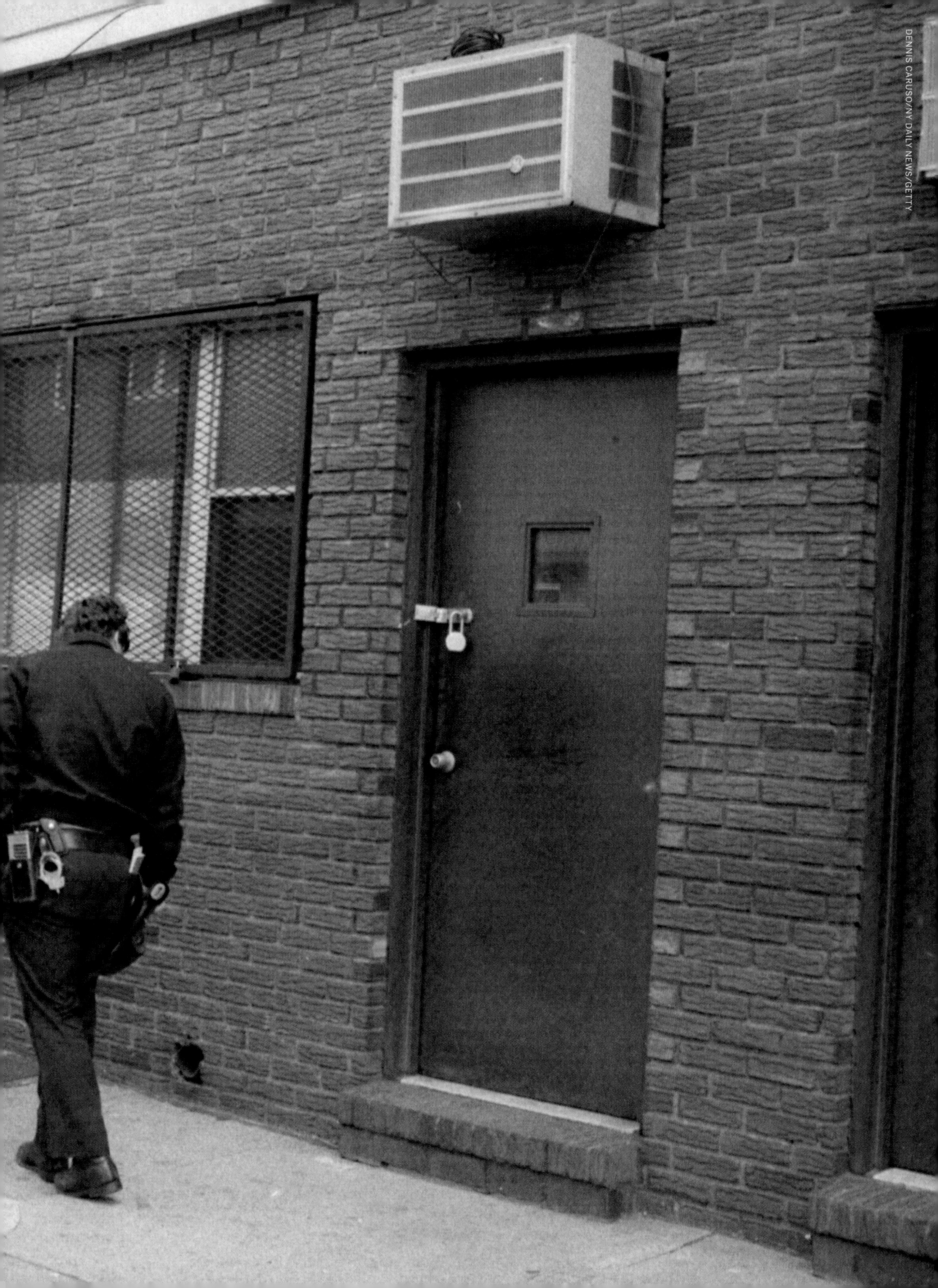

DENNIS CARUSO/NY DAILY NEWS/GETTY

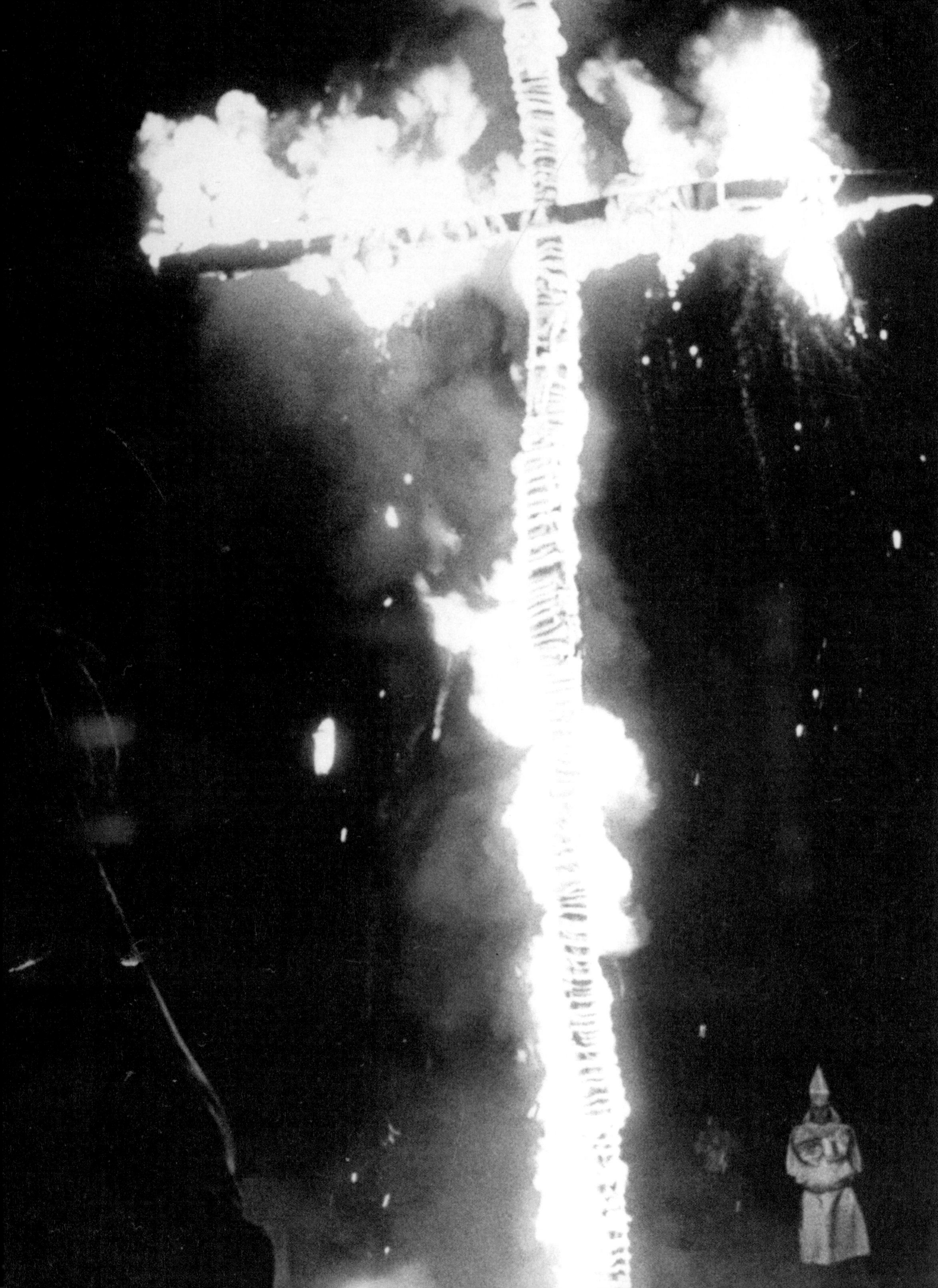

The Ku Klux Klan

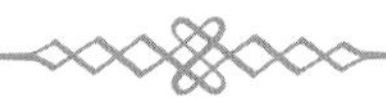

If the Civil War is seen as our nation's great crucible, and if liberty, freedom, equality and the pursuit of happiness are seen as paramount among our nation's founding principles, then the Ku Klux Klan can be regarded as our nation's great (if obviously abominable) homegrown secret society. It brought all those things into question.

The South in 1865 had lost the war—and thus the argument for slavery—and with that, the Klan grew like a virulent weed. As its founders might have wished, it has hovered ever since in the imagination, a perpetual nightmare.

We have suffered three distinct iterations of the KKK. The first one died out in little more than a decade. It was formed as a white supremacist terrorist organization in 1865 in Pulaski, Tennessee, by veterans of the Confederate Army, who chose the Greek word *kyklos*—"circle"—to signify their dedication. Klan groups spread throughout the South in a disorganized fashion, united principally by their shared dress: white robes, conical hats and masks. Although something of a ragtag movement, it grew to have a branch in nearly every southern state, with members engaging in criminal behavior, including murder, to restore what they saw as rightful white supremacy. In 1870–1871, the federal government fought back with the Enforcement Acts, and the Klan was suppressed. Smaller operations such as the White League and the Red Shirts carried on the cause.

The Klan was not yet destined for the history books. In 1915 it was resurrected and grew stronger than ever: more than 4 million members by the middle of the 1920s. It can be said that this Klan lasted until World War II. It has been succeeded, since the 1950s, by Klan 3.0, which might today number 5,000 subscribers.

Essentially a far-right white Protestant secret society given foremost to intimidation and occasionally to violence, it has added other grievances to its menu over time: anti-Catholicism, anti-communism, anti-Semitism. Its largest problem has been: It has no friend in the United States of America nor in the Constitution of our nation.

BETTMANN/CORBIS; ALBERT HARLINGUE/ROGER-VIOLLET/THE IMAGE WORKS

OPPOSITE: On July 25, 1975, a burning cross in the farmland of Morgan County, Indiana, signifies that the Klan is there. Top: Confederate Army major general Nathan Bedford Forrest was a cofounder of the Ku Klux Klan and served as its leader from 1866 to 1869. Above: "Colonel" William Joseph Simmons, seen in 1915, was responsible for the organization's second resurgence.

BETTMANN/CORBIS

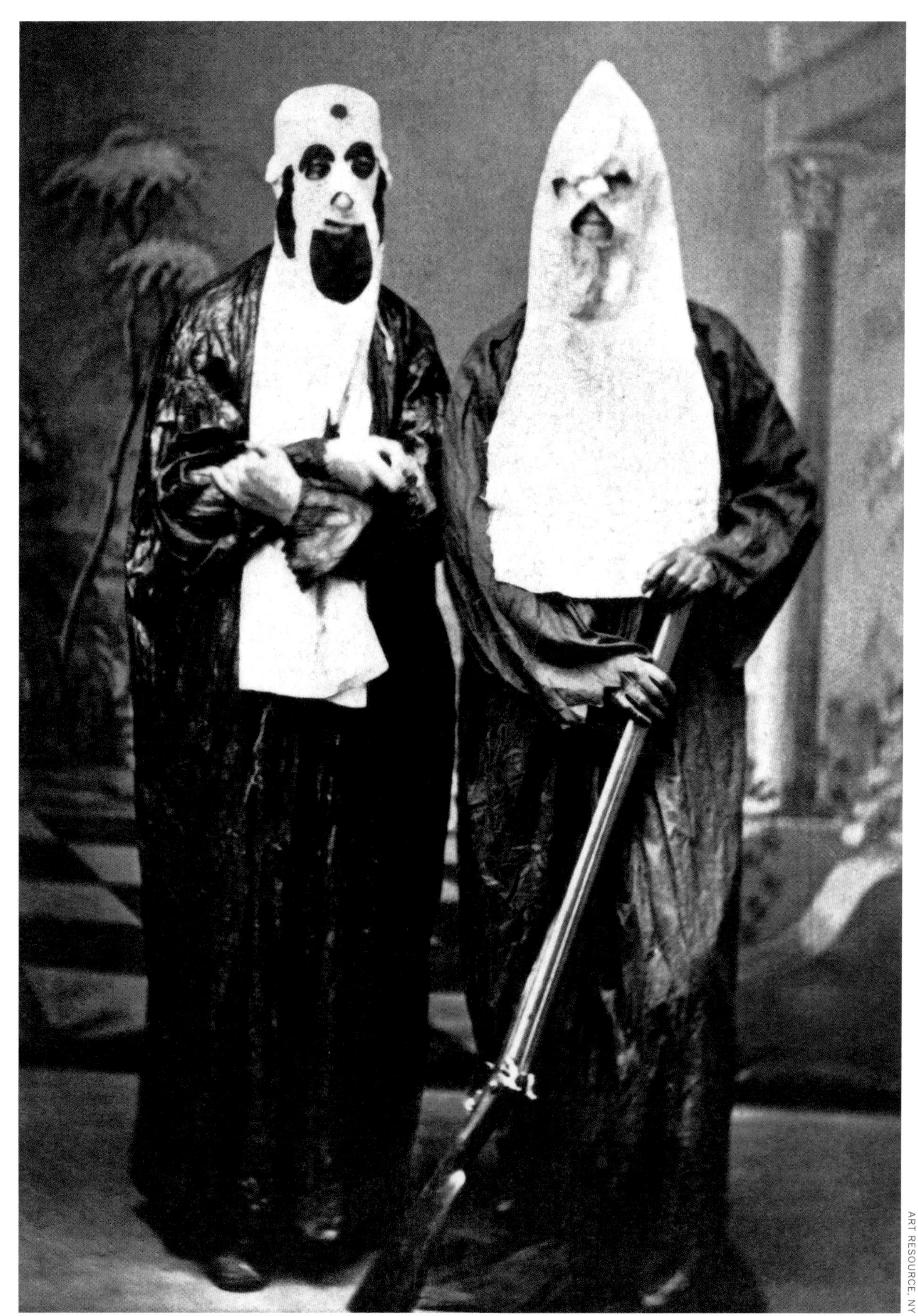

ART RESOURCE, NY

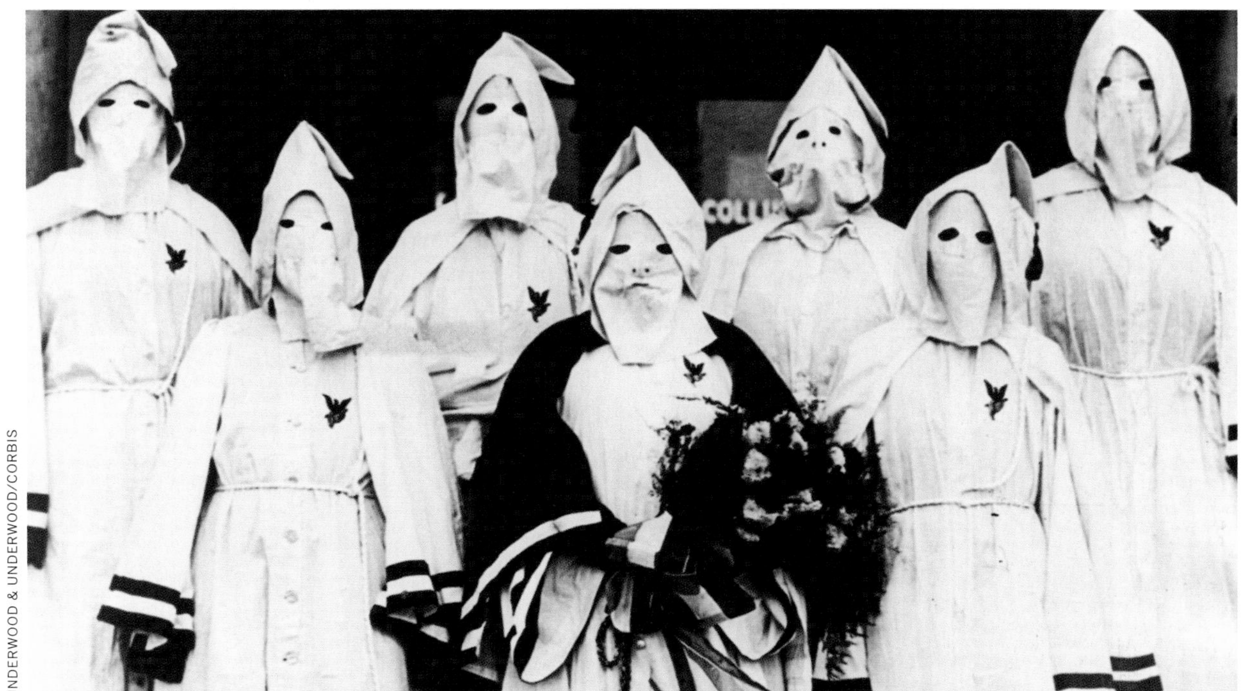

UNDERWOOD & UNDERWOOD/CORBIS

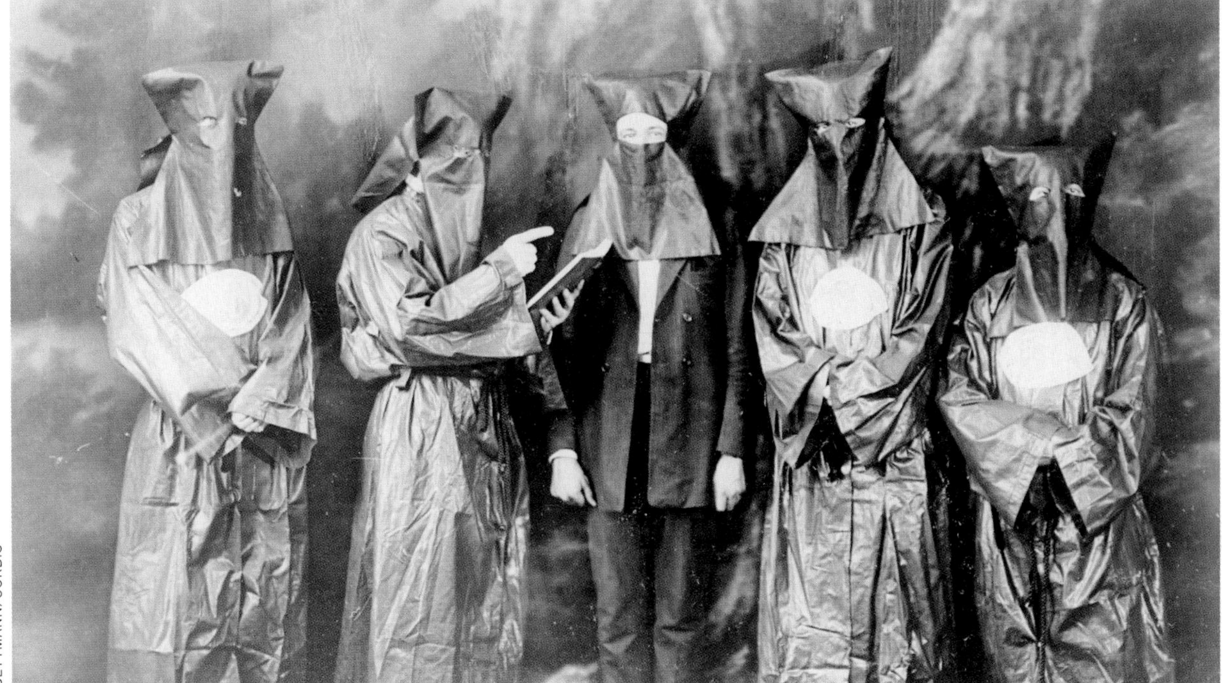

BETTMANN/CORBIS

OPPOSITE: A portrait made in 1868 in Alabama, during the Klan's first rising. Top: A picture made in Atlanta in 1922 during the Klan's resurgence. These are not men but women: members of the Dixie Protestant Women's Political League, which is to the Klan as the Eastern Star is to the Masons. The woman with the flowers is Mrs. E.N. Gibbs, who says, "We aren't dangerous, but Atlanta and Georgia and the country will hear much from us from now on." Above: A new member is sworn in to the Knights of the Invisible Jungle of the Tiger's Eye, a society founded in 1922 to combat the Ku Klux Klan. The Invisible Jungle knights wore gowns and masks to hide their identities—just as their foes did.

WHITE SUPREMACY!

Attention, White Men!

Grand Torch-Light Procession

At JACKSON,

On the Night of the

Fourth of January, 1890.

The Final Settlement of Democratic Rule and White Supremacy in Mississippi.

GRAND PYROTECHNIC DISPLAY!
Transparencies and Torches Free for all.

All in Sympathy with the Grand Cause are Cordially and Earnestly Invited to be on hand, to aid in the Final Overthrow of Radical Rule in our State.

Come on foot or on horse-back; come any way, but be sure to get there.
Brass Bands, Cannon, Flambeau Torches, Transparencies, Sky-rockets, Etc.

A GRAND DISPLAY FOR A GRAND CAUSE.

GRANGER

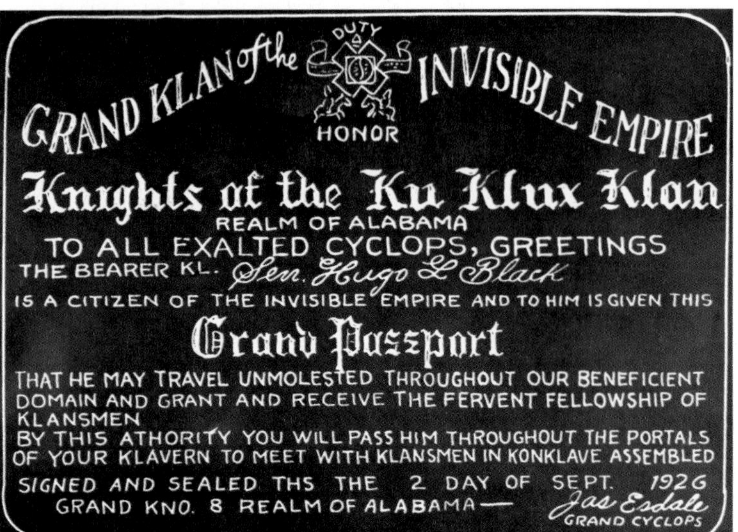
DUTY
GRAND KLAN of the INVISIBLE EMPIRE
HONOR
Knights of the Ku Klux Klan
REALM OF ALABAMA
TO ALL EXALTED CYCLOPS, GREETINGS
THE BEARER KL. Sen. Hugo L Black
IS A CITIZEN OF THE INVISIBLE EMPIRE AND TO HIM IS GIVEN THIS
Grand Passport
THAT HE MAY TRAVEL UNMOLESTED THROUGHOUT OUR BENEFICIENT DOMAIN AND GRANT AND RECEIVE THE FERVENT FELLOWSHIP OF KLANSMEN
BY THIS ATHORITY YOU WILL PASS HIM THROUGHOUT THE PORTALS OF YOUR KLAVERN TO MEET WITH KLANSMEN IN KONKLAVE ASSEMBLED
SIGNED AND SEALED THS THE 2 DAY OF SEPT. 1926
GRAND KNO. 8 REALM OF ALABAMA — Jas Esdale
GRAND CYCLOPS

BETTMANN/CORBIS

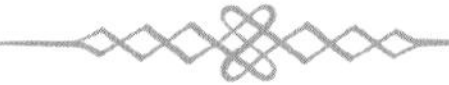

AS THE ITEMS on this page indicate, the Klan has always been a curious kind of secret society: wanting to travel anonymously, yet also wanting to shout from the mountaintops. This certainly has everything to do with its lawlessness—an individual could get himself busted—and with the fact that it is political in nature (we *need* to get our message out). But not all Klansmen have hid behind the mask, and some have been American civil servants of undeniable eminence. Opposite is Justice Hugo Black, a former Democratic senator from Alabama who was named to the Supreme Court by Franklin Delano Roosevelt in 1937 and became one of the most influential jurists of the 20th century. He is remembered today as a strong supporter of civil liberties and liberal policies generally. But in the 1920s, when a politician, he gave anti-Catholic speeches, joined the Klan and let everyone in Alabama know he was a member. He later said, with regret and contrition, "I would have joined any group if it helped me get votes."

CORBIS; INSET: ROGER-VIOLLET/THE IMAGE WORKS

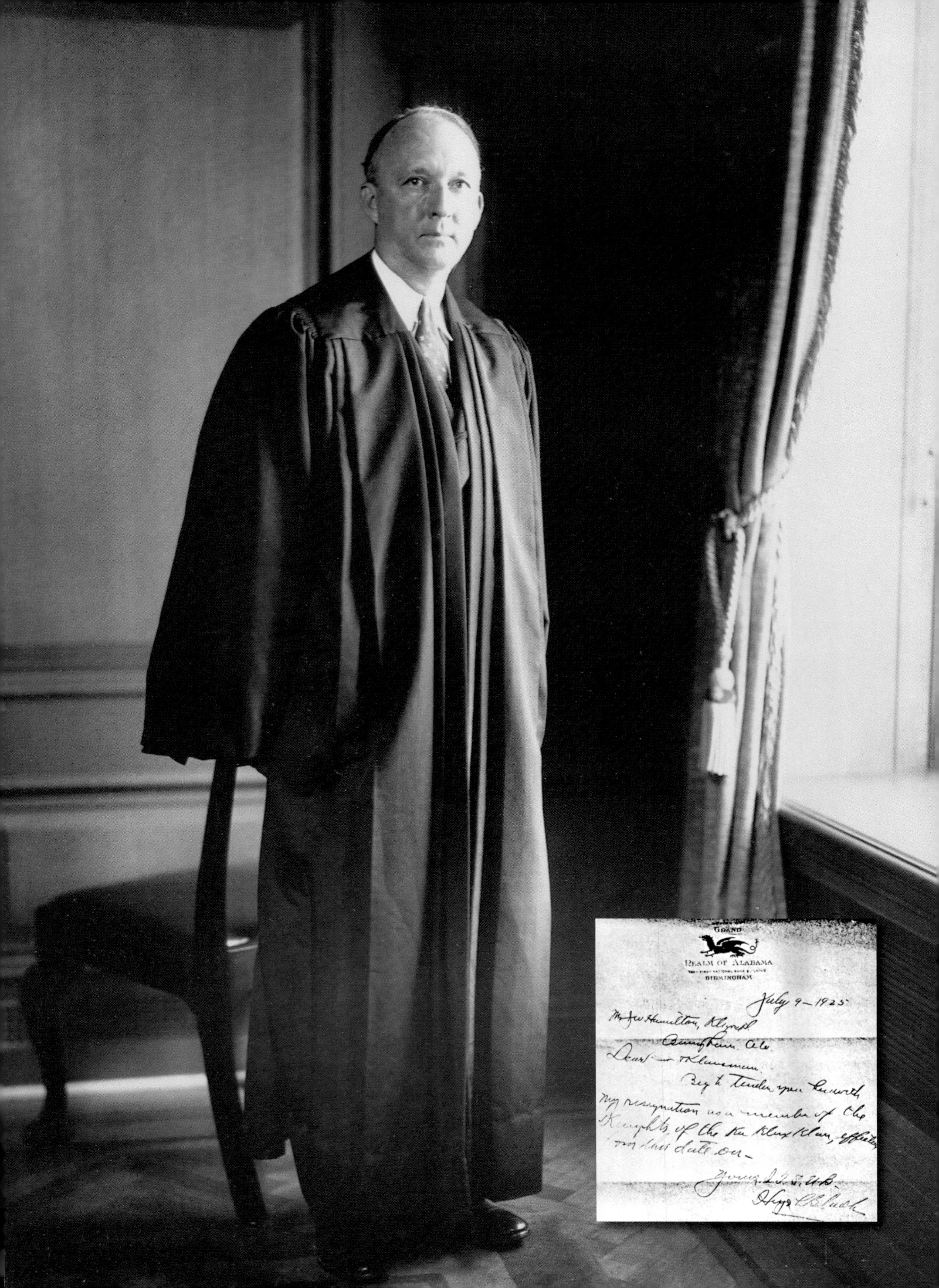

GRAND

REALM OF ALABAMA

BIRMINGHAM

July 9—1925

Mr. Jas Hamilton, Klygrapp

Birmingham Ala.

Dear Sir & Klansman:

Beg to tender you herewith my resignation as a member of the Knights of the Ku Klux Klan, effective from this date on—

Yours I.T.S.U.B.

Hugo L. Black

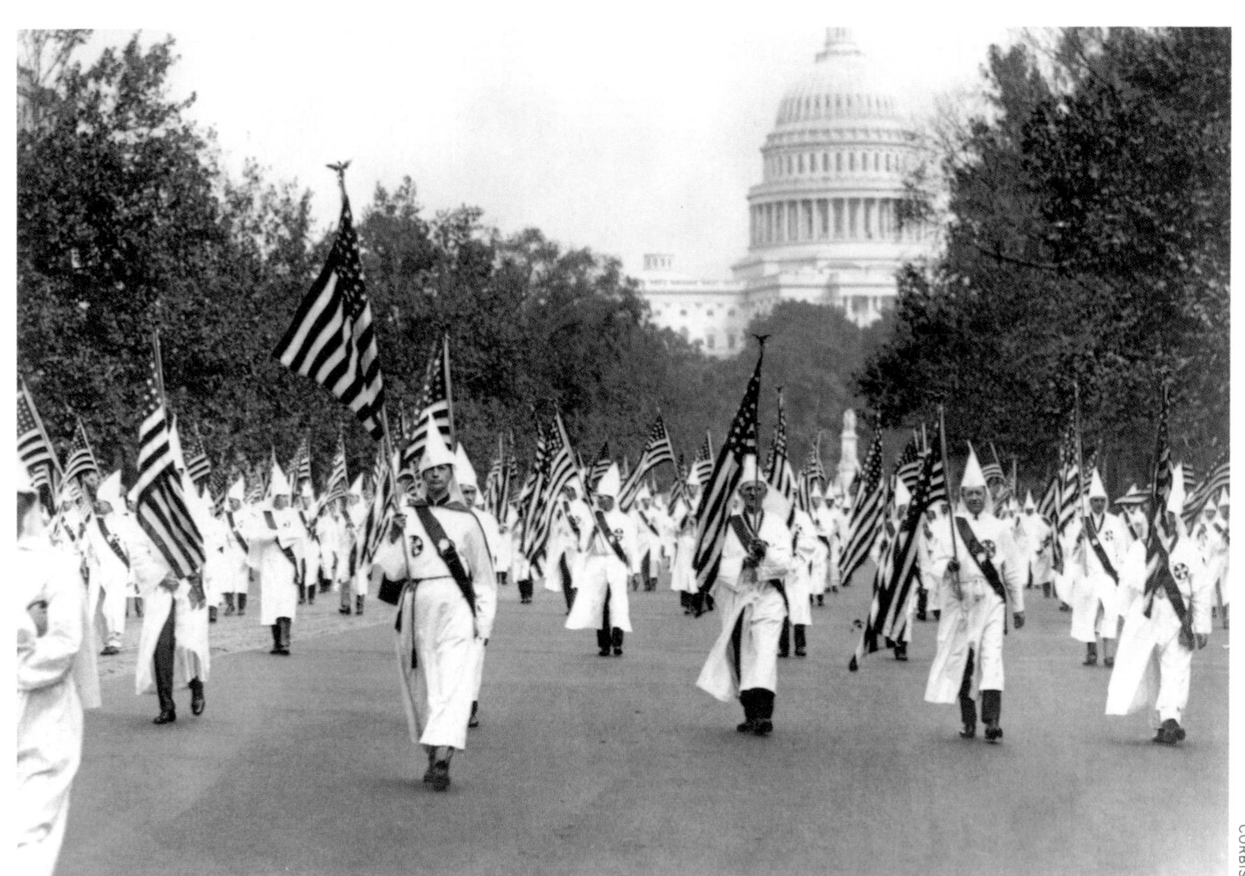

CORBIS

JIM LO SCALZO/EPA/CORBIS

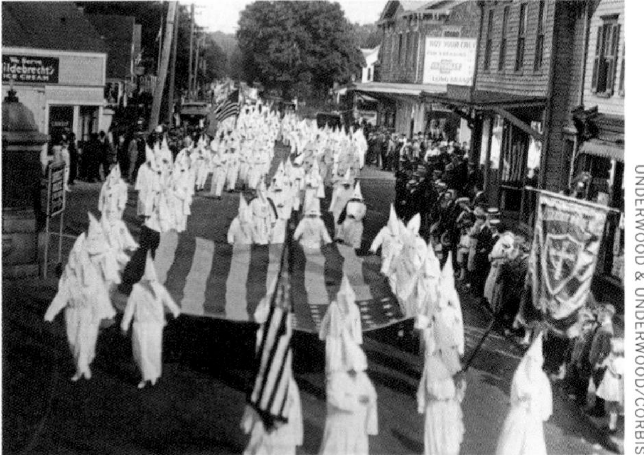

UNDERWOOD & UNDERWOOD/CORBIS

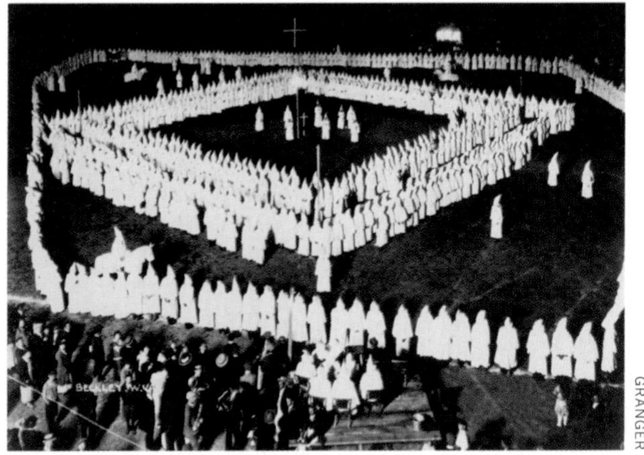

GRANGER

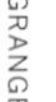

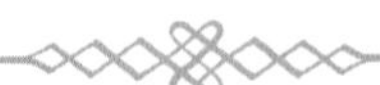

THE KLAN, yesterday and today. On this page are three photographs from the 1920s: KKK members parading on Pennsylvania Avenue in Washington, D.C., with the Capitol in the background (top); celebrating the opening of their new headquarters in Long Branch, New Jersey, on the Fourth of July in 1924 (above, left); and participating in another ceremony that same year in Beckley, West Virginia. Opposite, top: On May 28, 2011, two female members of the Knights of the Southern Cross Soldiers of the Ku Klux Klan don robes and hoods before the start of a cross-lighting ceremony on private property near Powhatan, Virginia. Three chapters of the Klan have recently reemerged in the state, holding rallies, lighting crosses and recruiting new members. Bottom: Near Stone Mountain, Georgia, another modern-day Klan cell enjoys a cross-burning, also on private land: the best way to stay out of trouble, even if it does turn the event into more of a party than a protest.

ROBIN NELSON/ZUMA/CORBIS

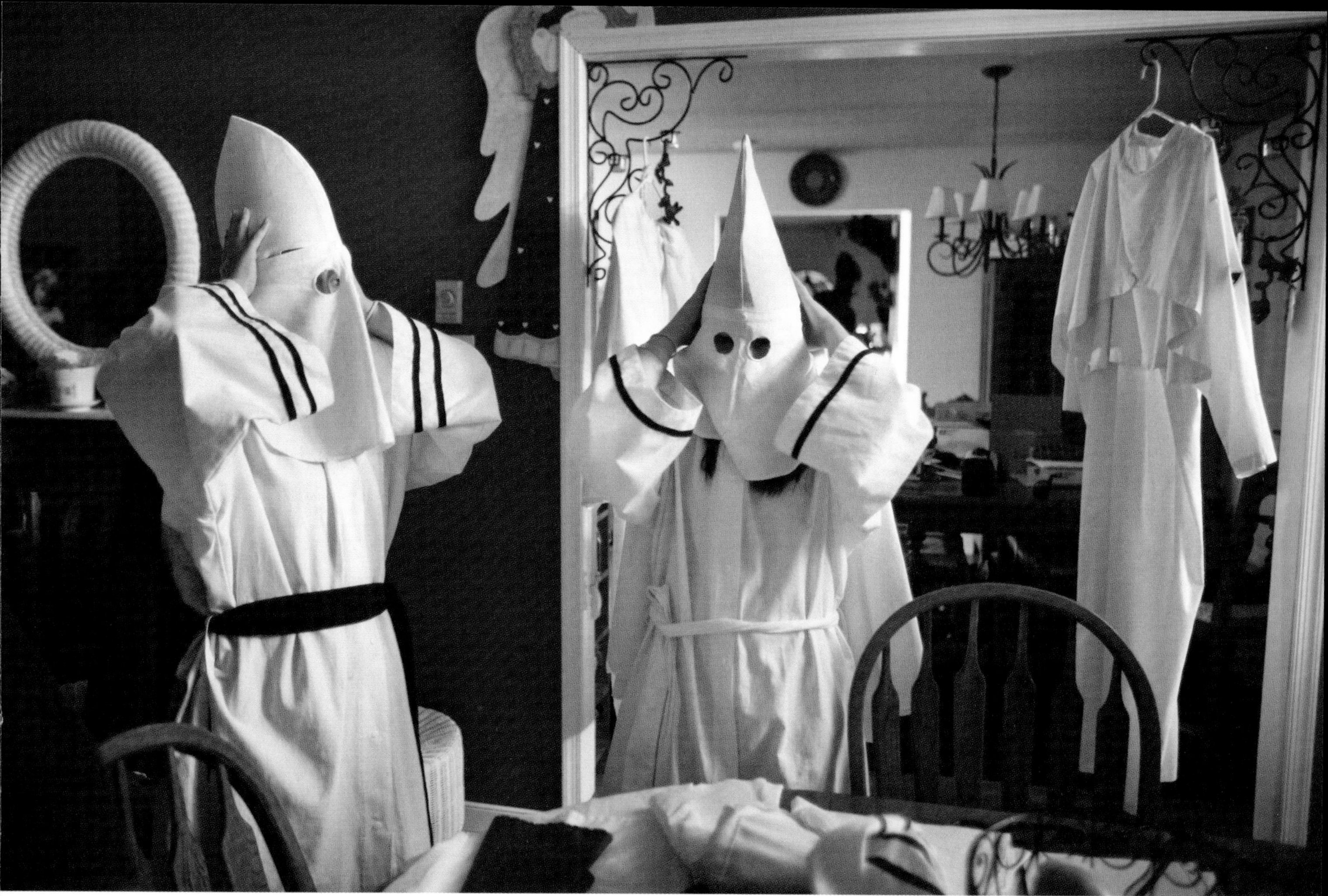

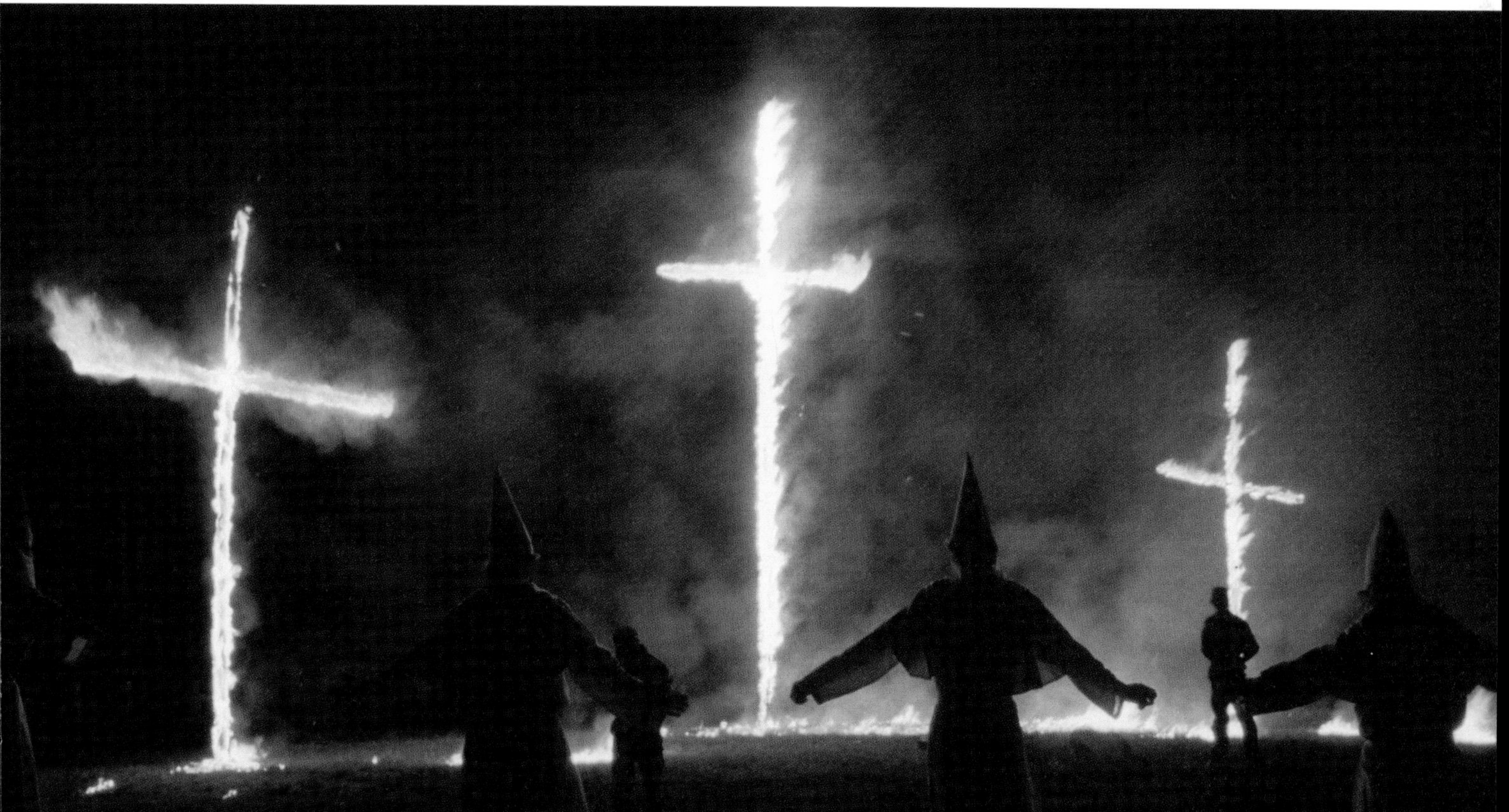

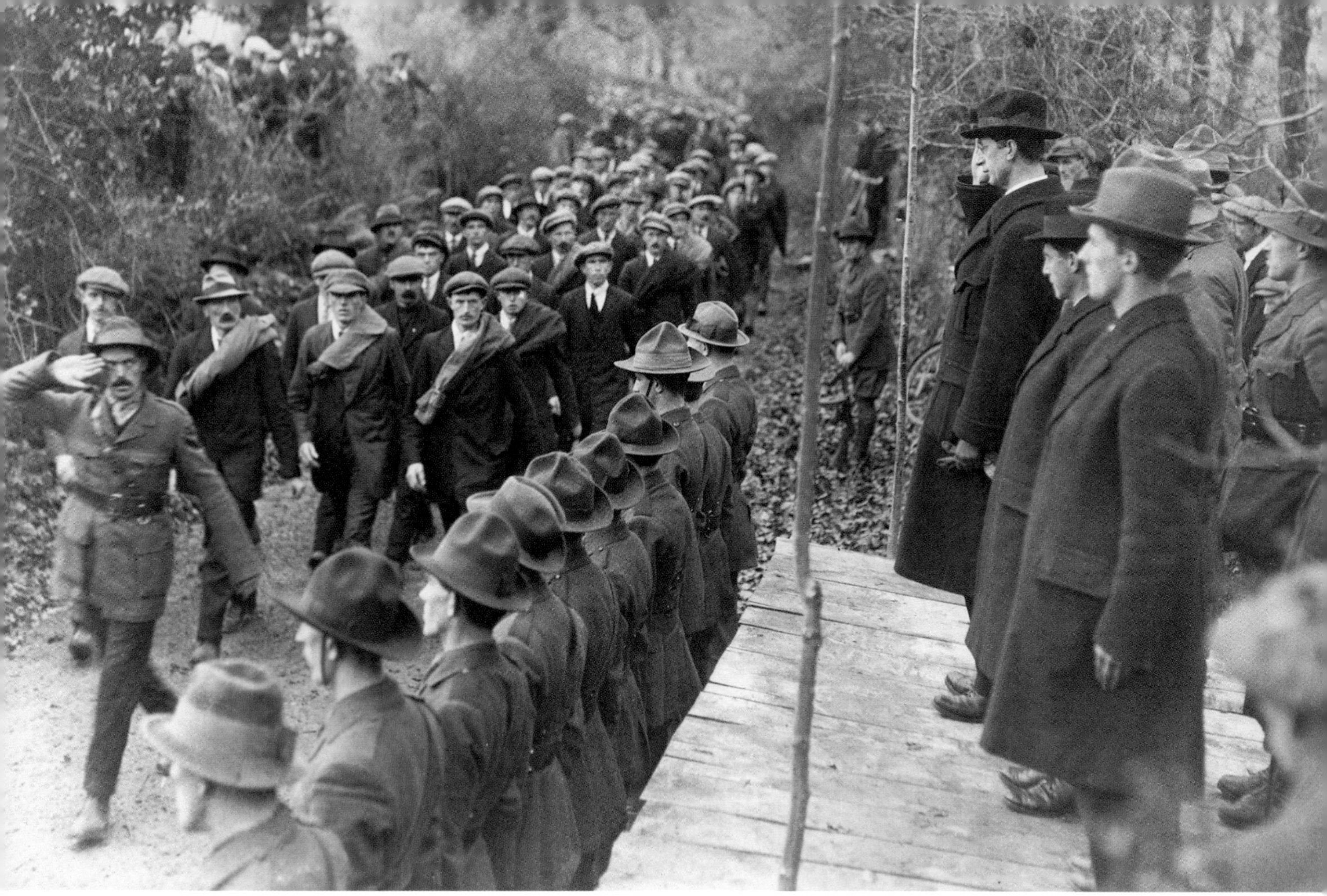

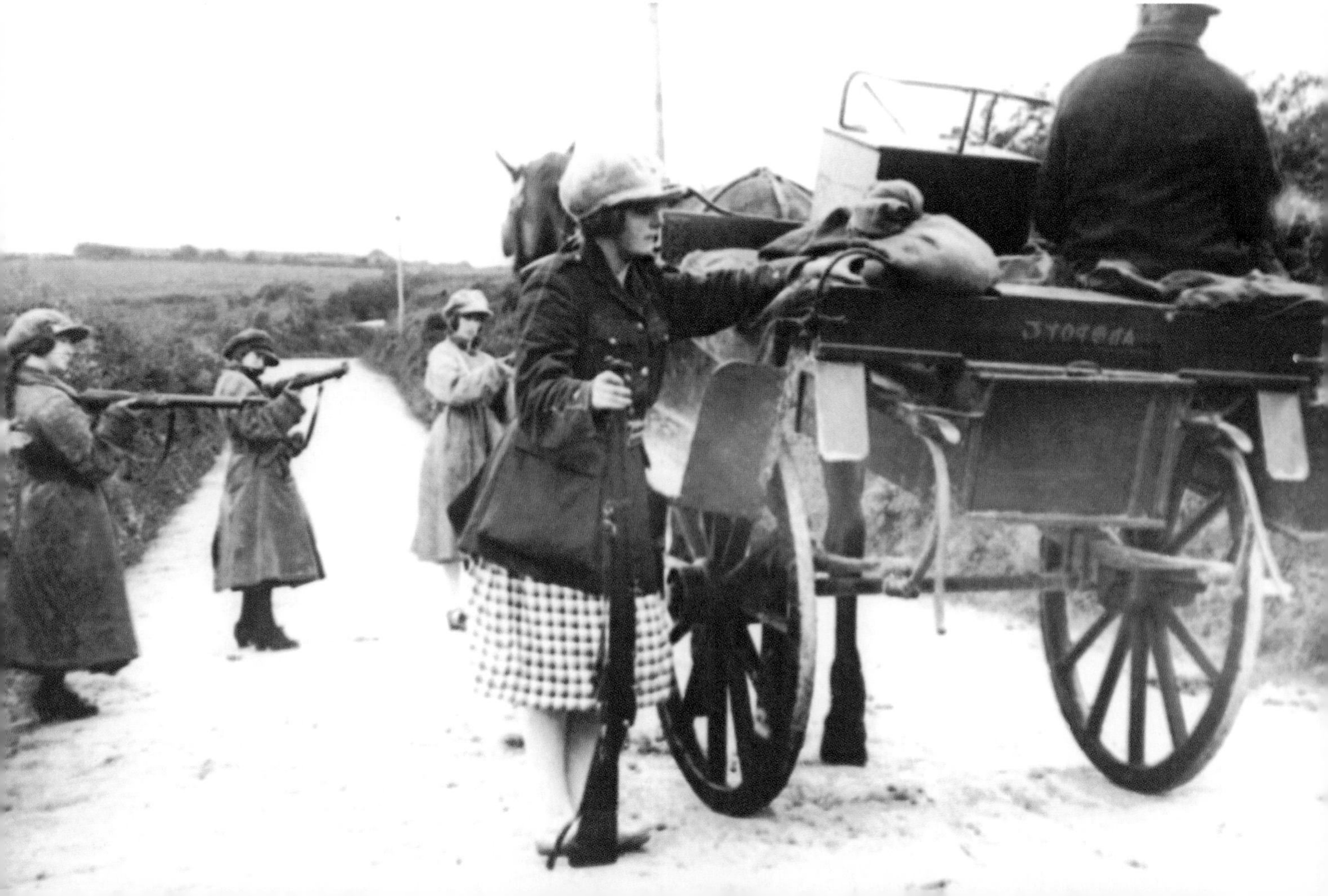

The Irish Republican Army

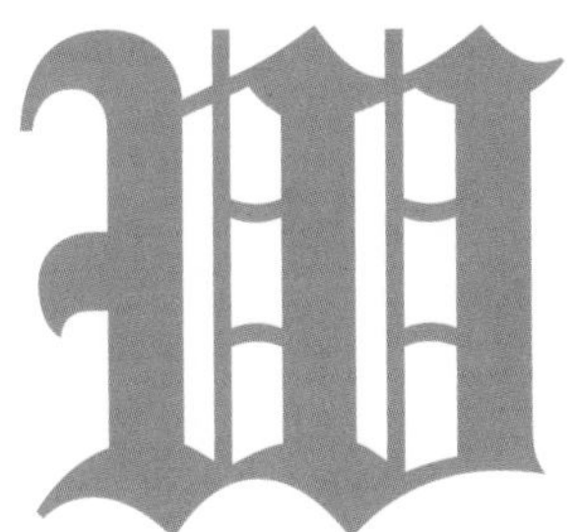

We have dealt in our pages with paramilitary groups, and others that are simply of a violent nature. But now we arrive at a secret society that calls itself an army. Is that a conceit? Hasn't it shown itself over time as essentially a terrorist organization?

First: Which IRA are we talking about? Not unlike the term *Rosicrucian*, the initials *IRA* have been applied to several semi-affiliated groups. We've had the original IRA, the Official IRA, the Provisional IRA, the Real IRA and the Continuity IRA. The famous IRA, which existed from 1922 until 1969 before splintering yet again, lost a civil war with the original IRA way back when.

As quickly as we can: There was an organization in the mid 19th century called the Irish Republican Brotherhood (IRB). It spawned the original IRA. That and all other IRAs have been, since their inception and in spite of their differences, dedicated to an independent Ireland (today's Republic of Ireland), and many have sought a unified Ireland: the north (today under British control) and the south (the Republic) rejoined.

The aggression of the IRB and others led to the Anglo-Irish Treaty in 1921 and to the establishing of the Irish Free State in 1922. For a brief moment, that state comprised the whole island, but six counties in the north of Ireland that were largely Protestant soon opted out—as they were allowed to do in the treaty—choosing to remain a part of Great Britain. Many in the original IRA were okay with the new formulation, but many were not. In 1922 and '23, the two sides fought a civil war—and the old guard, led by Michael Collins (who would be assassinated) prevailed, giving rise to the underground IRAs.

To be sure, the Irish Republican Army has always had a cause. But many innocents, including scores on the Republic's side who have been victims of violence exercised by their own countrymen, have been harmed.

Today, the Official IRA participates in a process that has led to a tenuous kind of peace. But groups such as the Real IRA and Continuity IRA continue with the bombing.

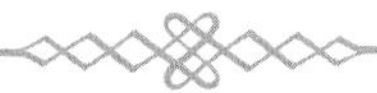

OPPOSITE, TOP: Circa 1920, Eamon de Valera inspects members of the Western Division of the Irish Republican Army at Sixmilebridge in County Clare during the Sinn Féin Rebellion. De Valera was a towering political figure in 20th century Ireland. In the Irish Civil War of 1922 and '23, he led the anti-Treaty opposition (which gave rise to the famous IRA) and in 1926 he founded the Fianna Fáil party. He thrice led the Irish Republic's government: from 1932 to 1948, from 1951 to 1954 and from 1957 to 1959. Bottom: On September 6, 1922, in the west of Ireland, the Irish Republican Girl Raiders hold up a mail transport (the script on the rear of the wagon is Gaelic for "post-car"), searching for government dispatches.

HULTON-DEUTSCH/CORBIS

AP

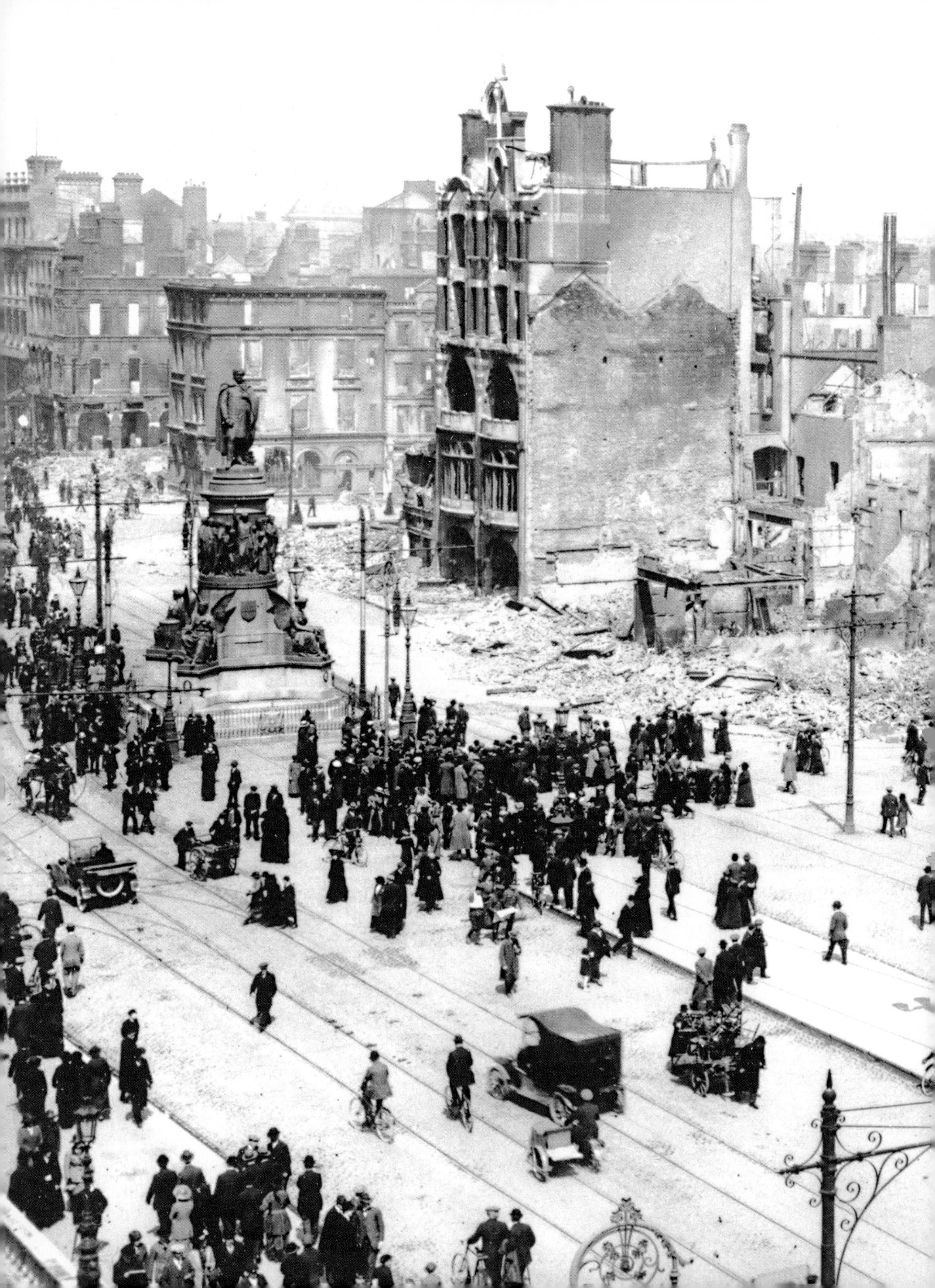

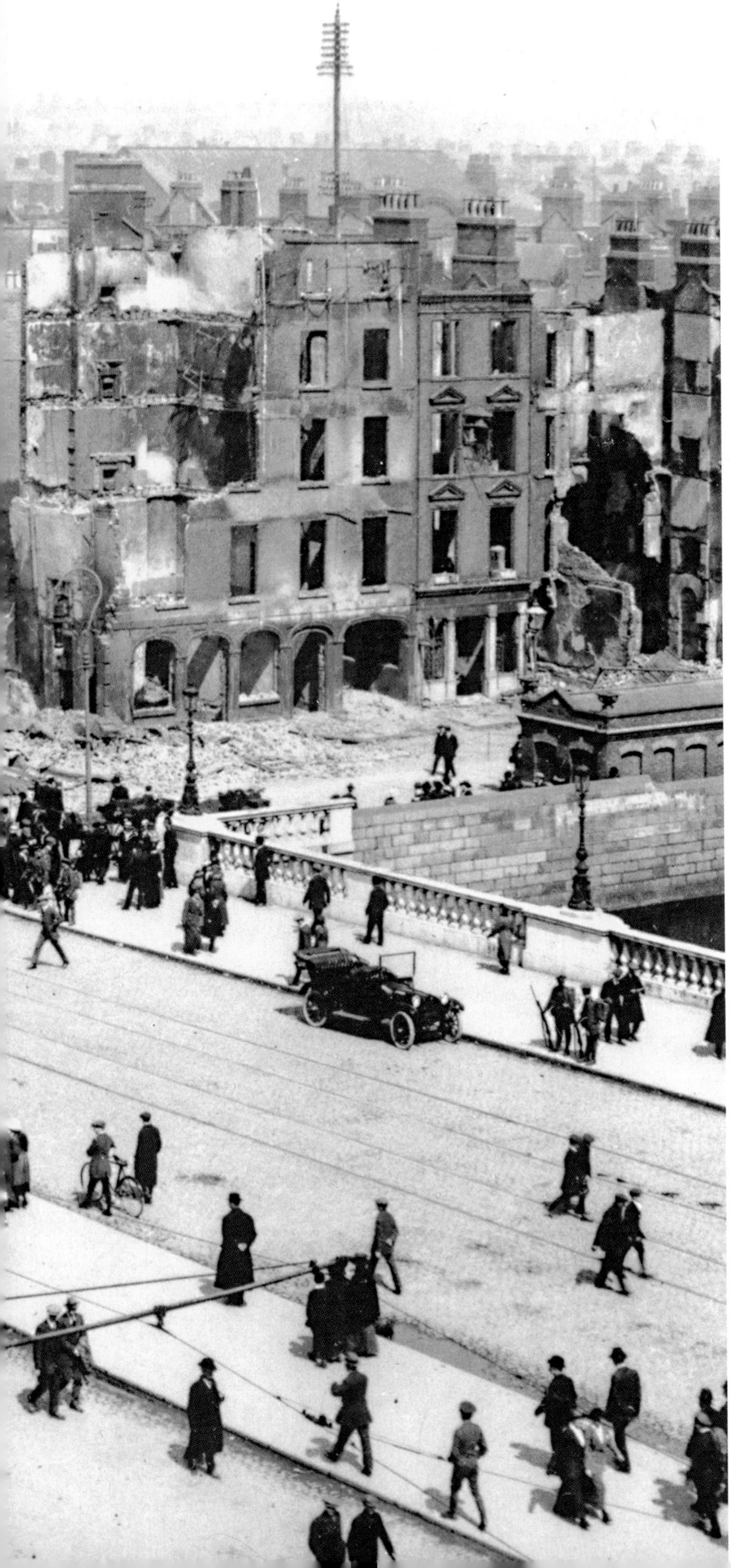

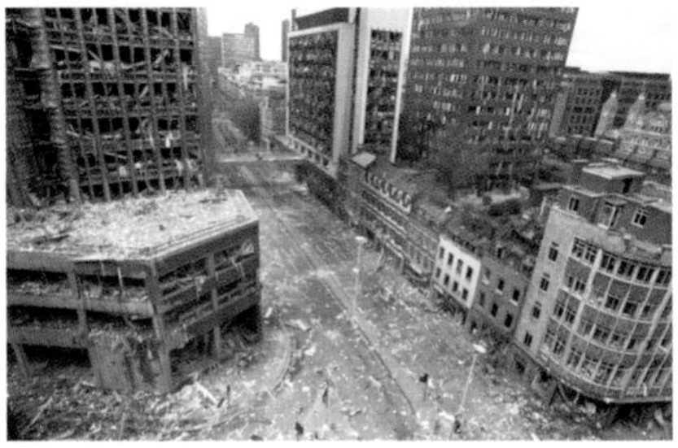

ANDRE CAMARA/REUTERS

THE FIGHT for Irish independence and then unification in the 20th century was marked by a steady stream of bloodshed—and constant heartache. At left is the destruction in Dublin following the Easter Rising of 1916, a seminal event in Ireland's history. Organized by the Irish Republican Brotherhood, the precedent organization of the IRA, the Rising saw nationalists seize control of several locations in Dublin and battle for nearly a week before being suppressed. Leaders of the movement were executed, but the Irish had been stirred, and the clock was ticking for England. In 1919, the Irish Republic was established, but Great Britain said no, and so began the Irish War of Independence, which the Irish would (largely) win. The IRA would carry on for many years because its leadership saw their task as incomplete: Even if there was now a nation called Ireland, the north was still part of the United Kingdom. The army hit the English whenever and wherever it could, exporting its violence not only to Northern Ireland but across the Irish Sea. Above is the wreckage after the April 1993 Bishopsgate bombing in London. Well over a million dollars in damage was caused but miraculously only one person, a journalist, was killed; police had received a coded message and were frantically evacuating the area when the tremendous truck bomb exploded.

AP

Chapter 5

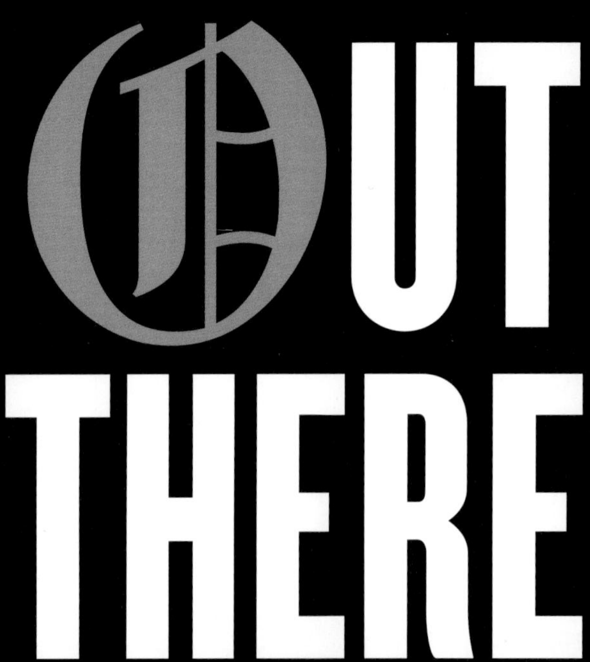

THIS IS ALEISTER CROWLEY, king of kooks. Obviously, he was content to be the poster boy for secret society mavens who might buy into the weirdo stuff. Unfortunately, this kind of fringe mentality could lead, in the bizarro world of secret societies, to abject tragedy.

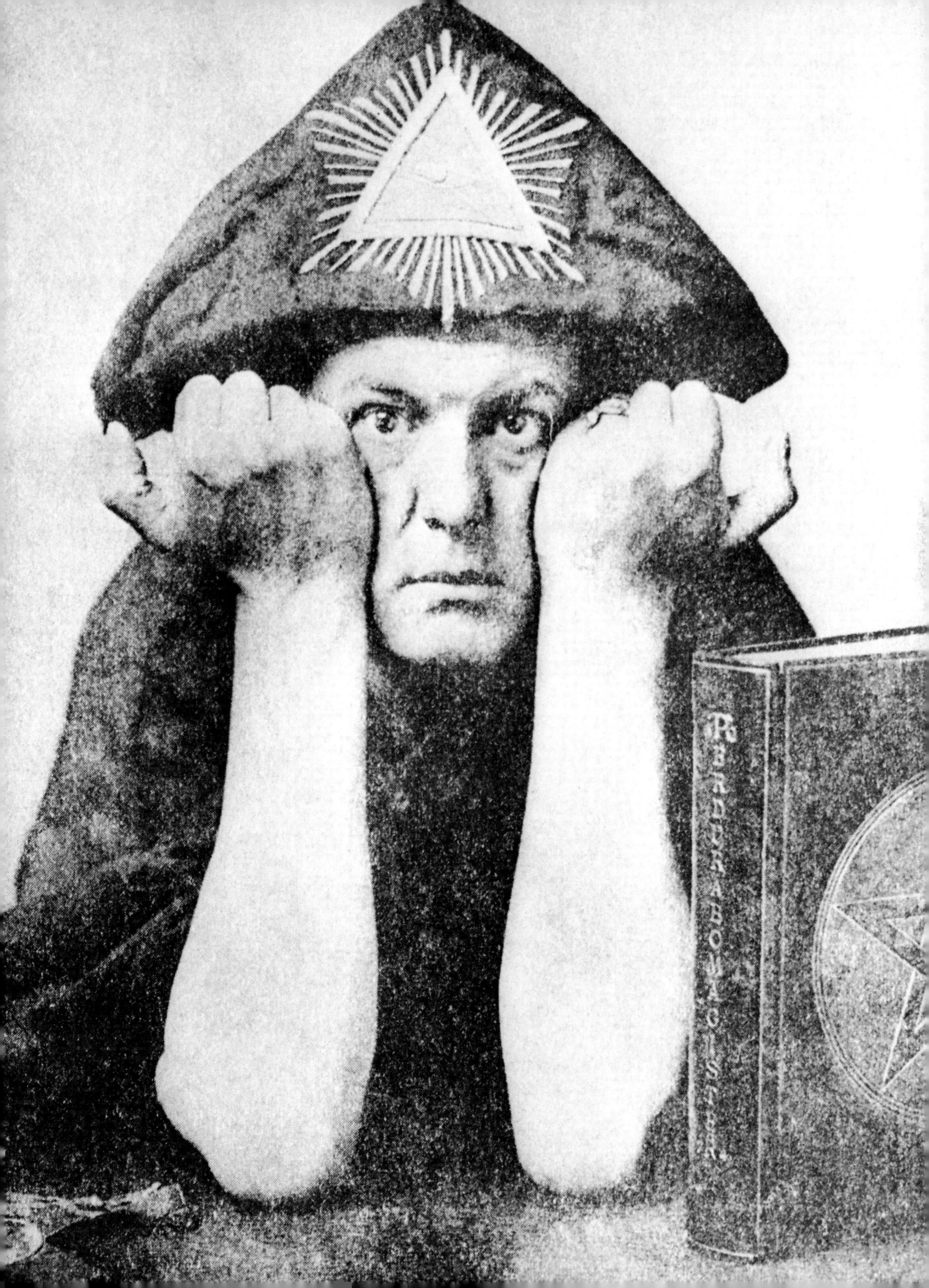

Cultists and Occultists

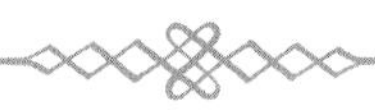

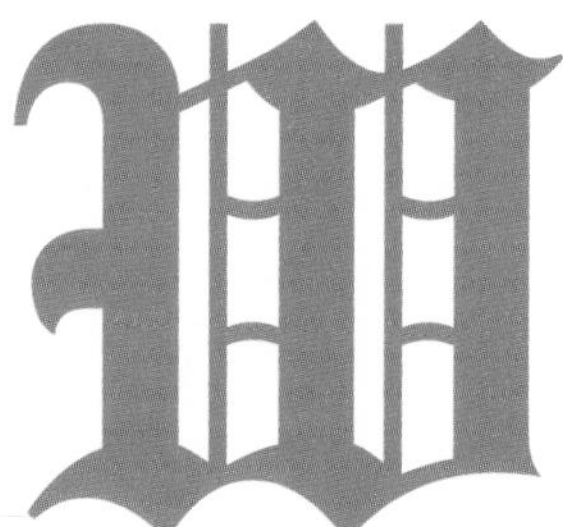

We have already encountered in our pages plenty of strange individuals and groups. But let's discuss a few that may be summarily discounted: Aleister Crowley and William Robert Woodman, for instance, almost dared society to discount them.

It's not that they were charlatans, but in terms of the temporal and/or sensible world, Crowley & Co. were carny magicians who took themselves and their magic seriously. This has happened over and over again throughout history, with far greater—and far worse—consequences than Crowley's or Woodman's goofiness would engender. Think: false prophets, fake messiahs. Manson's faithful, drugged on him and also on chemicals, committing mass murder. James Jones's colony drinking the Flavor Aid. The Heaven's Gate communal suicide in 1997 in California. By contrast, such as Crowley and Woodman did little harm, but what is of a piece is the slavish devotion to a trumped-up idol.

Who was Aleister Crowley? He was a nutcase of the first water, way into sex and the occult. Apparently, he had charisma and attracted disciples, including more than a few women. He fashioned himself, for their entrancement, the "Great Beast" (a nickname bestowed on him by his mother), and it can be assumed he behaved bestially. It remains historically astonishing how prominent his "religion," Thelema, was and even remains; a 2002 BBC TV poll ranked Crowley the 73rd greatest Briton of all time. He was born to the upper class, and became a member of the Hermetic Order of the Golden Dawn. From Golden Dawnian teachings, he would evolve his theories of Thelema, and would proceed to found his own secret society. He would lead his *Ordo Templi Orientis,* and would continue his career as a sexual experimenter (men and women), druggie (all kinds) and, ahem, social critic. "Do What Thou Wilt" was his hallmark. Today, many regard Crowley as the most influential occultist of all time.

As for the Golden Dawn: It was one of the esoteric societies closely related to Masonry. Among its cofounders in the late 19th century was Woodman, a prominent Freemason and Rosicrucian. He was a surgeon and a master gardener and a man of great refinement. Unfortunately, he is best remembered today as one of the Golden Dawn's initial Triad of Chiefs. It makes him seem silly, which he was not. Not necessarily.

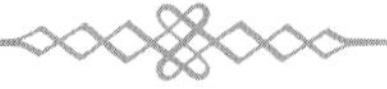

THIS IS Dr. William Robert Woodman, estimable Englishman and cofounder of the Hermetic Order of the Golden Dawn, which was only one of a multitude of neo-Masonic secret societies to blossom in Great Britain (and, veritably, around the world) in the extremely excitable, fertile 19th century.

R.A. GILBERT/BRISTOL, ENGLAND

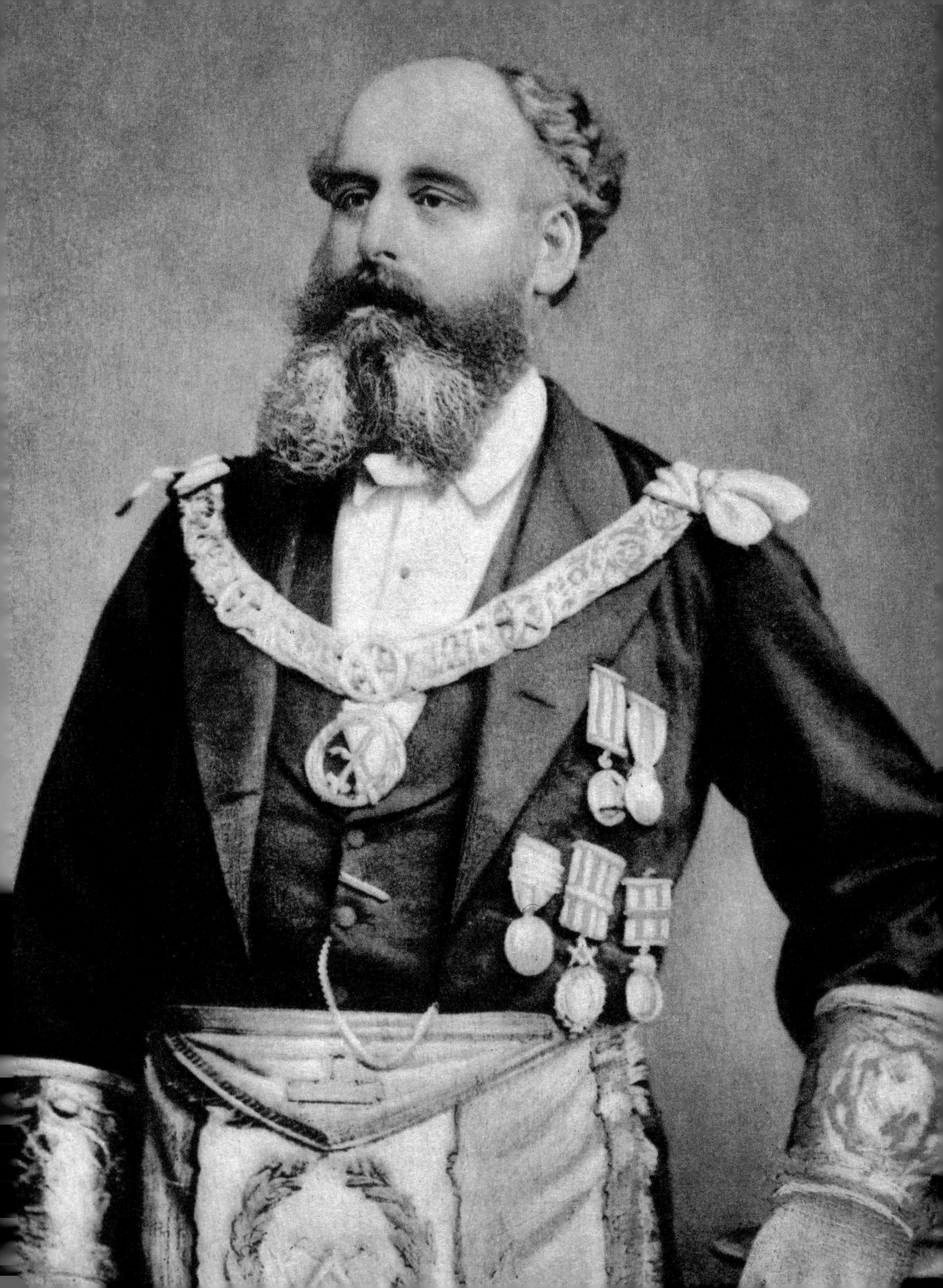

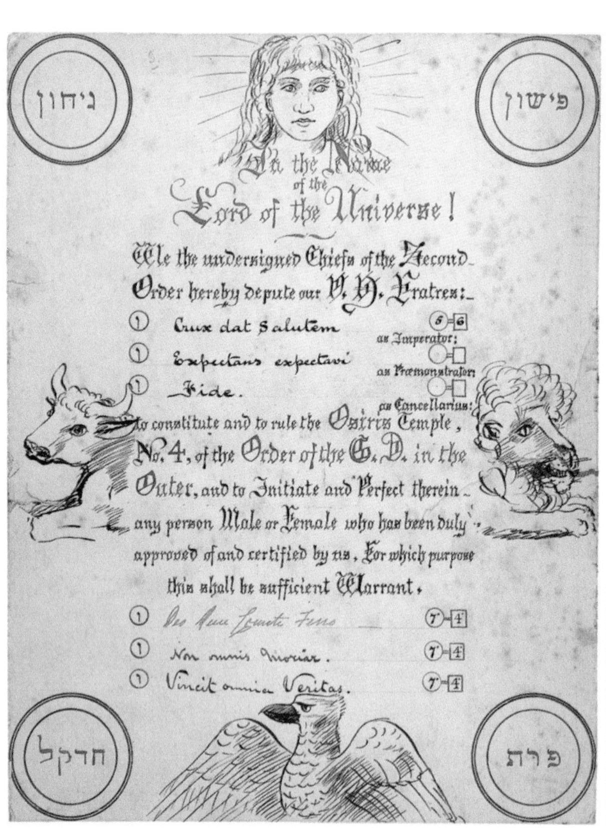

גיחון

פישון

In the Name of the Lord of the Universe!

We the undersigned Chiefs of the Second Order hereby depute our V. H. Fratres:–

① Crux dat Salutem ⑤-6 as Imperator:

① Expectans expectavi ○-□ as Praemonstrator:

① Fide. ○-□ as Cancellarius:

to constitute and to rule the Osiris Temple, No. 4, of the Order of the G. D. in the Outer, and to Initiate and Perfect therein any person Male or Female who has been duly approved of and certified by us. For which purpose this shall be sufficient Warrant.

① Deo Duce Comite Ferro ⑦-4

① Non omnis moriar. ⑦-4

① Vincit omnia Veritas. ⑦-4

חדקל

פרת

R.A. GILBERT/BRISTOL, ENGLAND

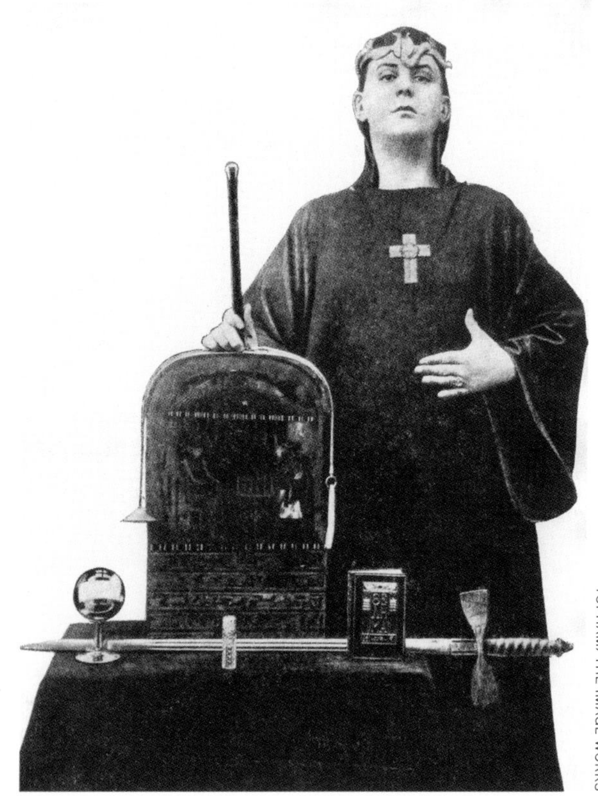

TOPHAM/THE IMAGE WORKS

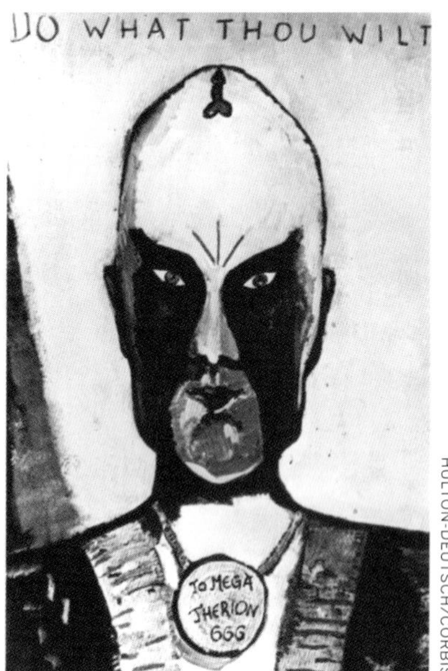

HULTON-DEUTSCH/CORBIS

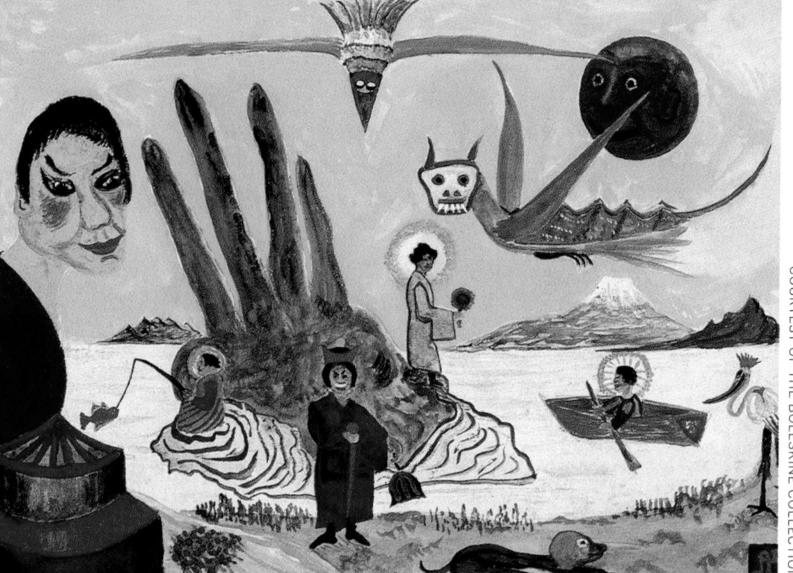

COURTESY OF THE BOLESKINE COLLECTION

WHEN DEALING with secret societies, a chapter entitled "Out There" could fill a book—but we choose not to have our chapter do so. Rather, we quickly point out that on the fringes of the fringes, such folks as Aleister Crowley have flourished. Above, clockwise from top left: The Golden Dawn charter; Crowley at his altar, magically robed and crowned with the Egyptian Uraeus serpent, and with his hand resting on the Stele of Revealing and his principal Book of the Law on the table; "The Island of Magicians," a 1921 watercolor by Crowley whose symbolism is meant to be intuitively appreciated; a Crowley self-portrait. Opposite: Crowley performing rites at his temple, with his disciples kneeling. In a phrase: Holy mackerel!

MARY EVANS/HARRY PRICE/THE IMAGE WORKS

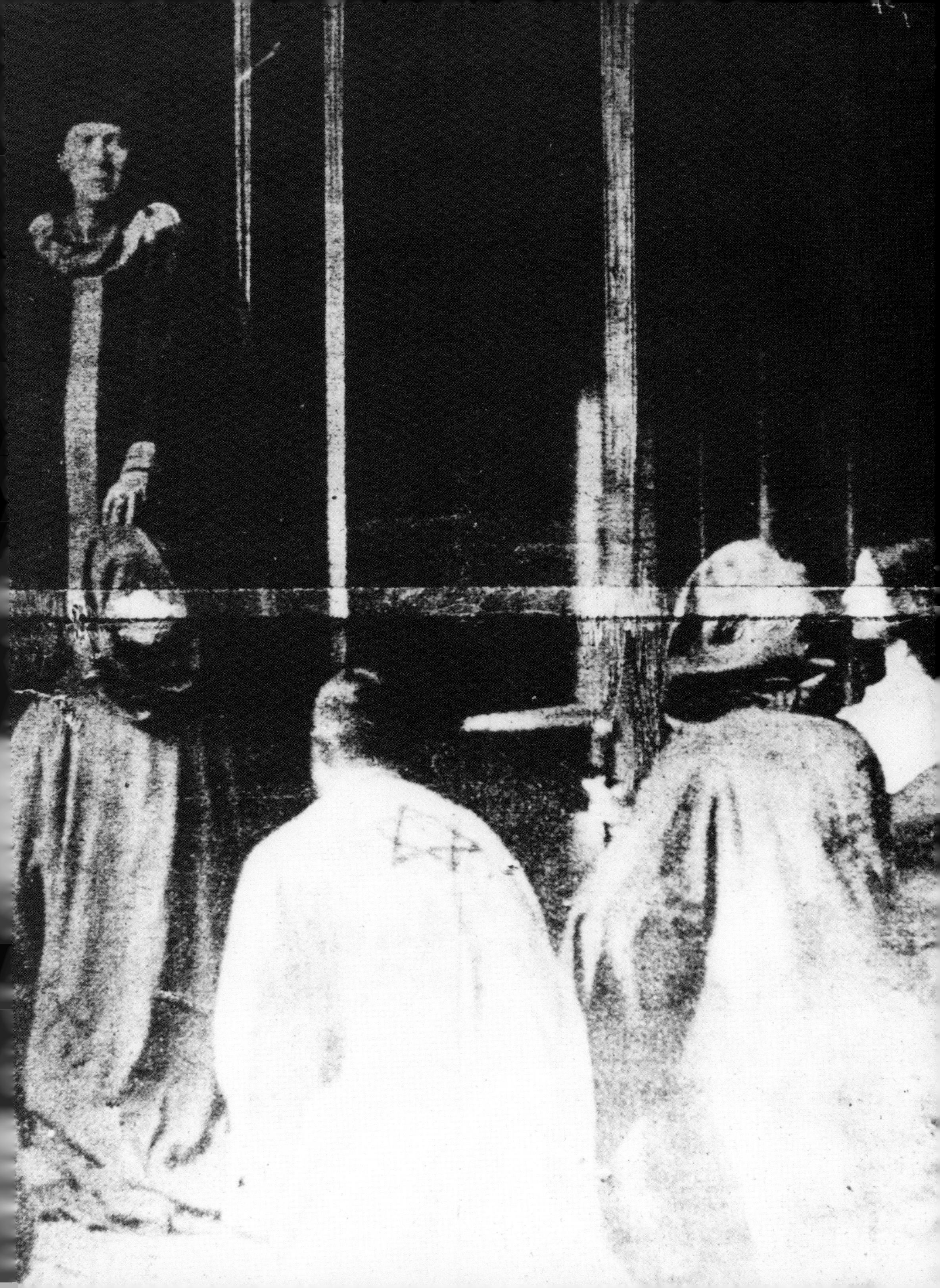

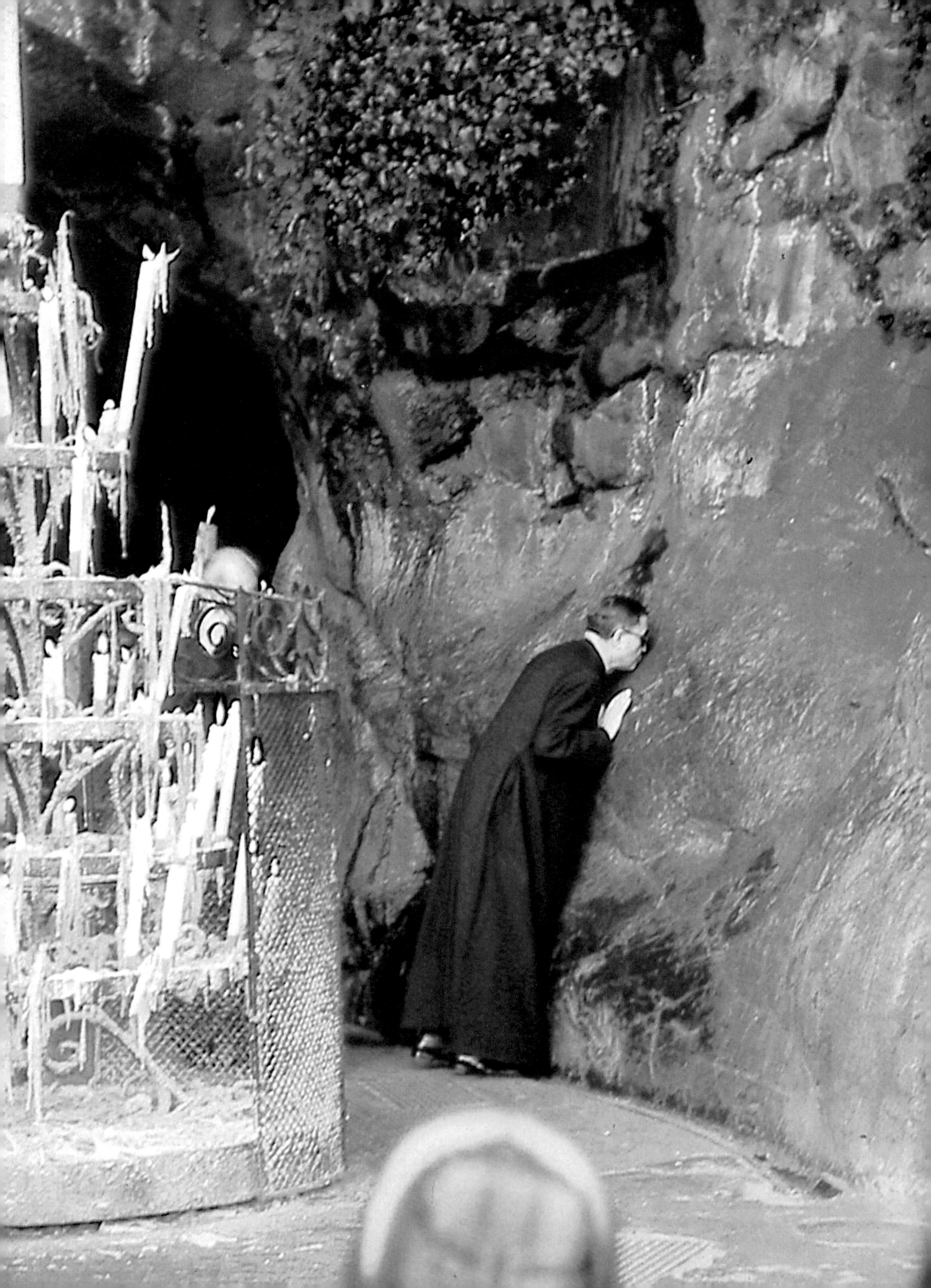

Chapter 6

What is Opus Dei?

JOSEMARÍA ESCRIVÁ DE BALAGUER at Lourdes on July 9, 1960. Born in 1902, this cleric was and remains the heart and soul of Opus Dei, an organization he founded within the Roman Catholic Church in 1928. He died in 1975 and was canonized by Pope John Paul II on October 6, 2002.

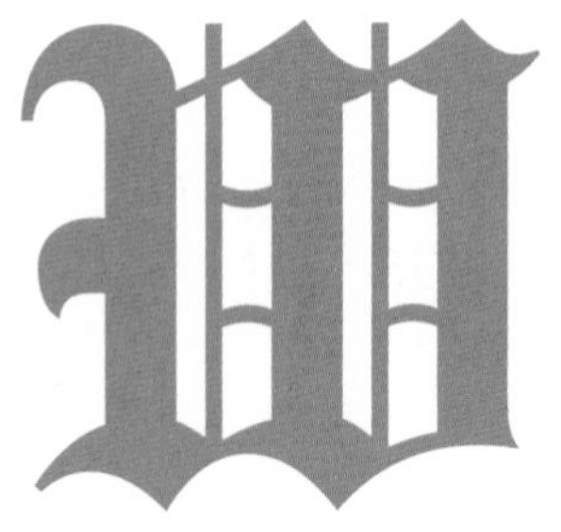hen dealing with secret societies, there are obscurities, fringe considerations (such as the Hermetic Order of the Golden Dawn) and then there are the big and inescapable subjects such as the Masons and the Templars and, yes, Opus Dei. Actually, this last one could be considered Roman Catholicism generally, a religious institution that has seen endless conspiracy theories attached to it like so many barnacles on a whale. Some seem to see St. Peter's Basilica as just an enormous, constantly churning generator of plots and stratagems.

Well before there was Opus Dei there were the Templars, of course, and also the Jesuits. This order within the Church, founded in the 1500s by Ignatius of Loyola, had long been considered suspect by those who consider everything suspect. These folks say that the 17th century "Secret Instructions of the Jesuits" outlines a plan to gain power within the Church, and thereby the world. Never mind that the *Monita Secreta* is considered a forgery, that Jesuit colleges and other institutions are among the world's best and most prominent, that brave Jesuits did more than many to save Jewish lives during the Holocaust (in excess of 150 Jesuit priests were killed in the effort). Never mind all that. An irresistible conspiracy theory is an irresistible conspiracy theory.

But as to Opus Dei: The words mean "the Work of God," and when 26-year-old Spanish priest Josemaría Escrivá de Balaguer developed his notions of enhanced Catholic spirituality in 1928, this was precisely his idea: for the lay faithful to take the lessons of Sunday Mass and make them present in their lives 24/7. If there was concern that they might slip in their worship, well, for focus, they could wear a cilice, a small chain with spikes, around their thigh on a daily basis, or undergo weekly "discipline" by lashing themselves. Certainly Escrivá himself submitted to such ritualistic reminders of Christ's sufferings, and his charismatic personality and dedication drew others to his order. Today there are perhaps 87,000 Opus Dei members worldwide and perhaps 3,000 in the U.S.

In 1982, Pope John Paul II declared Opus Dei a "personal prelature": a favored status not unlike that once granted the Knights Templar. In 1975, Escrivá died. Twenty-seven years later—a very short time—he was canonized by John Paul. Three hundred thousand of the faithful filled St. Peter's Square for the ceremony. Sales of Escrivá's seminal work, *The Way*, climbed to nearly 5 million copies in more than 40 languages. His collective writings have now sold several million more.

Ah, but in the way of our world, Dan Brown's *The Da Vinci Code*, with all of its Opus Dei intrigues and suspicions, has sold more briskly still.

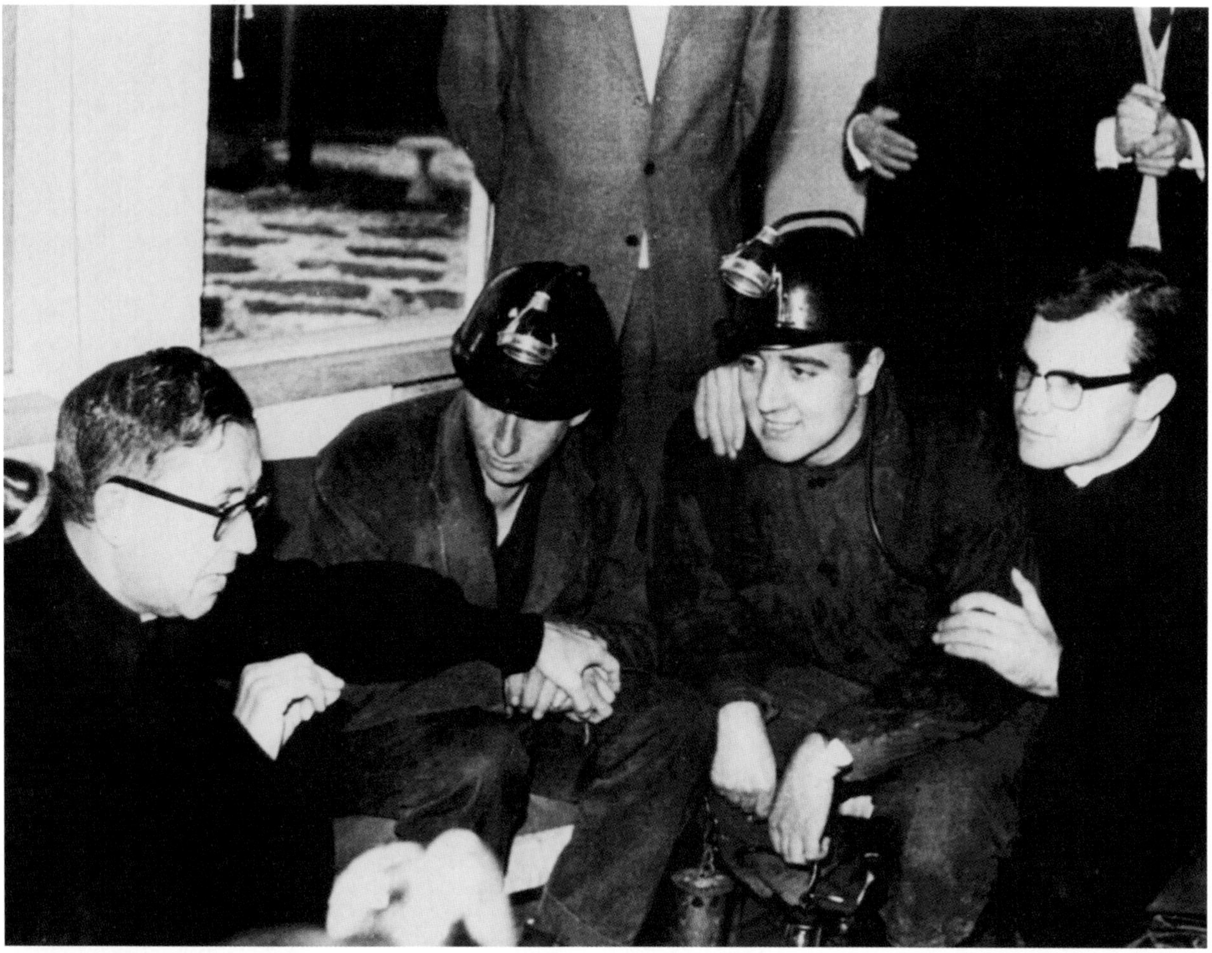

CLOCKWISE FROM TOP: RAPHO/GAMMA; ORJAN F. ELLINGVAG/CORBIS (2)

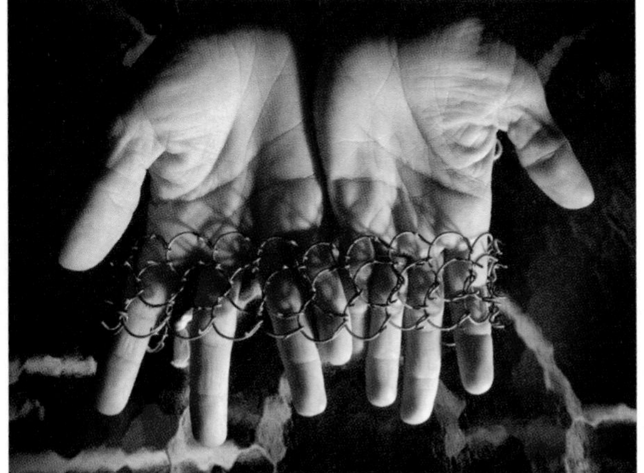

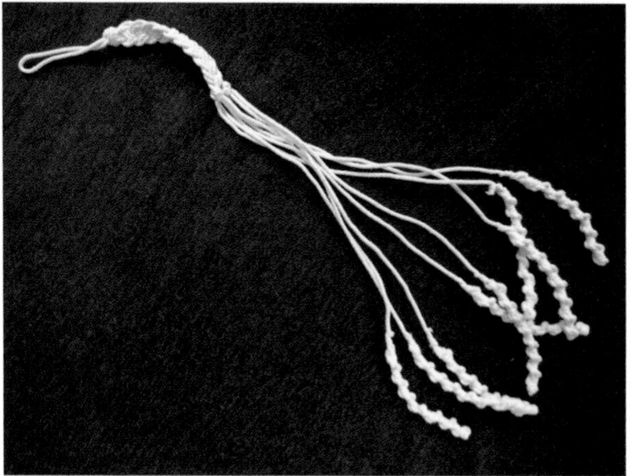

TOP: Escrivá and miners of the Asturias region of northern Spain in 1964. Among many suspicions of Opus Dei—and Escrivá—through the years were its (and his) coziness with the tyrannical Spanish regime of Francisco Franco. Above, left, is a cilice, and at right is the cordlike whip called a "discipline." Escrivá set the example. "Soon, I began to hear the forceful blows of his discipline," said one witness of an Escrivá exercise. "[T]here were more than a thousand terrible blows, precisely timed. The floor was covered in blood." Such scenes would make for quite a movie, and of course they did. Not all applauded, and today there are support networks for former Opus Dei members who have left the sect.

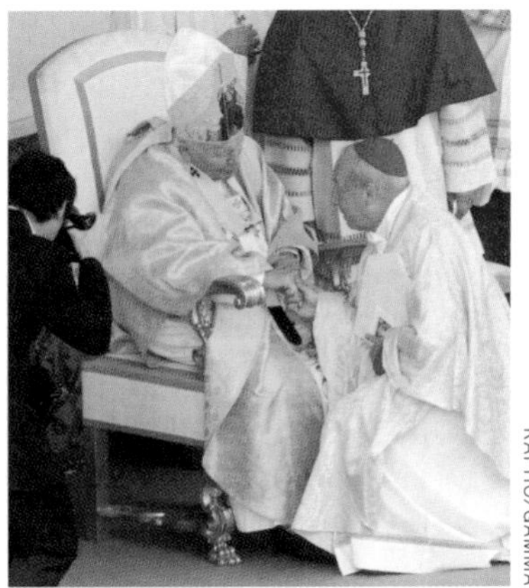

RAPHO/GAMMA

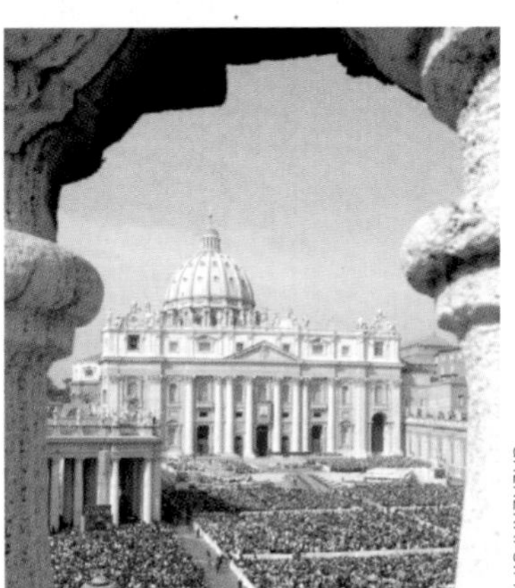

GALAZKA/SIPA

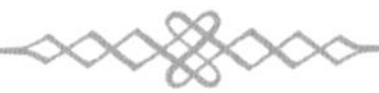

TOP: Opus Dei prelate Bishop Javier Echevarría salutes the Holy Father at the Vatican on October 6, 2002, at the canonization of Josemaría Escrivá de Balaguer, as crowds gather outside (above). Right: Members of Opus Dei convene at their headquarters; a bust of Escrivá is on display outside the meeting room. As for what constitutes Opus Dei's secrets: It is said to be wealthy. It is said to have outsize influence and to be ultra-conservative. It was said by *Harper's* magazine that Opus Dei is "an authoritarian and semi-clandestine enterprise that manages to infiltrate its indoctrinated technocrats, politicos and administrators into the highest levels of the state." Could that be so?

ANTONELLO NUSCA/GAMMA

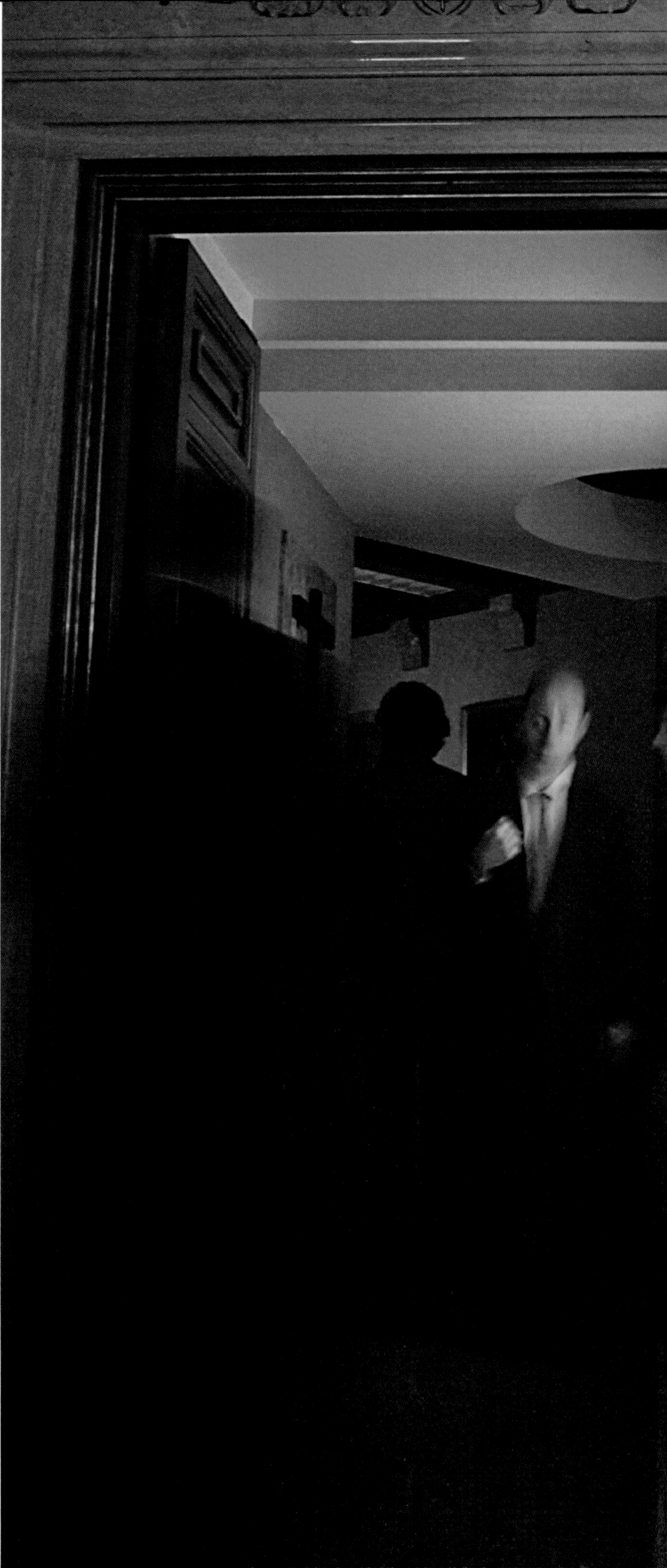

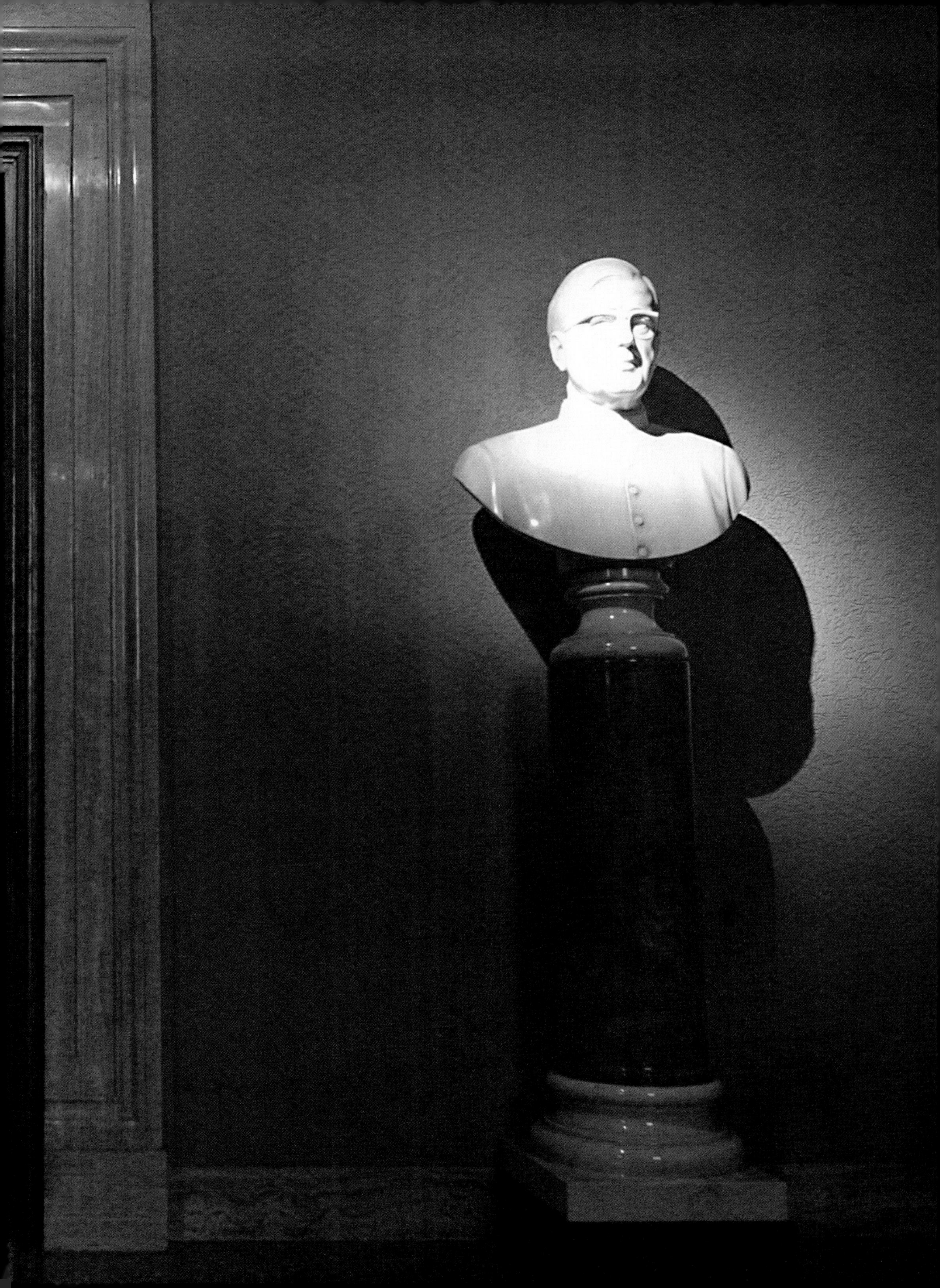

BOYS BEING BOYS

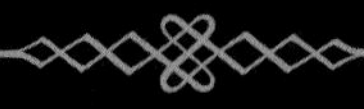

NO, THIS IS NOT going to be a chapter with nothing but flatulence jokes. It's going to deal with serious and hallowed American institutions like the Bohemian Club (opposite) and Skull and Bones. Very serious institutions, which occasionally nurture, or are patronized by, our greatest leaders, including several American Presidents. Make fun of such august institutions? Never. Not us. So, then: This chapter is not going to be just about schoolboy humor. We very much hope.

FT LIBRARY/UNIVERSITY OF CALIFORNIA, BERKELEY

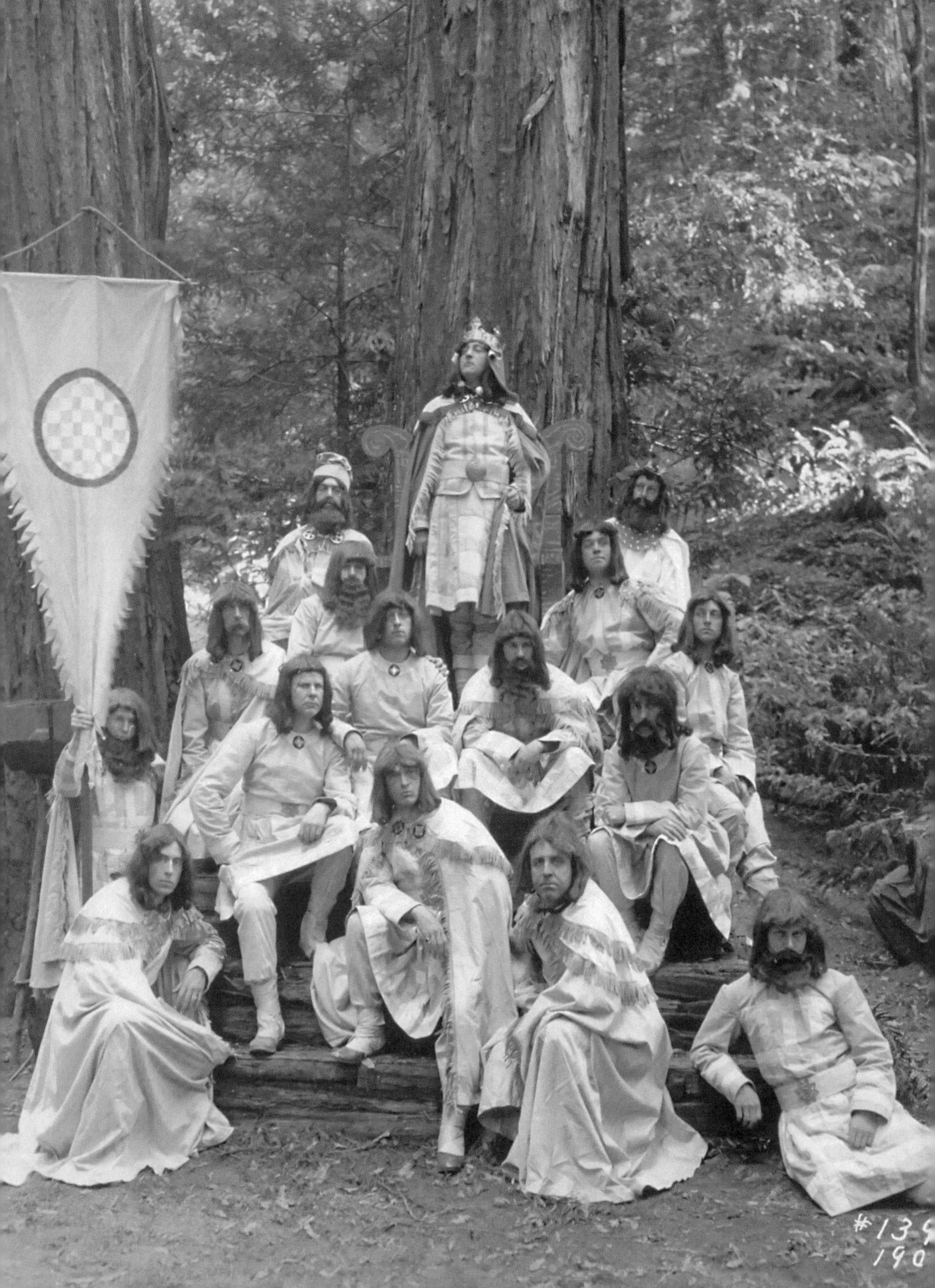
#13
190

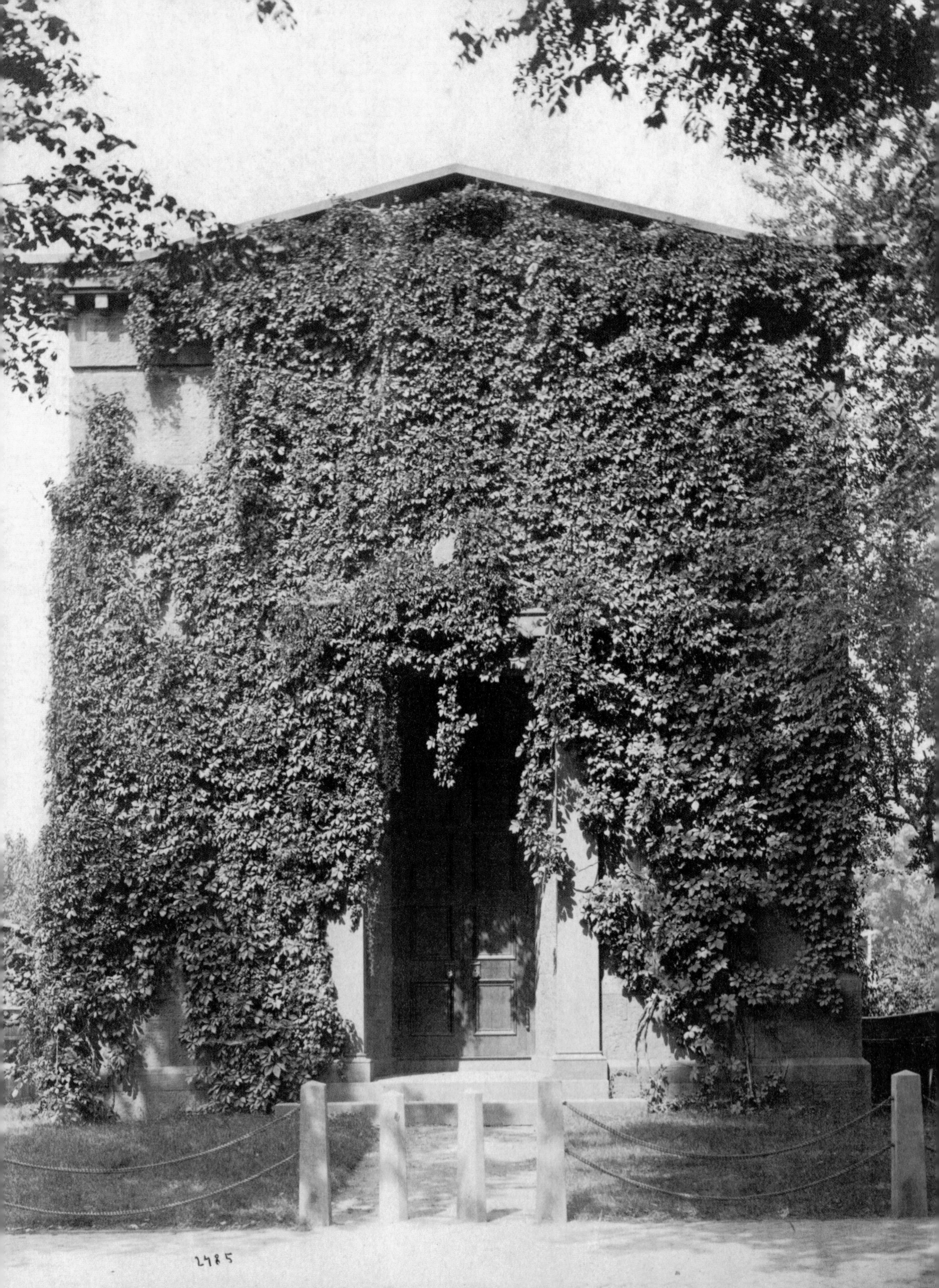
2485

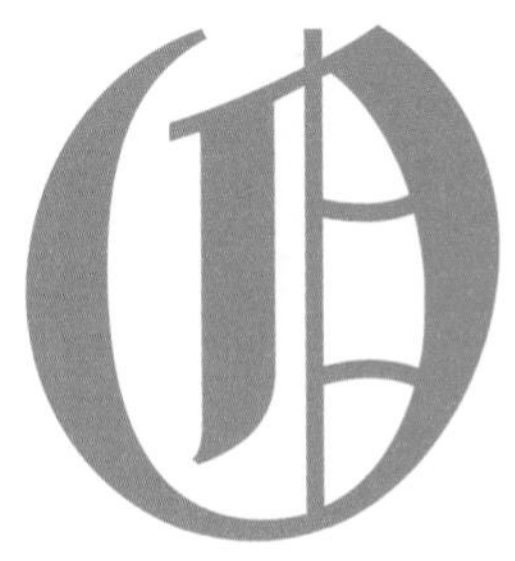

Opposite is the Tomb, headquarters of Yale University's Skull and Bones, certainly the most famous collegiate secret society in the United States, wherein never a flatulence joke has been . . . well, uttered.

But of course we can't know that for sure, because everything that has happened inside this imposing building has been, as the boys of *Animal House* would appreciate, double-secret. Not just secret, but double-secret, which makes "secret" seem, like, lame. Half-baked.

And yet we know everything about Skull and Bones! The thing about these ultra boys (or ultra-boys) fraternities is: For all their protestations, for however much they twist themselves into knots to not admit they're in the fold, they're really, really bad at keeping secrets. They're like the Templars, storming the gates: "Umm, well, sure, we're together and such, and we're Crusaders, and we've got the big red cross, but Templars? Oh, ho, ho: Not me. If I were a Templar I'd have secrets. And I would keep them from you."

In 2004, a Bonesman (that's what they call themselves) ran against a fellow Bonesman for President, when John Kerry (Yale 1966) opposed George W. Bush (Yale 1968). Everybody knew it; it was a great joke. The most fun question that could have been asked at any debate would have been, "Hey, Skull and Bones? What's up with that?" There has never been a less-than-five-minute answer at a presidential debate, never mind a not-one-second answer. The candidates would have hemmed and hawed and contorted. It's what Bonesmen do. Tim Russert did bring it up with John Kerry in a *Meet the Press* interview, during which Bush was not present, and when asked what he would or could divulge, Kerry laughed amicably and said, "Not much, because it's a secret."

Sure. Whatever you say.

But if so, if it's such a secret: Why does the wider world think Skull and Bones has within its Tomb not only Geronimo's skull but maybe that of Pancho Villa, too? Wouldn't those be secrets worth holding close to the vest? And why are there so many Skull and Bones photos floating about that we can more than fill a chapter in an illustrated LIFE book on secret societies?

Speaking of pictures: The Bohemian Club, a group of professedly adult male movers and shakers who gather annually in the Bay Area to plot the course of the free world (and otherwise party down), could surely profit by a more circumspect public relations firm. The evidence is on the prior pages and also forthcoming.

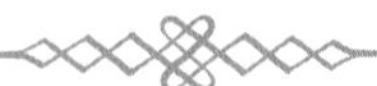

HERE WE HAVE Skull and Bones, drenched in ivy, as is fitting. On the following page, we have the several secret societies of that well-fertilized breeding ground of secret societies: Yale University in New Haven, Connecticut. This collection was depicted in a drawing by Alice Donlevy, who wouldn't have been allowed to enter any of them. At top is Psi Upsilon (Beta chapter) at 120 High Street; then at left we have our infamous Skull and Bones at 44 High Street; at right is Delta Kappa Epsilon (Phi chapter) on the east side of York Street, just south of Elm; and at bottom is Scroll and Key at 490 College Street. See! Not so secret.

MANUSCRIPTS & ARCHIVES, YALE UNIVERSITY

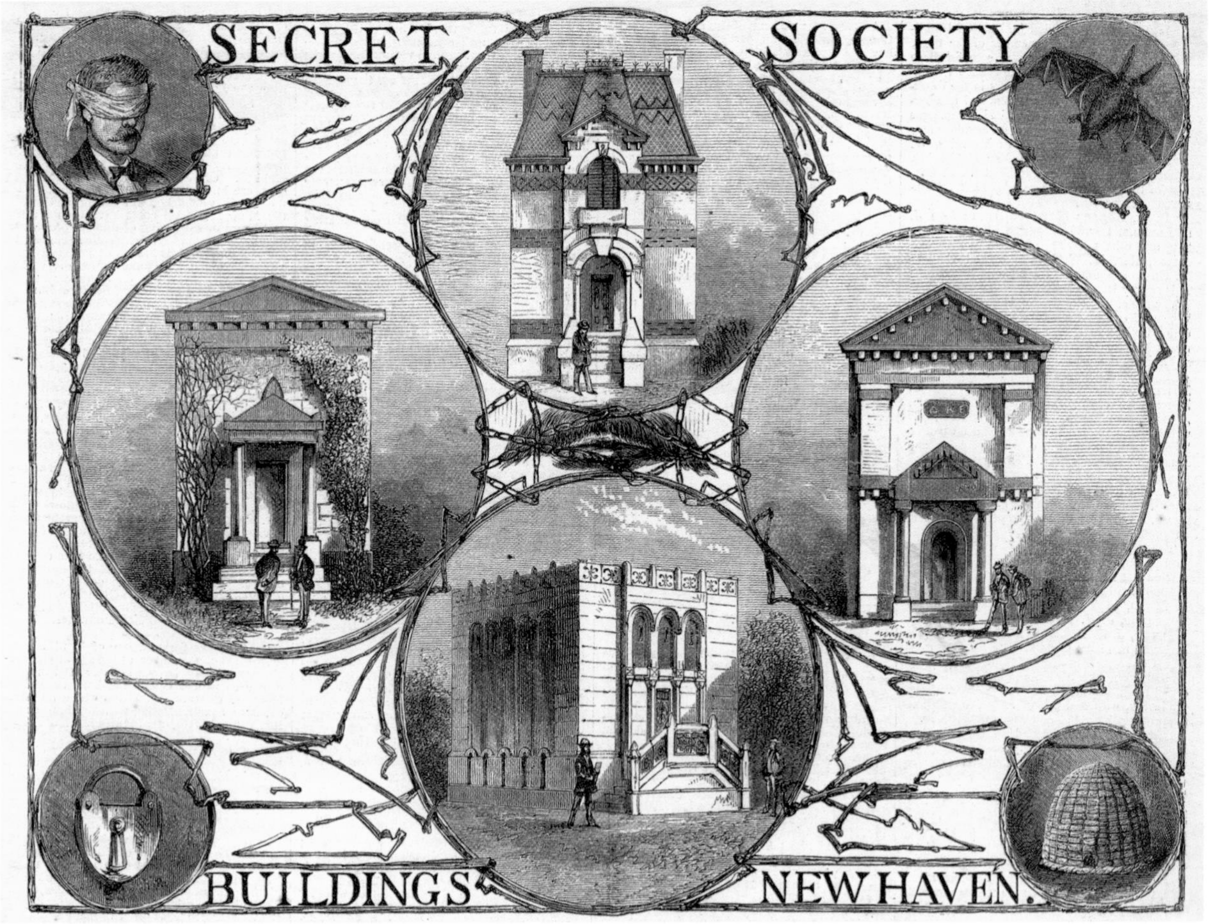

SECRET SOCIETY BUILDINGS NEW HAVEN.

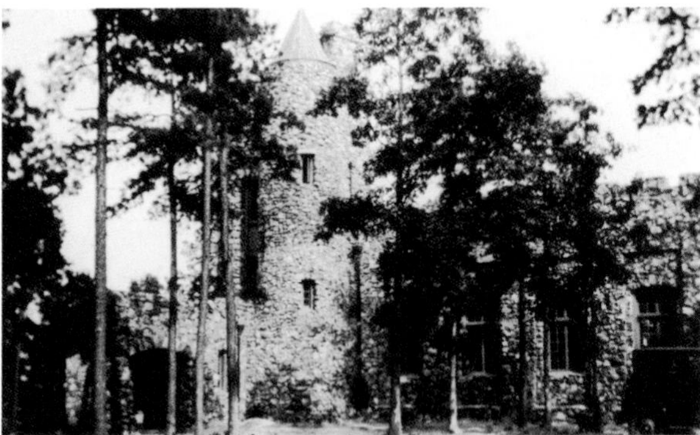

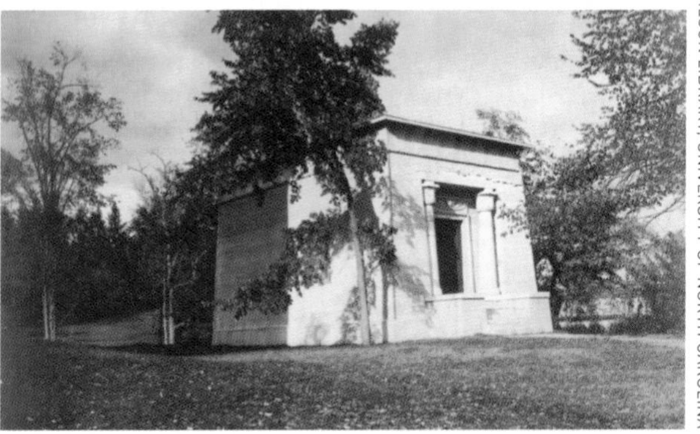

CLOCKWISE FROM TOP: MANUSCRIPTS & ARCHIVES, YALE UNIVERSITY; COURTESY DARTMOUTH COLLEGE LIBRARY; THE WILSON LIBRARY, UNIVERSITY OF NORTH CAROLINA

MANUSCRIPTS & ARCHIVES, YALE UNIVERSITY

BETTMANN/CORBIS

ABOVE are two of the way-coolest secret society edifices on U.S. college campuses: Gimghoul Castle, where the University of North Carolina's Order of Gimghoul convenes (left), and the Sphinx Tomb at Dartmouth College in Hanover, New Hampshire. It was rumored that Sphinx had the highest water bill in town because it had a pool in the basement; the myth was discounted because others in general society concluded that Sphincters seldom bathed. Opposite, top: Skull and Bones class of 1861. Bottom left: William F. Buckley Jr., a Bonesman of the class of 1950 whose brother James had been one too; William's son, Christopher, would be a class of '75 Bonesman. Bill Buckley gathered fellow alumni in an (unsuccessful) effort to sue Skull and Bones when it opted to admit Bones*women* in 1991. At center: An alum Bonesman and a Bonesman-to-be, the two George Bushes, circa 1946. At right: Bonesmen Kerry and Bush squaring off in Phoenix on October 13, 2004, in their final debate of that electoral season. The subject of Skull and Bones never came up. Hmmmm.

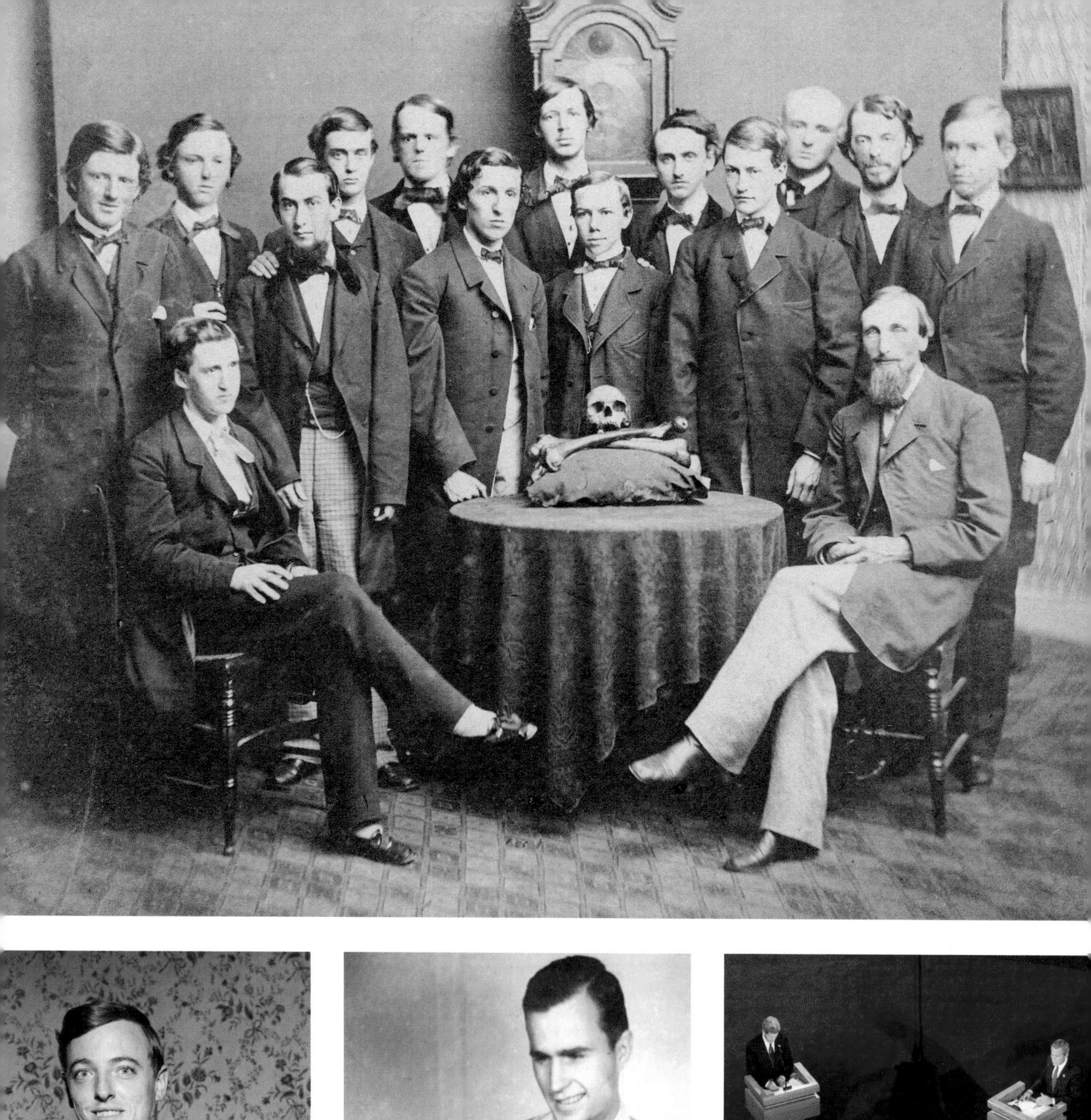

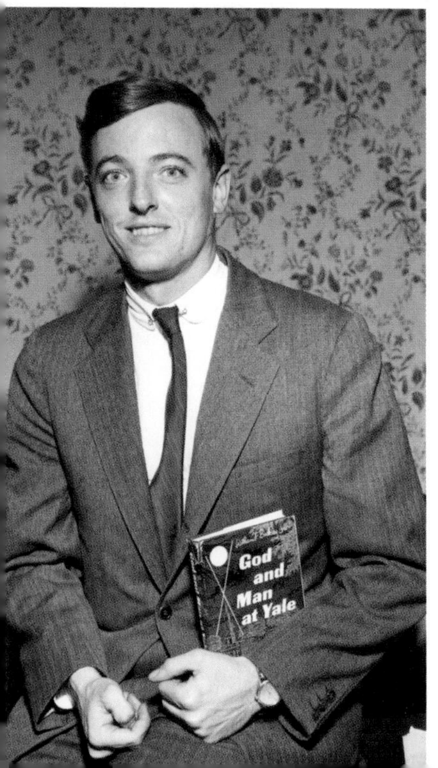

GEORGE BUSH PRESIDENTIAL LIBRARY

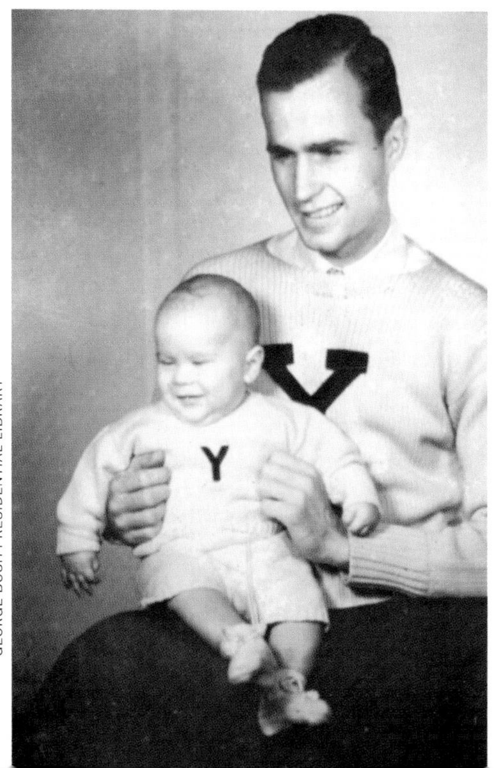

CHARLES OMMANNEY/CONTACT PRESS IMAGES

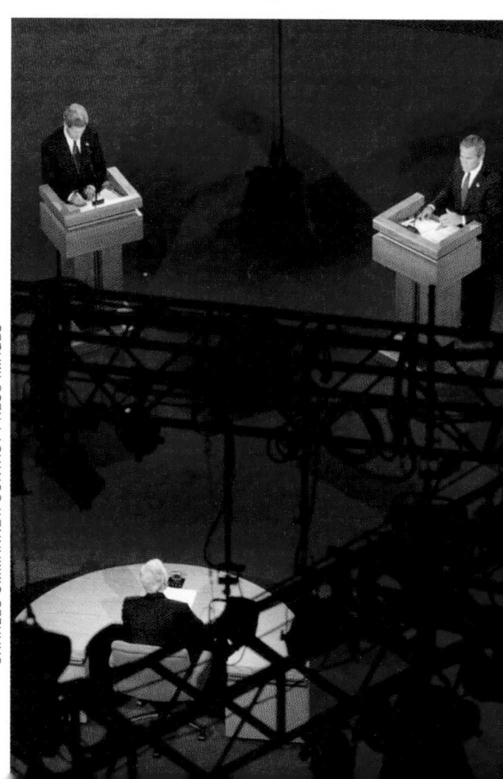

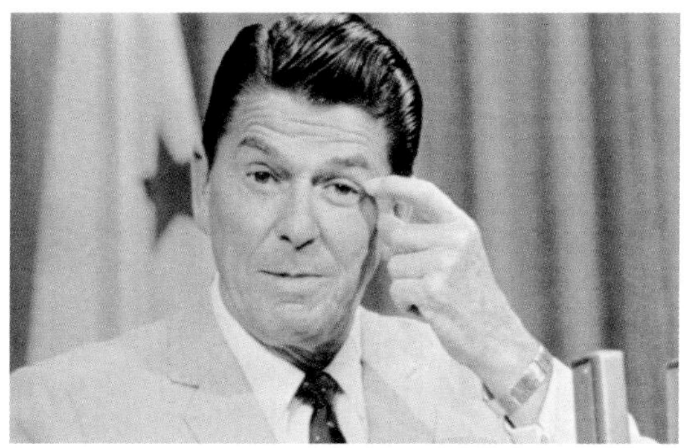

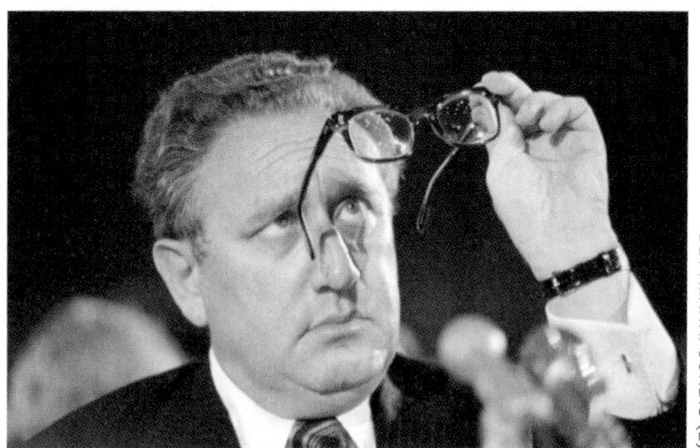

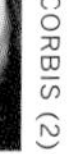

BETTMANN/CORBIS (2)

PETER PAN never wanted to grow up either, but we all love Peter Pan. So why do people make such unkind fun of the Bohemian Club and its antics at the Bohemian Grove? Well, for much the same reason that they enjoy Peter Pan: It's childish (and Grovers aren't supposed to be) and has been so since 1872. The argument here is: Give these guys a break. This is fun and harmless and, at the end of the day, like Pan and the Lost Boys, irresistible. These masters of the universe spend 51 weeks a year trying to move the world forward, some of those weeks schmoozing with their more "serious" secret societies like the Bilderberg Group or the Trilateral Commission. So surely they deserve some frolic. At top: Governor Ronald Reagan reacts in his hallmark "ahh, ummm" way when asked in 1967 whether he was heading for a Bohemian Grove gathering outside San Francisco. He didn't spill the beans on that occasion, nor ever did Henry Kissinger (above), a big Grover through the years. Before the hotshots started coming, the Bohemian Club movement was "arts" oriented (opposite), and still today, we can only presume . . . the play's the thing.

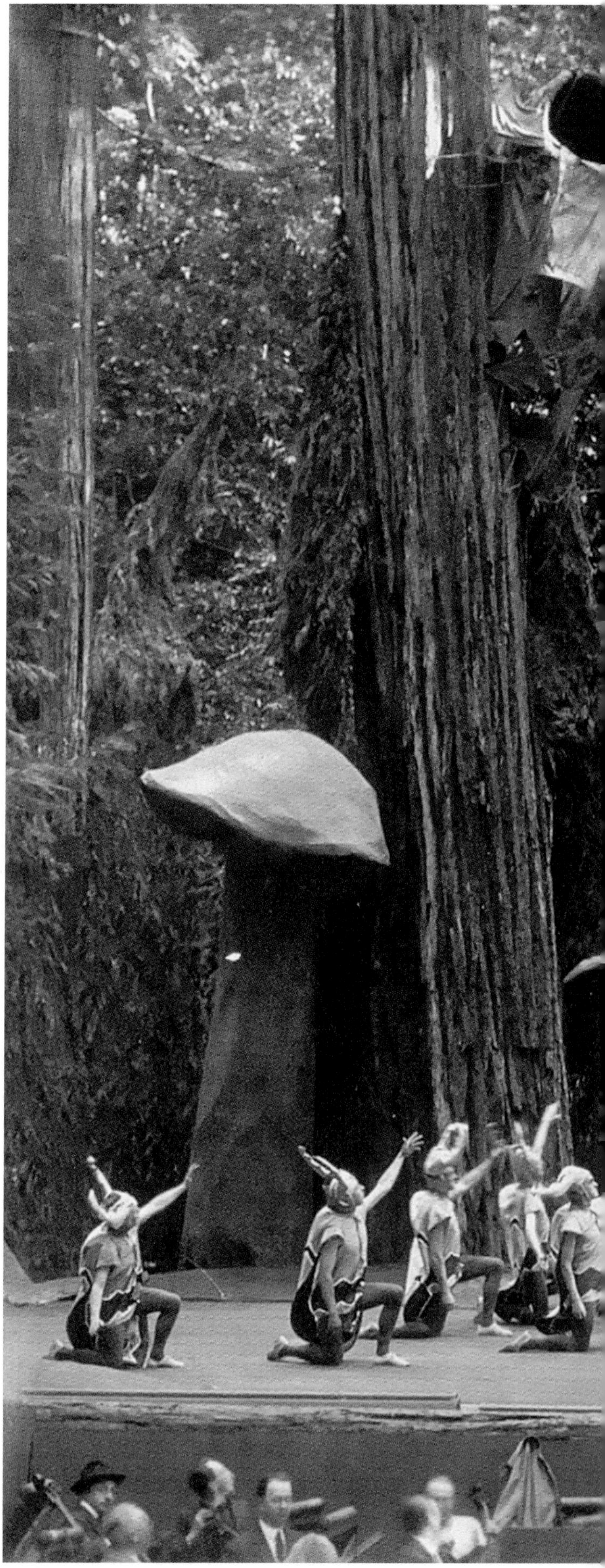

BANCROFT LIBRARY/UNIVERSITY OF CALIFORNIA, BERKELEY

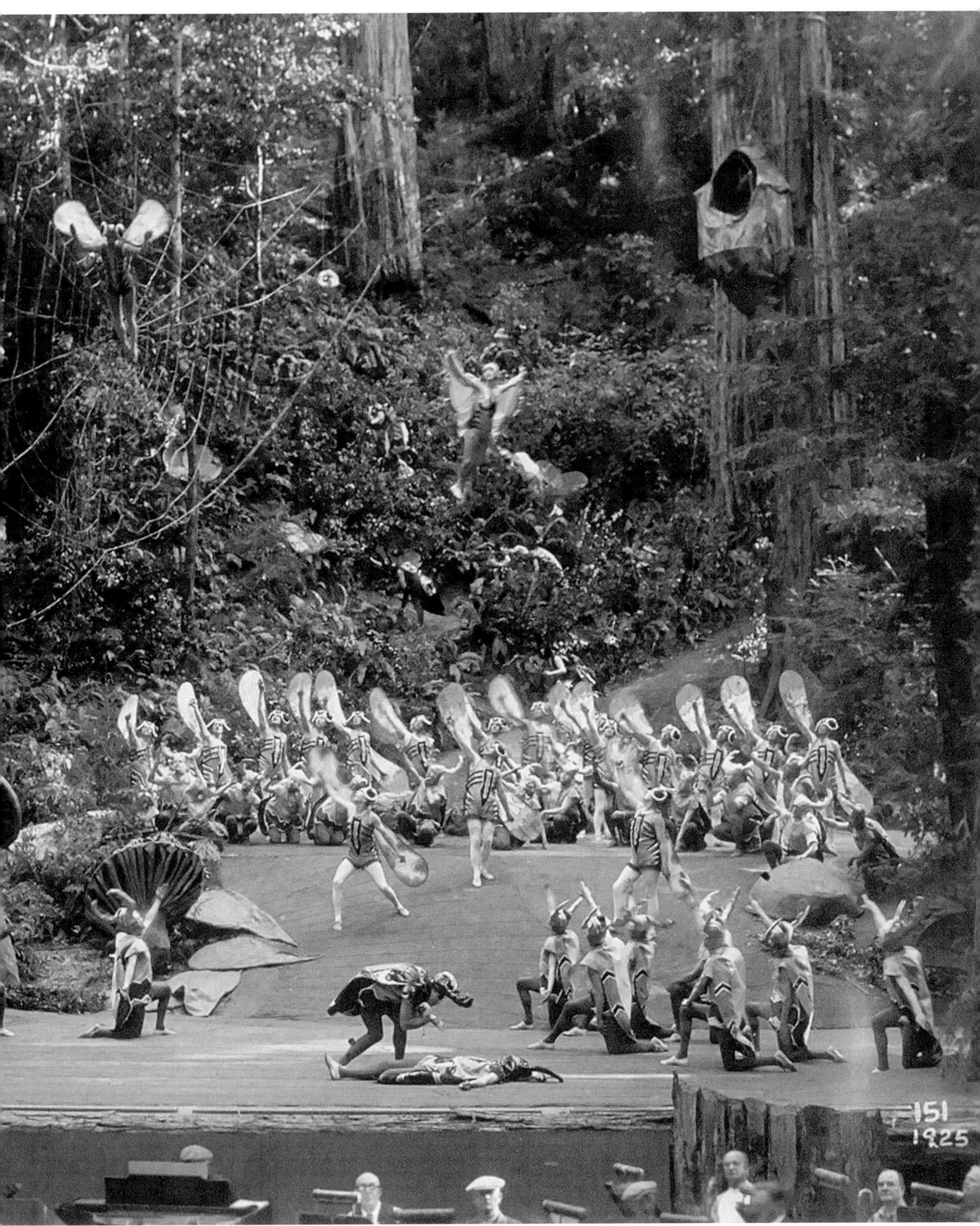
151
1925

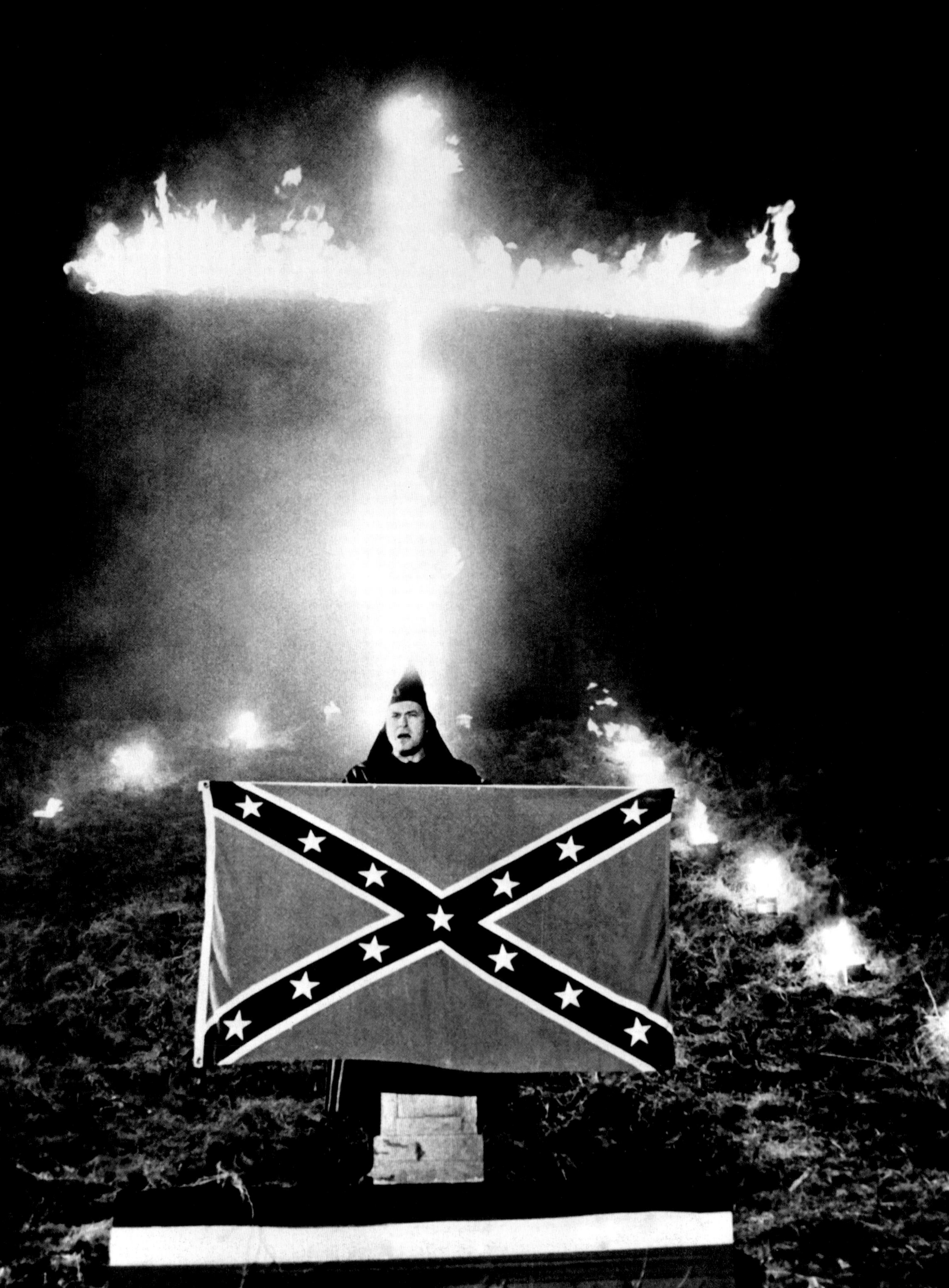

Chapter 8

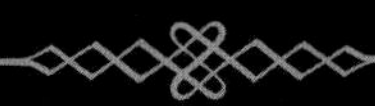

EXPOSED!

THE KLAN, which of course was purposely and vigorously visual from the get-go, was movie-ready for D.W. Griffith in the earliest days of filmmaking and has not gone a decade without being reinterpreted. This scene is from the fine 1975 TV movie starring Rip Torn (seen here) and Ned Beatty, *Attack on Terror: The FBI vs. the Ku Klux Klan.*

EVERETT

As the prior 100-plus pages of our book indicate, there exist precious few secrets in the wide, wide world of secret societies. We've got news, we've got pictures. That's the thing: Once you declare yourself a secret society, everyone else wants in on the secret. And the outsiders—which includes most of us—are going to expend substantial energy figuring out what it is. Eventually, we're going to get what we're after. And then we're going to shout out loud: "Hey, here's the secret!"

It can be presumed that the first book on secret societies was written shortly after the world's first secret society was formed; it would have been antiquity's equivalent of what happens today when Bernie Madoff goes south or Justin Bieber goes north: There's going to be an audience for such a book, so let's write it. There have been thousands and thousands of books written on secret societies since. To return to the authoritative work we cited earlier, Charles William Heckethorn's *The Secret Societies of All Ages and Countries: Two Volumes in One*: "This is not so much a second edition of my book on Secret Societies published in 1875 as an almost entirely new work.

"When the first edition was published, some of the societies had scarcely any history. Of the Nihilists, for instance, the account now given, recording their doings within the last eighteen years, fills many pages of this work. The story of other societies, active even then, such as the Fenians, had to be brought down to date . . ."

Heckethorn learned enough to fill more than 700 dense pages with inside tales on such as the Magi and the Mithraics, the Chinese metaphysics and the ancient Druids, Kabbalism and Gnosticism, the Freemasons and so on. And his second volume was published over a century ago. Think how much more fun stuff we've dug up since!

If it was galling for members to see their secrets parsed by such as Heckethorn, think how painful it must have been when the rise of Hollywood gave further vent to their intriguing and audience-pleasing narratives. Since D.W. Griffith first put the Ku Klux Klan on the silver screen, the exposition of secret societies has been a movie mainstay, securely in the file labeled: "People Love This Stuff." Herewith, a sampling.

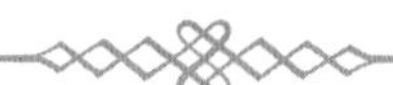

TOP ROW, left to right: D.W. Griffith's *Birth of a Nation*, 1915; Jackie Gleason and Art Carney as Raccoons in *The Honeymooners*, 1955; *Storm Warning*, with future real-world Bohemian Ronald Reagan (who in this movie prosecutes Klansmen) and Doris Day, 1951. Second row: *Stars in My Crown*, with Dean Stockwell and Joel McCrea, 1950; *The Intruder*, starring William Shatner, of all people, 1962; *The Molly Maguires*, with Sean Connery, 1970. Third row: *Angels & Demons*, with Tom Hanks as Dan Brown's Robert Langdon, 2009; *The Name of the Rose*, again with Sean Connery (and based upon the fabulous Umberto Eco novel), 1986; *Monty Python and the Holy Grail*, 1975. Fourth row: *Mississippi Burning*, starring Gene Hackman, 1988; *Indiana Jones and the Last Crusade*, 1989; *National Treasure: Book of Secrets*, starring Nicolas Cage, 2007; Fifth row: *The Hatchet Man*, with Edward G. Robinson, 1932; *American History X*, with Edward Norton, 1998; *The Da Vinci Code*, also with Hanks as Langdon, 2006. Bottom row: *Eyes Wide Shut*, Stanley Kubrick's thrilling investigation of cults, starring Tom Cruise and Nicole Kidman, 1999; *The Skulls*, about a well-known and thoroughly over-exposed Yale secret society, 2000; Angelina Jolie in *Lara Croft: Tomb Raider*, 2001.

FROM LEFT TO RIGHT, TOP ROW: KOBAL COLLECTION/THE PICTURE DESK/ART RESOURCE, NY; EVERETT (2). 2ND ROW: EVERETT; MARY EVANS/FILMGROUP INC/RONALD GRANT/EVERETT; EVERETT; 3RD ROW: EVERETT; BOB WILLOUGHBY/NEU CONSTANTIN/ZDF/KOBAL/ART RESOURCE, NY; EVERETT. 4TH ROW: ORION PICTURES/EVERETT; LUCASFILM LTD/PARAMOUNT/KOBAL/ART RESOURCE, NY; ROBERT ZUCKERMAN/WALT DISNEY/JERRY BRUCKHEIMER FILMS. 5TH ROW: EVERETT; NO CREDIT; COLUMBIA/SIMON MEIN/KOBAL/ART RESOURCE, NY; EVERETT; UNIVERSAL/EVERETT; ALEX BAILEY/PARAMOUNT

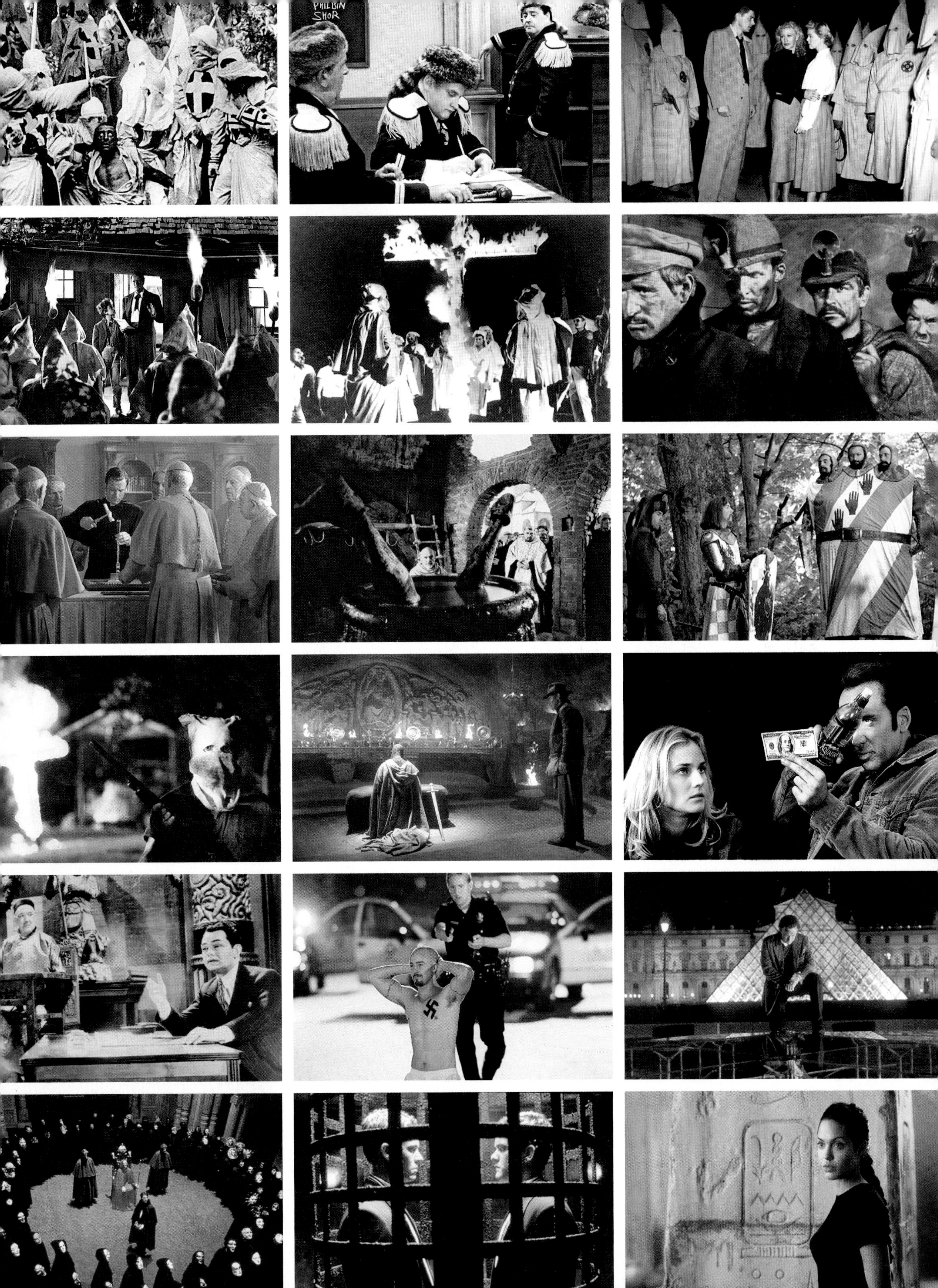
PHILBIN
SHOR

Just One More

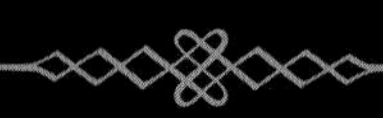

SENIOR SOCIETY

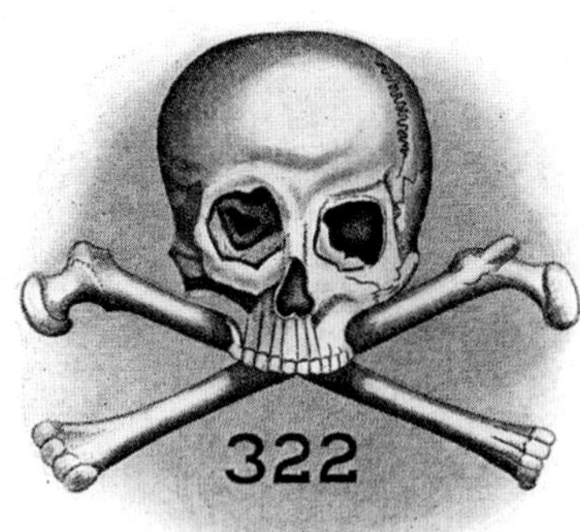

Lewis Greenleaf Adams
Henry Pomeroy Davison, Jr.
Briton Hadden
Frank Peavey Heffelfinger
John Morris Hincks
Francis Thayer Hobson
David Sinton Ingalls
Henry Robinson Luce
James McHenry
Morehead Patterson
Theodore Lee Safford
Joseph Weir Sargent
Alfred Coster Schermerhorn
DeForest Van Slyck
Daniel Robbins Winter

119

MANUSCRIPTS & ARCHIVES, YALE UNIVERSITY

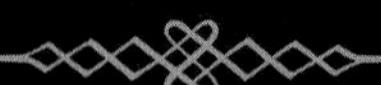

IN DAYS GONE BY (and who knows, maybe tomorrow?), running this as our last page could (or might) get the staff of LIFE Books fired.

What is it?

It is a super-secret roster of the 1920 class of Yale's Skull and Bones. Listed you will find Henry Luce and Briton Hadden, who are also editorial colleagues on the *Yale Daily News*. Upon graduating, they will team up and cofound *Time* magazine. Luce will go on to found *Fortune* and then LIFE. And our company will spin on and on, and merge with Warner Communications Inc., and then do that silly AOL thing and . . .

Did Luce and Hadden plot all this in the recesses of the Tomb in New Haven?

We cannot say.

Really, we can *not* say.

[illegible] dno ... qd in ... Post que

... dix qd in ... qd no. Post que ... et obseruabit ...

... fuit ... confessus ... accedet ... a sca eccia qua ipe pmiss

... qd ipe pateret madatis ecclie ac tenebit ...

... humilit petentem absolutois bnficiu a sca eccia ... in mia et ipoz nomine ac

de fratribus ... in tota normania, ... de Rupe preceptore francie apud ...

... ordinis militie templi per fratrem Almaricum de Rupe ...

militie Templi per fratrem ... ipe recipiens traxit ipm receptu ad prem

... ordis ... collum suum ... ipe recipiens osculat fuit recipientem in ore et in

... recepcois ... idem receptus osculat fuit ... et postea recepit plures alios fr

qd ... receptus, et postea recepit plures alios

... formam ... quam ipe fuit receptus, et de uicio sodomie et de capite idolatrico

de spuitoe sup crucem, de osculi, de uicio sodomie ... no uident ... audiuit quid ...

... qd alij fres qui sunt in eadem domo no uident ... audiuit quid ...

... qd alij fres qui fuit in eadem sua cofessione uolebat psistere

... predicta dixit qd no. Requisitus ... in eadem sua cofessione uolebat psisteri

... nec ... conscit ... fratrem ... modum et

... impendendum. Tenebat ... ad ecclie unitatem ... res

... et alijs suprascriptis, dixit qd ... uiginti octo annis ul circa qd ...

... Templi eidem recepto ostendit sibi quandam crucem depictam in quodam

... qd tu dicas si fuis requisit a frib; ... negatoem istam, si ego pro te ...

... predictam. Et cu idem recept ... nollet face posuit duas recapiens manu

... idolatrica ... osculi et alijs de quib; fres ... ordis fuit diffamati diligen

... odio aut Indiciane alicui ul ... aut ... confessione ...

... humilit postulanti, ... absolutois bnficium iuxta forma ecce ...

... preceptor domoz militie Templi ... francie ... preto ...

... Quadraginta sex annis ul circa in festo Magdalene ... preito ...

... qui fuit postea preceptor de ... duxit eu ad ... quandam capel

... cu ymago erat ibi depicta ... Et licet ... frat Johes ...

... sic ples et plures ... qui ... in ordie ... per que

... a cosortio mulierum et si no possent ... cotinie qd ipi ... se cum

... qd talia erat statuta siue puat ordis, et sperabit semp qd ille error ...

... consitatib; suis ... accidit ... qd ipe ... facer ... aud

... se cum alijs ... recapiunt qd no pot aliqd

... alijs nisi de seipo et illis quos recep ... ita secrete recapiunt ... Alemadum ...

... in Monte pessulani p fratrem petrum ...